The 21 Biggest Lies about Donald Trump
(and you!)

THE 21 BIGGEST BIGGEST LIES ABOUT DONALD TRUMP

(and you!)

Kurt Schlichter

REGNERY
PUBLISHING
A Division of Salem Media Group

Regnery® is a registered trademark of Salem Communications Holding Corporation

ISBN 978-1-68451-078-8
eISBN 978-1-68451-098-6

Library of Congress Control Number: 2020932589

Published in the United States by
Regnery Publishing
A Division of Salem Media Group
300 New Jersey Ave NW
Washington, DC 20001
www.Regnery.com

Manufactured in the United States of America

10 9 8 7 6 5 4 3 2

Books are available in quantity for promotional or premium use. For information on discounts and terms, please visit our website: www.Regnery.com.

Dedicated to Irina, J, and J

CONTENTS

Introduction

*D*efamation (n): A derogatory and deliberately false statement that causes the victim harm, either directly or *per se,* by the nature of the statement.

Libel is printed defamation; slander is spoken defamation. That's how a lawyer would put it.

Put another way, it's a lie.

Mark Twain once said that there are three kinds of lies: lies, damn lies, and statistics. He was right for his time, but today we're inundated with a fourth kind of lie, the kind of lie told about Donald Trump and you.

Our public square is filled with volley after volley of falsehoods that the left and its pseudo-conservative Renfields fire at our president and his supporters. There is no longer any argument or reasoned discussion, just lies. Editorial pages, the airwaves, and social media are all filled with hyperbolic accusations, making a scorched earth Yucca Flat out of rational discourse.

Crank your masochism meter to "High" and turn on MSNBC. Listen to the self-congratulatory panels preen, populated with third-tier guests whose diverse views range from "Donald Trump is Hitler II" to "Donald Trump is the Antichrist without the upside." It's all baloney, all the time. And it's getting worse.

Lies have always been a part of politics, but today defamation has replaced actual debate. It's almost quaint to see someone offer a coherent, thoughtful argument instead of spewing a spray of cheesy slander. When was the last time you heard someone provide a detailed, pointed critique of Donald Trump's policies? Not of his character or his alleged personal failings, but his *policies*?

It's been a while, hasn't it?

Now when was the last time you heard some establishment politician, media hack, or Twitter malcontent call Trump a "racist"? Well, probably the last time you heard or read an establishment politician, media hack, or Twitter malcontent.

Defamation is all the Trump-haters have left because the facts aren't working out for them. We have a booming economy (the viral tangent notwithstanding), no new wars, and a renewed faith in the American dream. By all objective standards, President Trump is leaving his mark as a great American president.

But when your goal is power, why concern yourself with facts, evidence, or bourgeois concepts like "reason?" The Trump-haters don't have a substantive critique of Donald Trump; they just can't stand his hulking, tweeting presence in the Oval Office. Each Trump victory represents another daunting obstacle to the establishment's unrestricted exercise of power. They believe they deserve to rule you, despite their manifest mediocrity, because they really want to. They're like spoiled children who just had someone take away their binky.

We want to be in charge damn it, and that Bad Orange Man is in the way.

Oh, and so are all of you who support him.

In their minds President Trump isn't the only problem. You are a problem too. You are in the way, and that's why every obnoxious libel that they print about Trump, every vile slander that they utter, every deliberate falsehood that they transmit, is not really aimed at Donald Trump. It's aimed at you.

You are the liars' target—you, who are not part of the club, who are not cool, and who do not initiate conversations by clarifying your pronouns like our betters do. You're their target because in 2016 you dared to flex your muscle. You dared to exercise your right to control the direction of your own society. You dared to hold accountable the elites that failed to achieve anything except failure for nearly a quarter century.

Trump is merely a symbol, an avatar of the righteous anger and resentment of the American people at our failed establishment. You are the final and most daunting obstacle to their real goal, unlimited power, and they will never forgive you for getting in their way.

Who are "they" anyway?

They are the authors, politicians, bureaucrats, writers, tweeters, talking heads, hipsters, millennials, movie stars, and aging rock stars who haven't had a hit since they wrote crappy songs dissing Ronald Reagan. They are the elites, the establishment, the globalists, and the ruling class who want to make sure you don't get a seat at the table.

We typically call them "the liars," if only for the sake of simplicity. So many groups, factions, institutions, and cliques have adopted the use of conscious falsehood as a strategy to defeat Donald Trump and the people he represents that it's hard to put them all in one group.

Sometimes the liars are the members of our political establishment, the power brokers Trump challenged. Sometimes they are the elites, the self-designated betters whose self-professed wisdom, morality, and virtue prompt them to lecture, hector, and scold those they consider their inferiors. Sometimes they are leftists and their weak sisters the liberals, while sometimes they are people who posed as conservatives until Trump's ascent revealed their grift. Sometimes they are the media—but I'm speaking in circles. We've already covered liberals, and there's no need to be repetitive.

You see, there's a method to the liars' mendacity. Their unprecedented defamation campaign has a purpose. It's not just meaningless bluster: the liars want to build a false narrative that morally disenfranchises you. *You* are bad people living in a bad country presumptuously exercising rights to which you are not entitled. As that weird Swedish climate change kid might say, "How dare you! HOW DARE YOU!"

Defamation is a weapon, designed to reinforce a narrative that will make you shrug, accept your own manifest unworthiness, and submit to your betters. It might even work, at least for a little while. After all, most Americans are nice people and would never think to call someone a racist or a homophobe or a religious nut bent on imposing some sort of handmaiden-themed theocracy unless the accusation were true. So, when someone says those things about us, our natural response is to wonder whether our accuser may have a point. We care, and in the narrative judo of modern American culture, our opponents use that against us.

In 2016 we elected a guy who doesn't care. Not even a little. Donald Trump is a guy who was born without a shame gene. Thankfully, it makes him impervious to their defamation. Could you imagine Mitt Romney under the pseudo-moral pressure Trump thrives on? He couldn't show his ripped belly fast enough. With one sentence at that 2012 debate, Candy Crowley practically decked him out in a diaper and a leash. Just think how fast he'd submit if everyone he knew in his social circle started up on him.

Not Donald J. Trump.

Call him racist? Trump doesn't care. To resurrect an ancient meme, he's a full-on honey badger when it comes to people's lying about him. He has a bottomless well of self-confidence and is delightfully free of self-doubt, which drives his enemies bonkers. Not only does he know he's not a racist in any intelligible sense of the word, he also knows that his administration has done more for minorities than any of his predecessors. And he's a brawler. Instead of hanging his head in shame, he punches back.

Call him sexist? Or a sexual predator? Again, he doesn't care. He's interested in results, and as far as his playboy days that were splashed across the covers of New York tabloids a couple decades ago, he regrets nothing. Oh, it drives his enemies up a wall when they accuse him of tagging a series of Playboy bunnies and pneumatic strippers and then a significant number of his supporters respond by offering him a figurative high-five.

Call him anything you want, and what does he do? He shrugs and counterattacks because he's been called worse things by more impressive people, and now he's president, and his opponents aren't. He leaves them broken and gibbering on *Morning Joe*, bellyaching about the latest "bombshell" that's totally going to do him in as he marches inexorably to his likely reelection.

Instead of playing "Hail to the Chief," Trump ought to have a guy follow him around to play those sad trombone notes every time he returns fire after yet another defamation.

Wah, wah, waaaaaaaaaaaah!

Ordinary Americans don't have Trump's bully pulpit, his media savvy, or his almost inhuman ability to not give a damn in the face of the vilest calumny. But we remain the target of the elites' lies. One day, Trump will go. (Though think of how much fun it would be to watch the meltdown that ensues from a half-serious effort to repeal the Twenty-second Amendment.) We will remain, and unfortunately the liars will remain too. They think of the Trump presidency as an unprecedented and wicked interregnum in their campaign for total power. Once he is out of the picture, our would-be elite overlords expect that it's back to fundamental transformation as usual. To make sure that happens, they'll do anything to suppress and tame us *mere* citizens.

Hence the attempt to control the narrative through the deployment of the mass defamation that we see today.

The intense defamation we are subjected to 24/7 in the media and popular culture is more than just *malum in se*. It poisons our society. Think about how our society was meant to operate. Look at the Founders, those slave-owning white men who created what was, until lately, the most successful experiment in government by and for the people in human history. While they could dish it out hard, the political model they bequeathed us relies on the possibility of argument and debate. It is built upon a foundation of reason and the premise that when a rational citizen is confronted by facts and arguments that demonstrate the superiority of a policy, he can be persuaded to support it.

The defamation approach the modern left takes offers a different model. Instead of trying to persuade, the defamation model rejects the possibility of calmly changing hearts and minds. When there's no persuasion, there is only force. And so, the model values expedience over anything else, calling for whatever it takes to accumulate power for one's political allies.

You could never win over a people through lies. The fact is that when someone is lying about you, and knows he is lying about you, and does not give a half-damn that he's lying about you, he will never change your mind.

But the liars don't want to change minds. They want to shame you, their enemy, into submission. Their purely *ad hominem* debate style does not seek to convert the slandered. Rather, because the lies are so obvious and hackneyed, they want to force the uncommitted to accept the narrative or crush any spirit of resistance in the victim.

Defamation breeds solidarity among the liars. By accepting defamation, you become more integrated into the liberal Borg collective. A liberal might howl that "Trump is a racist of such all-encompassing racism that Jim Crow himself would decry his manifest racism!" The fellow traveler down the road of defamation receives this insight, ignores the fact that there was no racist dude named "Jim Crow," and further ignores the fact that if there had been a dude named "Jim Crow," he certainly would have been a Democrat, and simply nods. There's no need for evidence, argument, or reasoning over whether the claim is objectively true. Objective truth, as you learn when running up a couple hundred grand in student debt getting a degree in Pan-Gender Colonial Oppression Rap, is itself a tool of evil and oppression. So, you don't demand that the claim be true; truth is beside the point.

When you're one of the liars, something is true when it's useful to your agenda. Accepting Official Truths like "Trump is racist" is a pleasing act of solidarity, so it must be true. It allows you to luxuriate in the warm embrace of mindless belonging, even when your career in heated beverage preparation and distribution isn't going as planned. It relieves you of the painful duty of thinking and measuring and testing, while alleviating the terrible risk of being labeled a wrong-thinker and bad person who doesn't wholeheartedly accept the Official Truth.

Look at what happened to Ellen DeGeneres when she exchanged pleasantries with George W. Bush at a football game. She interacted with the former president of the United States without throwing a fit, tizzy, or tantrum and was lambasted for it. The narrative, the defamatory Official Truth, is that this hapless, maudlin squish is not merely an officially-designated bad person; he is a racist, warmongering, murdering fascist who would make Mussolini retch in abject disgust.

Oh, the people on Twitter were so very disappointed with Ms. DeGeneres for not acting like a fool in the presence of a creature unapproved by liberaldom. In an all too rare outcome, the amiable TV hostess did not come crawling upon her belly like a reptile to beg the cultural establishment for forgiveness for her sin of behaving like an adult, despite the fact that she got bushels of grief.

Defamation is a tool of discipline, and the Woke Inquisition will mercilessly scourge anyone who fails to abide by its dogma. Sadly, most people do not have dump trucks full of money to comfort them when the high priests of political correctness show up with torches and pitchforks demanding blood. Ordinary people can't even be sure that they'll keep their jobs.

The defamation model is the precise opposite of the reasoned discourse the Founders took for granted when they crafted the Constitution. Reasoned discourse is the basis upon which our entire government rests. And when you replace a foundation of concrete with one of wet sand, you'll make the whole damn thing collapse in upon itself.

Our society was built on the idea that free citizens can inquire without fear into the facts surrounding the problems they face. Weighing the arguments of competing advocates leads them to the best solutions, freely chosen through a process of debate and deliberation.

Two branches of our government are entirely dedicated to this concept. In the judiciary, you literally have courtrooms where lawyers present evidence, make arguments, and, in the case of factual determinations, try to persuade juries of citizens to make a decision based on a rational consideration of what they hear. As for matters of law, the judges, considering precedent, statutes, and arguments, reason their way through competing opinions. At least that's what is supposed to happen. Obviously, Hawaiian judges are an exception.

And then there is the legislative branch, where in the federal government and in forty-nine of the states, excepting those unicameral weirdos in Nebraska, you have a House and a Senate (or the equivalents). The legislative branch allows us citizens to choose representatives and send them off to hear debates and come to decisions, presumably based on reason. Again, it does not always happen that way, even in eras where defamation is not the primary mode of discourse, but at least there was a chance of its happening.

There's no chance now, though. The left, which controls both sides of the establishment, is all-in on defamation as the primary mode of political discourse today.

Trump can't just be wrong. He has to be evil. Which means *you* can't just be wrong. *You* have to be evil. And, of course, evil people are banished from polite society and from the levers of power. Weird how that works out really well for the liars in the political establishment.

Eliminating the very process that makes our system of government function means that we lose our rightful claim to a government that serves the people. Instead of self-rule, you get California, which is just an adolescent version of the adult Venezuela that West Coast liberals aspire to. In California, you get decrees from on high—thou shalt not have a real car, charge rents beyond what we allow, or suck through a straw that doesn't melt into goo while you sip your cruelty-free iced tea. There's no debate about whether these things are good ideas or bad. They're good, full stop, at least among the unchallenged elite, and as a result, the rest of California's citizens live with an endless series of petty and not-so-petty impositions and oppressions about which they had no say.

Reasonable discourse assumes that people can change their minds. But you can't change your mind about disintegrating straws because, well, everyone knows that plastic is bad. The world is going to end in twelve years unless we do something, and banning functional straws is doing something. If you want to sip your drink with the same efficiency as some punk in the fifties then you must want global warming, hate Gaia, and not want your children to live on a functioning planet. How can anyone argue with that?

The defamation model assumes that the opposition is morally corrupt. Critiquing their policies is just a cop-out and a dodge and likely proof that you yourself are evil too.

The defamers claim to *know* we are bad, so they don't feel the need to investigate any further. It is written. And if you are one of the liars, there's no possibility of changing your mind because the Official Truth is holy writ and moral sanctity itself. To change your mind is, by definition, to embrace evil.

Our current elites define truth as whatever supports the narrative they advance. Once integrated into the narrative, lies become the Official Truth and unchallengeable. In fact, challenging the lies proves the perfidy of the wrong-thinker. Just look at the "climate denier" tag. You are not only bad because of your selfish greed for cheeseburgers and your ownership of an SUV which is literally killing the planet, but you are a million times worse because you refuse to accept your own complicity in this unfolding terracide.

That's not how a free republic is supposed to function; it's how tyranny is born. In the defamatory model, lies are impressed upon the masses without their consent from the top down, while in a free republic the people's will bubbles up through their representatives who put it into action. If you ever doubt the tyrannical will of the left, just look at how they try to impose their morals—or lack thereof—on the rest of the country.

It's no shock that the masses are the target of constant defamation. The masses are truly an inconvenience to the elites who would rather run things according to their own prejudices and preferences without having to deal with annoying input from the plebes. The defamation paradigm gets rid of the people's pesky dissent. It aims to silence and shame the masses into obedience. It's an exercise in raw power.

Our society was designed to eliminate the rule of power and impose the rule of law. Customs and norms, rules and procedures, rights and remedies were all baked into the system. And it was supposed to be a *system*. The pieces interconnect and intertwine. The individual components of the system—the primacy of reason, the importance of debate, the respect for due process and rights—mutually reinforce one another. But when you start removing pieces of the system that you don't like anymore because they give the other guy a voice, it's like political Jenga: remove one or two pieces and the structure may stand, but eventually the whole edifice will collapse.

Defamation may be an effective way to wield power in the short term, but it is ultimately toxic to the system our Founders envisioned. It is not going to work in the long term. The elite cannot reasonably expect that when they adopt a new mode of governance (in this case by embracing defamation), ordinary people will continue to use reasoned debate to address their grievances. Come to think of it, maybe they do expect that to happen. Maybe they do expect that they can adopt a new set of rules for themselves while their opponents just keep on keepin' on as if nothing had changed. After all, our elite, for all their pretensions of cosmopolitanism, are the most parochial ruling caste in our history. Its members don't understand history or human nature because neither was taught to them when they bought their degrees from our failing academia. They do know a lot about microaggressions, though.

Human beings don't tend to sit back and take grief. They don't tend to shrug when faced with unreasonable demands for obedience. They don't willingly toss away their self-rule because some pierced sophomore from Wellesley is "literally shaking" over the refusal of a guy who drives a Kenworth ten hours a day to concede his white privilege. Oppressed people get mad, then they get even. And a cultural elite where the majority of its members has never been in a bar fight might not be ready for a scenario where their preferred manifestation of power—words—has to compete with the preferred manifestation of power of those they want to keep down.

Mao observed that power flows from the barrel of a gun, not from a snarky tweet that gets retweeted 2100 times. And in our country, only one side of the growing divide has guns.

Defamation stirs up a unique kind of fury in its victims because of its sheer injustice. Here's the thing: the notion of fairness is deeply ingrained in the American psyche. Our culture is replete with references to it: "Due process," "Tell your side of the story," "Have your day in court." The idea that you can be convicted without having a chance to prove your innocence (though the idea of the presumption of innocence is another strand of our American DNA) is anathema to us.

Defamation is designed to circumvent those protections and convict you before you have a chance to stand up for yourself. The new defamation model shifts the burden of proof from the accuser to the accused. But be careful: trying to prove your innocence doesn't exonerate the accused; it merely compounds your guilt. It's evidence that you aren't contrite or don't regret the actions of which you are accused.

Take the hoary racism charge as an example. Some human drumstick on *Face the Nation* announces that "Trump is obviously racist." In a reason-based paradigm, the proper response would be to reply, "Because…?" and politely pause to give the accuser a chance to provide actual evidence. But in defamation world, the charge *is* the evidence. The accuser sits back with a smug look—game, set, match.

If evidence mattered, Trump could point out innumerable pieces of compelling evidence that show he isn't racist. He could point out his friendship with various members of minority groups. But that's not going to help. For some bizarre reason, being friends with members of minority groups is inadmissible and is a "racist" response. It is the old "some of my best friends are [fill in the group]" claim. Close friendship would seem to be compelling evidence that one is not racist, but according to the new rules, it's further proof that you are indeed a racist.

This is a theme we shall see again and again as we delve into the specific lies about Donald Trump and, by extension, you. A baseless accusation establishes a crime, but then even when the exonerating evidence is overwhelming, it is deemed inadmissible. At the same time, the accusation becomes the evidence of the crime. Why would someone call Donald Trump racist for no reason?

Look at the Brett Kavanaugh debacle. Thirty-five years after the fact, a woman insists—against the claims of her own friends who were with her at the time—that a grubby encounter took place at a house she didn't know, at a time she can't recall, with a guy with an unimpeachable track record of integrity. In a normal era, such a laughable accuser would not get the time of day. In our era, she gets canonized a secular saint and, having miraculously overcome her fear of flying, she now gets feted and lauded as a great heroine for…waiting a third of a century to offer shaky claims against a guy the establishment disapproved of. The fact that a couple of the other accusers either admitted lying, or effectively admitted lying by choosing judicial system–involved grifter Michael Avenatti as their legal counsel, just makes it worse.

Remember, believe all women, except ones complaining about Joe Biden's dastardly digits. Don't believe evidence; believe charges because of who makes them and because of their utility in achieving whatever political goal you have—be it taking back the White House or keeping it open season on fetuses.

Trump and Kavanaugh's response to the lies teaches a powerful lesson. They knew that the left would never abandon their lies. Kavanaugh's accuser could come out, put her hand on a Bible, and attest that she had been lying, and they would still claim, "See, I told you he was guilty!" But by standing strong and confronting the liars, you can convince normal people of the truth.

That's what Kavanaugh did. After the media informed us that his accuser was credible and compelling, Brett Kavanaugh came out and set the record straight. Facts matter to ordinary people of good faith, elite narratives be damned.

The defamation is only getting worse. The lies are multiplying, and we must be prepared to make our case to people of good will. The power of the media's deception means that we must fight every charge with courage. If we don't dispute their lies, accusations soon become verdicts.

It's annoying and frustrating, but in the end, defamation is a loser's game. Winners don't bludgeon their opponents into submission; they convince them by the strength of their cause. The fact that the left has gotten so desperate is proof that they are losing their grip on power. Defamation is not about truth; it's about power. By bringing their lies out into the open for all to see, we'll take away their power and strengthen our resolve to stand up to their attacks.

Let's get to the lies...

CHAPTER 1

Trump Is a Racist...
and You're a Bunch of Bigots Too!

Donald Trump is racist, as you may have heard once or twice. So very, very racist. He's the most racist of racists because of course he is. It's obvious, you see, from all the racism he is having. It's so obvious that there's no need to even list examples of his racist racism. He's racist, and racism is the alpha and omega of his racist movement.

And that makes you racist too. You've probably heard that since you came out as a Trump supporter. You are so very, very racist. You voted for Trump because of racism, you keep supporting him because of racism, and you probably have "RACIST" tramp-stamped just above your coccyx.

You might be shocked to hear that you are motived by racism. You don't think that you're racist, or that Trump is racist, or that you voted for Trump because you're both racists, but that's the story according to the Democrat Party, the mainstream media, the cultural elite, and all those riled-up college students running around our nation's campuses with their piercings and their daddy issues.

Trump is racist, and so are you. It's true, damnit. It *has* to be true. Racism *must* be the foundation of everything you believe.

Stop laughing. This is *serious*.

Except it's not serious, not anymore. There was a time when a lot of people really were racist, a time when cruel stereotypes and crude prejudices abounded and were openly expressed in public. But that time has long passed, and to most Americans the term "racist" has morphed from a soul-shaking accusation to a cynical lie used to stifle debate and compel obedience. Now, it's a cheesy punch line.

In millions of SUVs across America, the kids who used to screech, "Ashleigh is on my side of the seat!" to their harried moms are now howling, "Ashleigh is racisting at me!" and everyone laughs.

Leave it to the cultural left, the very people who pride themselves on their racial wokeness, to turn the serious accusation of racism into a joke. But that's what happens when you spend decades baselessly defaming your fellow Americans: you turn charges that we should take seriously into gags.

Remember the story of the gender non-specific youth who cried, "Wolf?" For decades, liars cried "racist," but when people looked around and noticed how few racists were wandering about America, they realized it was baloney.

But it's not baloney to the liars. To them, it's not even truth. It's more like a premise, a foundational notion, upon which all the other stupid notions they hold dear are built. As a result, the notion does not rely upon evidence or argument. In fact, challenging the notion of universal racism with evidence or argument is...you know where this train is headed.

Next stop, Racismburg—all aboard!

Donald Trump is racist because of course he is—how could he not be? He's bad, and racism is bad, so he must be racist. That's how their reasoning goes. But that's not reasoning in any meaningful sense; it's the opposite of reasoning. Reasoning uses facts and evidence to draw conclusions, whereas this works backwards from the conclusion to construct facts and evidence, a way of thinking we will see repeated over and over again.

Again, there is such thing as "racism." You may have heard some casual epithets tossed around in everyday life. But if you are older, you probably once heard folks stating loudly and unequivocally that certain racial groups were better than others—or worse—and not in the harmless manner of a comic observing that white people are often awkward dancers. No, there was real hate out there, ugly and vicious, stupid and cruel.

In the past, people's racial prejudices informed their personal lives and their politics. Lyndon B. Johnson—a Democrat, for those of you who went to public schools or to college in the last couple decades—famously had a, shall we say, negative view of black people. Other Democrats—again, if you were the victim of modern education this will come as a surprise—were even more forceful in their anti-black agenda, turning water hoses and vicious dogs on black Americans, and occasionally murdering them.

But let's fast-forward a half-century and some change to today, a time long after Democrats enshrined racism into law in the Jim Crow South. Things have changed for the better. When was the last time you personally heard a racial slur directed at a black person in a public place outside of a rap concert or some local chuckle hut?

It's been a while, hasn't it?

A whole generation of Americans has probably never heard those grotesque racial slurs used in anger. Race relations have gotten so good that the race-hustling liars are losing business. Now, when some slur is scrawled on a campus wall, we just begin the countdown until the inevitable revelation that it was a hoax designed to raise "awareness" of something that barely exists perpetrated by some social justice jerk.

America should get great credit for deciding, as a society, that we reject real racism. Many other countries haven't done the same. In societies around the world, racism is out in the open, loud and proud. And does anybody acknowledge our massive cultural achievement?

No. Instead, we hear about how the third decade of the twenty-first century is bubbling over with molten race hatred. You got nothing on us, early-nineteenth-century American South!

Weird, right?

Yes, that's one way to put it. Another way is to call it what it is: a bold-faced lie.

What does calling someone "racist" even mean anymore? We can get a clearer picture by taking Donald Trump as an example. What does it mean when the liars call President Trump "racist"? How exactly is he "racist"? What effect does this alleged "racism" have on his policies?

Those are good questions, and it is probably racist to ask them.

Here's the big secret: they don't have an actual definition of "racism" because not having a real definition is useful when you just want a tool to bludgeon your political opponents.

It was not always like that. Once, there was a general understanding that "racist" was a condition we could objectively diagnose.

Use racial slurs? Check!

Embrace and act upon nefarious stereotypes of people of other races? Check!

Are a member of the KKK? Check!

Well, that certainly seems to characterize a prominent and powerful politician of recent years, and it's not Donald Trump. That would be Democrat Senate Majority Leader Robert Byrd of West Virginia. You know, Hillary Clinton's senatorial mentor and noted KKK Exalted Cyclops Robert Byrd? He was a real paragon of racial unity. In a 1944 letter to Senator Theodore Bilbo, a fellow Democrat, Senator Byrd explained:

> I shall never fight in the armed forces with a negro by my side.... Rather I should die a thousand times, and see Old Glory trampled in the dirt never to rise again, than to see this beloved land of ours become degraded by race mongrels, a throwback to the blackest specimen from the wilds.

That's racism. Has Trump ever done or said anything even remotely close to that? I'd say we should look at the evidence, but there isn't any.

Is there a single recorded incident of Trump using racial slurs? If there were, you would have seen it about ten thousand times by now. In terms of damage, it would have made the *Access Hollywood* tape look like a cute kitty video on Facebook. It would have destroyed him. Trump's controversial comments regarding the willingness of women in his orbit to succumb to his charms almost took him out. Imagine what would happen if a Trump version of the Byrd–Bilbo Dialogues leaked.

There have been rumors circulating in the media ether that a tape like that exists, outtakes from *The Apprentice* where Trump let his Klan flag fly, so to speak. Tom Arnold, famous if at all only for not being good enough for Roseanne, has seen new life as a semi-professional Trump hater, and he spent a long time trying to dig up the goods. As with his comedy career, Arnold's efforts came to nothing. The fact is, dozens of media elites would drool over the opportunity to release anything reinforcing the "Trump = Racist" lie. The fact that we have yet to see any "bombshell" tape is compelling evidence that no such evidence exists. Plus, Trump has spent a lot of time on camera, *a lot*, and as we saw with his conversation with Billy Bush, he is not exactly guarded with his comments. If the great white supremacist whale that is the Trump racist-remarks video is swimming in the depths, one of the Trump-hunting Ahabs surely would have harpooned it by now.

There is just no evidence whatsoever that Trump uses racial slurs. But what about Trump's having views that characterize other races as inferior?

Well, there's… uh… okay, there's none of that either. And it's not as if Trump has ever been shy about going in front of a mic or tweeting his innermost thoughts. If he thought along the lines of noted Democrat icon Robert Byrd, odds are he would have made that quite clear in an all caps tweet by now.

The simple fact is that no example of Donald Trump's saying racist things is anywhere to be found in his voluminous public record. We would know if it were. Oh, would we know it.

But, of course, a lack of evidence is not a problem. After all, it's clear that Trump is racist because the liars said so. The narrative says that the bad man is racist, and the narrative cannot be wrong. What would we believe if we couldn't believe the narrative?

Our useless elites have three lies in their race-baiting playbook. First, they try to amplify the few actual racists in our country. There are undeniably a few obscure tiki torch–waving geeks marching around with their incel loser friends. At their largest gathering to date in Charlottesville, they numbered less than a thousand. But instead of portraying these dorks as a fringe movement, the media makes them seem commonplace. The racist losers love to play along: they're eager to bask in the spotlight the media shines on them. But the fact that these fringie weirdos get prime time coverage shows how few racists exist for the media to call out.

The second race-baiting play is the most common, where the liars consciously make false accusations to slander a rival. Look at Jussie Smollett or the Covington kids. Today, this is standing operating procedure, and it is not limited to Democrats. The Never Trump contingent, outraged and humiliated because actual conservatives saw through their grift, have adopted it too because True Conservatism™ means adopting the cheesiest and slimiest aspects of the left in order to enhance your own personal power and prestige.

Just look at how often leftists and Never Trumpers call the president racist. They all know it's a lie, but they say it anyway. And most of their supporters know it's a lie, but they still clap their flippers like trained seals.

The third kind of racism accusation is not just stupid, it's clinically insane. By this charge, some people are inherently racist because of their own race. If you're white, you're racist, and there's nothing you can do about it but atone for your racist sins. (Your sex and your preference don't help either—those cis white males are the *worst*.)

Wait, doesn't the idea that you have evil characteristics and should suffer poor treatment solely because of your race sounds a lot like…racism? See, what you thought was racism, well, it's not racism. In fact, it's racist to define racism that way. The new racism is much more flexible and much easier to use against opponents since it is completely untethered from any actual hatred of other races. It's the social justice warrior definition, SJW racism, and it's everywhere.

SJW racism theory holds that racism is not racism except when it is directed upwards on the hierarchy of racial oppression, where the powerful are at the bottom, and the oppressed are at the top. Under this definition, the supposedly more powerful identity groups can only be racist to less powerful identity groups.

Obviously, that leads to a lot of jockeying for position on the SJW identity pyramid. It may seem counterintuitive, but people want to be more "oppressed." When an oppressed racial group attacks other groups further up the intersectional food chain on racial grounds, they aren't racist, they're "empowered." In typical game theory, people compete with one another for higher positions of power. But in the social justice Grievance Olympics, less is more. The more you and your group are oppressed, the more points you can cash in to increase your own power.

There's plenty of competition for the "most oppressed status," but one thing all the identities agree on is that people of pallor are the least. They are the universal oppressors and the least oppressed. But fear not—anyone can be white if it the elites need them to be. Remember George Zimmerman, who shot the young thug pounding his head into the sidewalk? He was Hispanic, but that was awkward, so he became "white Hispanic." That way, he was a privileged oppressor and token of American racism. When his heritage almost derailed the narrative, they created a new one for him.

Phew, that was close.

And don't forget about anti-Semitism. The actual premise of "racism" used to be race, but it's now pretty much any identity that involves your great-great-grandfather's being from somewhere else. This means the "racist" rainbow includes anti-Semitism, to the extent the liars care about that. Trump, and you, are massive supporters of the Jewish state, yet the liars still find a way to call you both racist anti-Semites. With your support, Trump moved our embassy to Israel's capital, something no other president would do despite his promises. Trump's own daughter and grandchildren are observant Jews. Plus, there's not a word out there in his massive public record indicating anything but love and respect for the Children of Abraham. Of course, such overwhelming evidence cannot acquit him of the charge, just as no evidence is needed to support the charge. But hey, Trump is anti-Semitic because, well, that helps the narrative.

And while Trump hates Jews, he's also a raging Islamophobe. They try to base this one on a policy decision, but unsurprisingly the substance of the charge is bogus. Within weeks of moving into the Oval Office, President Trump signed an executive order banning visitors from several predominantly Muslim countries such as Iran, Iraq, Libya, Somalia, Syria, Sudan, and Yemen. But Trump didn't ban the listed countries because of their Muslim majorities; the listed countries are hellholes packed with violence and anti-American hatred. All of them are now or were recently embroiled in war, and only Sudan's doesn't involve American troops. Moreover, the policy allowed Muslims from Indonesia, Pakistan, Saudi Arabia, and every other Muslim-majority country on earth to travel to the United States. If Trump was trying to ban Muslims, he did a poor job.

When push comes to shove, anyone who voted for President Trump because he thought he was a racist must be disappointed. Before the Chinese coronavirus pandemic hit in early 2020, Trump's policies had driven minority unemployment rates to their lowest point in half a century. If Trump is a racist, he isn't a very effective one. This must be truly disappointing to him and to you, because of all your racism.

There is only one logical conclusion to draw: Trump is not a racist, not by any commonsense definition of the term. And as we've shown, you would have to accept the ridiculous SJW definition on faith to even begin to build a case. While white liberals with graduate degrees might be willing to buy into this notion—since the unspoken assumption is that they and their kids will not be the targets of the racial retribution envisioned by the SJWs—others are not so patient.

If racism is wrong, then it's wrong regardless of whether someone is a member of a group college professors consider "empowered" or not. The moral argument against racism, reinforced by Judeo-Christian notions of the dignity of the individual and the universality of natural rights, is incompatible with the SJW reappropriation of the term. The older view, put best by the Reverend Dr. Martin Luther King Jr. in his March on Washington speech, is that it is wrong to judge a human being by the color of his skin rather than the content of his character. That argument continues to resonate with Americans because it is so obviously and manifestly true. Plus, it applies to everyone. In that sense, it is fair.

The new notion of "racism" is a reversal of the principle that this country was built on. Under the old definition of racism, the one that ordinary folks still believe, the new definition is itself racist, insofar as it begins from the premise that people's moral standing rests on the basis of race.

And it is unfair. Evenhandedness is important. You can convince people to give up advantages and resources and to otherwise act contrary to their strict self-interest if you can convince them that fairness to others requires it. People don't patiently stand in the checkout line at the grocery store behind that nimrod who still uses checks because they enjoy standing there perusing the *National Enquirer* headlines. They don't push their way to the front of the queue, because the other person got there first, and it's not fair to cut. It's human nature.

That's why people don't cheat most of the time. Most of the time, people play by the rules and hope to get the results they deserve. They believe that the rules should be the same for everyone, that we are created equal, and that the system should reward merit.

The SJW racism rules are not fair. Their definition of racism rejects fairness as an ideal. Some identities are afforded special rights, dispensations, and protections, while others are subject to sanctions. And it's done under a vague, secular mask of morality. Except—one of the disadvantaged might wonder—why am I forced to play by different rules than someone else? And why am I always in the wrong no matter how well I adhere to the rules?

See, that's one of the problems: even if you follow the rules, the liars may end up calling you a racist anyway. And according to their definition, they would be right. For SJWs, nothing you do as a white person can remove your racist nature. It's a bizarre twist on Christianity in that the racial sinner, in the SJW's eyes, cannot be redeemed through acts. You cannot overcome your race, your place on the pyramid o' oppression, simply by not being racist. No, you need grace—the grace that the SJWs bestow upon those who believe in their dogma. You can even buy indulgences by giving money to their charities or getting a degree in race studies.

In other words, you have to accept their neo-Marxist ideology in order to be saved.

Race is the original sin. You were born the wrong race and will not be in a state of grace until you completely submit to the oppression merchants. Acts don't matter; only faith can redeem you. The SJWs call it "unconscious racism." "Unconscious racism" means that you can be a racist without even knowing it. It's not volitional. It's not a choice. It's not who you are as a person, but what you are as a racial identity. Which is, of course, exactly what people rejected when they rejected traditional racism.

While Donald Trump simply ignores the SJW definition of racism, he wholeheartedly embraces the traditional definition of racism, as do his supporters. Normal people look at a game where the rules compel them to lose and to beg forgiveness for what they never did, and they refuse to play. But when you refuse to play, they only call you racist more, not because you discriminate against certain races, but because you utterly refuse to. You refuse to buy into a hateful new paradigm of bizarre regulations and intersectional relationships designed to ensure the cultural and political power of a bitter band of Frankfurt School kids.

Your refusal is poison to their entire worldview. The racism lie can only succeed when its targets accept it. Otherwise, it's just a pack of pinko professors, hipster doofuses, millennial internet geeks, and other liberal losers whining in the darkness.

One of the beautiful things about Trump is that his decades of battling the lying New York media market have made him utterly immune to the urge so many conservatives have to submit to the lie, humble themselves, and seek absolution.

He knows he's no racist. He knows you are no racist. And he knows that whatever he does, the liars will lie about your and his being racist. And so, he refuses to play their game. You should too.

CHAPTER 2

Trump Is Stupid...
and You Idiots Are Too!

I don't tell war stories often, not because I'm particularly humble, but because my wartime duties largely consisted of running a heavily armed carwash out in the middle of the desert. Epic tales of decontamination operations are a bit esoteric for most crowds. But I have one story that applies to one of the more tiresome lies about Donald Trump and his supporters—that they are dumb.

It's early 1991 in the Arabian Desert. The Persian Gulf War—that would be Iraq 1.0—was about to begin. I was with VII Corps, the greatest, most powerful military formation in human history. VII Corps was one of the two armored corps (about 100,000 strong each) tasked with defending West Germany from the Soviets back when we all agreed that the Russians were the bad guys. After the Berlin Wall fell and Saddam Hussein launched his invasion, VII Corps got shipped out to liberate Kuwait. We had the best equipment, the best trained troops, the best leadership, and the most sophisticated battlefield operating systems of any force ever assembled.

And we prepared to fight what we assumed was an enemy of equal strength.

The Iraqi Republican Guard consisted of Saddam's best troops, elite warriors skilled in Soviet tactics and operating cutting-edge Soviet equipment that they had maintained to the peak of readiness. VII Corps was going right at these forces, and we were projected to take heavy casualties in a hard slog against a motivated, effective foe.

VII Corps crossed the line of contact and blasted through the Iraqis like they were not even there, annihilating brigade after brigade until the Iraqi side of the Arabian Desert was a junkyard of smoking T-72s and smashed BTR-60s. Thousands of ragged conscript Iraqi soldiers surrendered in droves, while the ones who kept fighting faced certain death. I watched it unfold from the VII Corps main command post. The war was over so fast that my platoon never got to move north.

How does that anecdote relate to the big lie that Trump and his supporters are a bunch of dummies?

Because underestimating your enemy is a grave strategic error.

Always prepare to fight the strongest possible opponent, not the one you hope to face. *Overestimate* your enemy, don't underestimate him. Don't be George Armstrong Custer, who surveyed the rolling hills at Little Big Horn and decided that he and his cavalrymen could easily take on Elizabeth Warren's ancestors. That went poorly.

The idea that Donald Trump and his supporters are stupid is not just a strategic mistake, it's manifestly untrue. Yet our lying elites cannot resist the temptation to slander their political rivals. Why? Because our elites rest their claim to rule on qualities they attribute to themselves— "goodness," "sophistication" and, of course, "intelligence."

Those elites may have made decades of mistakes, but hey, they're *smart*. That's why they come up with increasingly abstract ways to justify their position in society. It's not as if they can fall back on a list of stunning achievements. Taylor Swift? The opioid epidemic? Grindr? Those are not exactly comparable to putting a man on the moon.

Excuse me, a non–gender specified human person on the moon. We don't want to forget their accomplishment of creating an exhaustive vocabulary of woke terminology.

Posing as smart is central to the elitist liars' self-image. Calling everyone who disagrees with them a slack-jawed moron is crucial to their self-worth. Just look at their entertainment. The Stephen Colberts and Jon Stewarts of the world make their audiences think that they are part of an exclusive coterie of witty, urbane, intelligent people. The audience laughs even when they don't quite get the joke, clapping along because they want to be part of the club. If you get the joke, you're smart. You've identified yourself as one of the cosmopolitan citizens of the world, nothing like those backwards American rubes in flyover country.

You know, like Trump and those buffoons who voted for him, many of whom truly believe the Jesus and Moses stuff. Those parochial know-nothings don't understand white privilege, or how socialism works, or that the Pilgrims were pretty much running a slave market at Plymouth Rock. Isn't that what the *New York Times's* "1619 Project" said?

It's fun to look down on others. It's also flattering. Every time the elites insult us with some lie about our tragic cerebellum deficit, they build themselves up. They reinforce their own aura of superiority. But that's not worked out particularly well.

See, Trump is a lot of things, but he is certainly not dumb. And his supporters are also many things, but you couldn't call them dumb. Well, I guess you *could*, but you'd be dumb to do it.

Oh, there are certainly idiots who back the president. Trump won over sixty million votes, and statistics demands that some of them are half-wits and nimrods. But no reasonable, rational analysis would find that his average voter is a nincompoop.

Yet their opponents assume that, and it has worked out poorly for them.

If President Trump is so stupid, how did he beat Hillary Clinton? In fact, he did more than beat her. He pummeled her, in large part by winning Midwestern states she fully expected to win. The Smartest Woman in the World™ was beaten by someone she considers a drooling idiot.

So, what does that make Hillary?

Isn't it possible that perhaps the person who beat you is not, in fact, your inferior? Maybe he's your superior. Maybe he's smarter, more capable, and better than you, and maybe he just proved it by getting what you both wanted.

The sound you hear is liberal heads exploding.

Trump looked at the situation and saw vulnerabilities in Hillary's strategy, then exploited them ruthlessly to take the Oval Office. Hillary looked at the situation, decided that the ordinary rules didn't apply to her because she is so darned intelligent, canceled her trip to Wisconsin, and ended up doing morning drive radio hits on "Captain Kooky and The Geebo's Morning Zoo."

She flushed the biggest gimme election in American history down the crapper, and Donald Trump pulled off the most amazing upset in American history. And Trump's the dumb one?

Maybe it depends on how you define "smart." We could call intelligence the ability to use brainpower to achieve goals. But that wouldn't work for the "smart" people; they haven't achieved anything!

So instead of admitting that you're an idiot, why not get rid of embarrassing metrics that focus on real-world accomplishments and develop an obsession with credentials instead? Our elites collect this diploma and that internship, and, bedecked with all these badges and ribbons, they present themselves as accomplished. But what have they actually *done*? Today, degrees from the most prestigious university often mean little more than a high-end liberal brainwashing. Once you matriculate, unless you get booted out on a trumped-up harassment charge or come out as conservative, you're pretty much a lock to graduate. Some college students work hard, take advantage of the opportunity to learn and grow, and graduate knowing how to think. They may even have learned some things to think about. Others just come out knowing how to "feel," whine, and fetch lattes.

These are not indicia of intelligence. They are bad habits that would have been stamped out if academia had not become such a joke.

The only thing you can be certain of when presented with an academic credential from a prestigious university is that its bearer was an overachieving sixteen-year-old who aced his SAT, or that his dad was a Democrat senator who got his kid into the Ivy League with a phone call to the dean of admissions.

Speaking of the Bidens, is there anyone out there who has the word "smart" pop into his head when he sees Joe Biden? If not for the amazing luck that allowed him to stumble into the Senate, then into the White House with Obama, he probably would be spending his days at home eating Malt-O-Meal and watching his stories on the TV.

The smart people insist that Joe Biden is smart, but Donald Trump is dumb. Let that mind-blowing notion ricochet around your head for a while.

One factor that makes the "Trump and you are dumb" lie irresistible to elites is that Trump rejects the kind of intellectual posturing that they adore. His doesn't try to project his intelligence by carrying a David Foster Wallace novel into a Starbucks, front cover out so everyone can see that he's carrying a David Foster Wallace novel. Trump has no interest in whether you think he's got brains. He has a great deal of interest in winning. He's cunning and cagey, with a clear and comprehensive understanding of human nature. His natural talents were honed not by Wharton, but by his real estate development work, a field where failures suffer real consequences.

That's an important distinction between Trump and most of the elites. Trump's intelligence (and yours) has metrics. It has deliverables. But for the elite, intelligence is often demonstrated by a much-retweeted tweet. It's amusing that Donald Trump is the undisputed master of Twitter. He seems to delight in being better than the elite at the things they find important, like social media and winning national elections.

The elites' species of intelligence frequently delivers nothing but meaningless self-validation. In academia, esteemed teachers never have to build anything. They're never held accountable for anything. A good teacher, a bad teacher, an innovative researcher, a leftist scholar regurgitating stale Herbert Marcuse leftovers—it's all the same. With tenure, nothing matters. You've got a gig forever. In real estate, you go bankrupt when you screw up.

Hollywood is another elite bastion of stupidity masquerading as smarts. In Hollywood, most of the actors are secretly ashamed that they never went and got those fancy degrees and diplomas that the suits who surround them have. They think that if they just mimic the shrill wokeness of their credentialed liberal associates, they can be part of the smart set too.

It's so unnecessary. Actors, at least good ones—so we can leave the Kristen Stewarts and Mark Hamills out of this discussion—are not necessarily intellectually inferior. They just focus on different things than, say, someone who minored in Mongolian Transsexual Poetry. And, arguably, that focus requires more intellectual effort than the man-bunned grad student's unreadable dissertation.

The "Trump and his supporters are stupid" lie privileges—there's that word—the kind of intellectual effort that the liars are most comfortable with. Those exercises usually end up being of the navel-gazing ilk.

Sometimes it's law. Lots of people think lawyers are smart, but hang around a few courthouses and watch the morning motion-calendar circus, and you'll be rapidly disabused of that notion. Passing a bar exam requires little more than a few weeks of sleepless nights, some luck, and a few handfuls of Adderall.

People think teachers are smart. Again, interview a few millennial applicants and see if you still believe that an education degree indicates a particularly sharp intellect. And what about bureaucrats? Oh, they're all geniuses. Most of the "smart" set are white-collar types who push paper from one cubicle to the next and imagine that their lives have meaning.

It's not that they're all dumb, but a lot of them aren't smart in any meaningful sense of the word. That's why they cower behind their credentials when they're confronted by an argument that makes them uncomfortable.

By any objective criteria, Donald Trump has managed to demonstrate his own intellectual aptitude by regularly defeating those who consider him their inferior. And he loves to rub it in—remember the "very stable genius" business that sent his opponents into paroxysms of outrage a few dozen outrages ago? Moreover, his tweets are filled with typos, malapropisms, and bizarre capitalization choices that must be as agonizing as fingernails on a chalkboard to the smart set hate-reading his mini-missives. Maybe he just likes to torment his foes. Do not underestimate the chance of that.

The stupidity slander is even more obnoxious when directed at his followers. It is also self-defeating because you cannot possibly reach out and appeal to people you call "idiots." Ask yourself: have you ever seen a Trump voter who said, "Yeah, I'm going back to the Democrats because they respect me?"

Trump voters are not necessarily smart in the way the smart set defines "smart." They care about degrees and prestige. And while studies have shown that a lower percentage of Trump supporters have advanced degrees, the credentials often aren't worth the piece of paper they're printed on, much less the two hundred grand they cost. So, what evidence is there that support for Donald Trump correlates to intellectual inferiority?

None.

Part of this is a class issue. The credentialled gentry largely support the Democrats, alongside some of the simpering sellouts of the Republican Never Trump contingent. They find Americans who build or drive or fight for a living to be lesser beings fit only to serve and obey. That predated Trump, though at one time the Democrats claimed to be the Party of the Working Man. Now it's the Party of the Non-Binary Who Works at Google.

Lots of people who labor in tech are smart, though only in their narrow band of expertise. There are plenty of Silicon Valley types who drive their Priuses down Interstate 280 to Cupertino and know how to code but can't change their own tire. If, by some stroke of fate or cosmic justice, civilization were to come crashing down, would you rather be the guy who invented the Twitter Blue Check or the guy who knows how to trap a juicy squirrel with a field-expedient snare?

Not too long ago, we smelled gas around my yard. With my three advanced degrees from institutions of such selectivity that most Santa Monica helicopter parents would wet themselves at the thought of their progeny's getting admitted, I formed a plan.

I called the plumber because he knew what the hell he was doing, and for all my fancy book-learning, my intervention probably would have blasted my neighborhood flat.

"Smart" is often just the ability to perform adequately in a given context.

Think of farmers, those sturdy tillers of the soil. Put aside the fact that a good number of them have actual agriculture degrees that involve science and not terms like "colonialist hegemony" or "patriarchal paradigm." Even without Ivy League sheepskins, these are guys who literally have to skin sheep. Can you skin a sheep? Can you raise a sheep? Can you tell a sheep from a goat? I think one of them, maybe the goat, eats tin cans or something.

And can you tell what plant goes where, or when it has to be planted, or what you have to do to make it grow? And those are only the horticultural aspects of farming, which requires more than just the growing of food and husbanding of animals. What about the business side of it? You have to figure out your costs, calculate your potential gross, and make deals, all while jousting with an invasive federal government.

I couldn't be a farmer. Unless you are a farmer, and I hope there are farmers reading this, you probably couldn't be a farmer either. But because the farmer may not have devoured the latest novel that Oprah selected for her book club, or because he does not hold all the same lockstep views as the nonconformist rebels who make up our elite, he is not stupid. Perhaps angry little Mike Bloomberg thinks farmers are dumb, but no one piloting a John Deere tractor spent a billion bucks to win the American Samoa Democrat primary.

The same goes for a truck driver, or a cop, or a car dealer, or a soldier. The noxious lie that these people are stupid only reflects the status insecurity of people who often make and do nothing of substance but want to retain—at least in their own minds—their delusion of superiority.

They want to look down on those unsophisticated simpletons who follow Jesus or read the Torah. They want to look down on those unsophisticated simpletons who tear up when the flag passes by. They want to look down on those unsophisticated simpletons who refuse to join the weather cult. They want to look down on those unsophisticated simpletons who defend their country.

And sometimes, the defamers paste the "dummy" label onto Trump supporters not just because of their cheesy class prejudices, but because they think that voting for Trump is itself self-defeating stupidity. They purport to know and understand the interests of the Trump voters better than the Trump voters themselves. What amazing hubris.

Truth be told, the people who look down upon Trump supporters are themselves the best argument for supporting Donald Trump. Their contempt for their countrymen is reason enough to elect someone, anyone, other than whomever these jumped-up snobs prefer. In what world would people vote for their own oppressors?

That would be, well, stupid.

Trump does not think his supporters are stupid. He sees them as he sees most everyone else, as people pursuing their own self-interest. In their case, that self-interest is not sending their kids off to fight some objective-free war in Whocaresistan. That self-interest is an unemployment rate approaching zero and reining in a government that wants to dictate how they worship God.

The liars, you see, believe that you are entirely unfit to govern your own life, let alone the country. That's what they mean when they refer to you and other Trump supporters as stupid. Since you don't have one of their fancy degrees, you don't know what's good for you. Their condescension is the unspoken assumption undergirding the progressive nanny-state ideology that Hillary Clinton embodied. In the end, only the woke elect have the smarts to get a say.

Remember, if we allow the wrong people to participate in politics, they might run Facebook ads that swing the election. Scratch that: the elites don't call advertisements they don't like ads anymore, they call them "disinformation" and want to regulate them off the face of the earth. It's their new boogeyman, and the backwards need their wise moral betters to distinguish between "the truth" and "fake news" and save them from themselves. And, just by happenstance, those wise elders will share all the views of the liars who want to defame their fellow Americans. How convenient.

Hillary and her sobbing supporters said the same thing in the wake of her humiliating defeat on November 8, 2016, and they didn't even have the decency to be subtle about it. But these geniuses, these people who were so much smarter than everyone else, overlooked the implications of their position. If Hillary lost in the Midwest because the natural Hillary voters who would have otherwise voted for her were so dumb as to be manipulated by some online clickbait posted by Macedonian troll farms, isn't she really saying that those natural Hillary voters are dumb people? That those idiots were "with her" by right?

That does not seem smart.

Trump keeps coming up against the people who think he is dumb, and he keeps on beating them. When will they learn? Imagine if they were as smart as they think they are. Imagine if they did what VII Corps did and fought a stronger enemy than they were facing, rather than a much, much weaker one. Perhaps they might occasionally celebrate a victory themselves.

But don't hold your breath. The ongoing lie that Donald Trump and his supporters are stupid is not based on facts or evidence, and it can't be reasoned away. It's too central to the liars' egos. They have to be "smart," because they need something to tell themselves to ease the sting of failure.

CHAPTER 3

Trump Hates LGBT People...
and So Do You
Cisgender Monsters!

Let's assume that Donald Trump actually hates LGBTQ-whatever-whatever-whatever people. He doesn't, and you don't, but once again anything that's "bad" according to the liars has to be one of Donald Trump's defining characteristics (and yours too). So, let's get past the troublesome, narrative-derailing facts and get to the substance of the claim.

Let's start by defining our operative acronym. What is LGBTQ-whatever-whatever-whatever anyway?

The "L" is "lesbian," and supposedly Trump hates lesbians. Duly noted, though of all guys Trump seems the least likely to dislike lesbians. They have so much to talk about.

"G" is "gay." Trump hates "gay" people? Does this include lesbians, which would make the acronym redundant, or is this just gay males? Why not "GP," for "gay people?" Really, doesn't defining people as either "lesbian" or "gay" impose some sort of binary paradigm upon them?

"B" is for "bisexual." Got it. Always smart to keep your options open.

And "T" is for "trans" or "transgender," which is strange because the "T" concept is not like the others. A trans person may or may not be

L, G, B and/or Q. If you want to be exact, trans is not a sexual preference, it's a gender identity. And exactness is really, really important to the people who care about this stuff.

That's why we have "identities" that are cocktails of made-up genders and sexual preferences—"two spirits," "non-binaries," and "intersex" identities that you need a masters in gender studies to understand. And then there are the extremes: pansexual pretty much covers everything, while asexual means you once wrote for the *Weekly Standard*.

Just kidding. Real asexuals choose to be without romantic partners.

LGBT is often followed by a "Q," for "queer," which is a nasty slur but has apparently been reclaimed by some people to identify themselves. But wait, sometimes the "Q" is for "questioning." Those "Qs" must have no idea what the hell is happening sex-wise. So maybe it should be LGBTQQ, just for the sake of being thorough.

So, now that we have defined our terms, we are…right back where we started. The baffling nomenclature of sexual identity leaves those of us who haven't stepped foot on a college campus in a few years puzzled and confused. Unsurprisingly, that includes many gay people who simply want to mind their own business without fussing over precise categories defining their situations.

Of course, the fact that this is all a head-scratcher for most people means that most people are…wait for it…homophobic, which itself seems a pretty limited term. Shouldn't there be a catchall for people insufficiently versed in the arcane typology of human desire and self-definition?

But "homophobic" will have to do, and our moral betters are dead set on calling you and Donald Trump homophobes.

But is he really? Are you?

Let's break this down again by starting with "L."

Where does Trump stand on lesbians? Has Donald Trump ever even mentioned lesbians? Are there any tweets out there slamming lesbians? Sure, he's tweeted a lot, and it's easy to forget specific mini-missives, but writing something about lesbians would have triggered a five-alarm media inferno. True, Trump has exchanged barbed words with Rosie O'Donnell, but there are myriad reasons to dislike that belligerent harpy besides her erotic inclinations.

Trump's Twitter record doesn't say anything about lesbians. How about his political record? Well, Trump famously supported gay marriage before Barack Obama. That's not to say opposing same sex marriage is homophobic, but the liars often use that as a right-think test which Trump supposedly fails.

We also know that Trump nominated Judge Mary Rowland, an open lesbian, to the U.S. District Court for the Northern District of Illinois. Did he forget that she's a lesbian, or does he not harbor bigotry against our sapphic citizens? Of course, "facts" and "evidence" don't actually prove or disprove anything when it comes to slandering the president.

Are the rest of us who support Trump down on the "L?" How many times have you been around like-minded conservatives and gotten into long discussions of the perfidy of women who dig other women? For me, that would be zero. This has happened to me no times. One could imagine an agitated speaker haranguing a gathering of conservatives about the lesbian peril, and the men replying, "Women making out—oh yeah, we gotta put a stop to that pronto."

No one cares. Ellen does not draw our ire. She seems nice, and we're happy to have her in our homes. Some of us have lesbian relatives, friends, or co-workers. Others just shrug. Still others think it's hot. But as far as being on The Big List of Things That Rile-Up Trump Supporters, chicks digging other chicks would be way down at the bottom.

And just like that, we arrive at "G"—"gay." Again, Trump's not shy about expressing controversial opinions, but you would be hard-pressed to find the tweet where he took on gay men. If he thought it, we would know it. Remember, Trump is a rich New Yorker, and his wife was a supermodel. It's safe to say he's met a couple gay people. Yet, despite the instant fame and publicity it would bring, there are no gay people testifying about Trump howling, "I rebuke thee, ye sodomites!"

Donald Trump bears no secret grudge against gay men—thinking he does is just plain silly. The man famously nominated Ric Grenell as our ambassador to Germany, a position of central importance to President Trump's plan to recalibrate our relationship with Europe. So far, His Excellency has been the administration's point man on prodding the euroweasels to pull their NATO weight and not to cavort with the mullahs in Tehran, and his appointment as acting director of National Intelligence provokes widespread wailing and gnashing of teeth in D.C.

Why do I spend so much time talking about Grenell? Because Mitt Romney, prior to botching a winnable campaign against Obama, famously fired Ric from his foreign policy team for being gay. Plus, the example of Ric Grenell would fully exonerate President Trump and his supporters if the charges were accusations subject to falsification. Full disclosure: Ric Grenell lives in the same town as the author, and the author and his wife have often been out to dinner with Ric and his husband. It's weird to stumble upon an ambassador to a major European power browsing through the produce section at Trader Joe's. Fuller disclosure: the author is willing to bet money that the first openly gay president will be a Republican and will additionally bet that his name will be Ric Grenell. More on that in a later chapter.

The author doesn't just support Ric because he sees him out shopping; lots of hard-core conservatives support him as well, including thousands of grizzled veteran non-commissioned officers who adore Ric's total support for our troops and utter fearlessness in confronting America's timid allies. Take that, knuckle-dragger stereotypes. This is part of the long evolution in how conservatives see gay Americans. Twenty years ago, Ric couldn't be on the Conservative Hot 100 list and moving up the charts with a bullet. But this is not twenty years ago.

Many on the right have embraced the small but growing cadre of gay conservatives. Sure, there is still some reticence about gay marriage, particularly among religious conservatives, but much of the hesitation stems the fact that the Obergefell decision mandated marriage as a constitutional right from the top down. Nothing that the Founding Fathers wrote makes any mention of same-sex marriage; pointing that out doesn't mean that you harbor a grudge against gay people. Regardless, gay conservatives have been in the fight, and they are now part of the team.

The relationship between gays and the Republicans, which remains the party of necessity for conservatives in the Age of Trump, has long been fraught. Here's a shocker: there have always been gay Republicans. Most of them were just pretty good at hiding it from the public, but we always knew it. We just considered them "ours" and never held it against them.

It was like that in the military. I was dealing with gay soldiers in the 1980s, and while it was technically possible to get booted out for homosexuality, gay soldiers who didn't make their sexuality their superiors' business—unlike the guy caught with a boy in his wall locker during a weekend inspection—flew under the radar. Loyalty trumped acceptance. "Sure, he's gay," people thought, "but he's our gay."

"Don't ask, don't tell" (DADT) was the general rule long before Bill Clinton signed it into law in 1993, and afterwards nothing much changed. We all knew who was gay in our unit, and the policy worked well, at least for those of us who were not gay. That's why so many of us approached the 2011 repeal of DADT with trepidation. My concern was chaos in the ranks and double standards in discipline. I was a lieutenant colonel and former battalion commander by then, and I knew I could deal with a straight soldier's disruptive sexual shenanigans, but would I get the back-up from the top to discipline a gay soldier's?

President Obama signed the bill into law, and in those days—before the Trump Exception™—unelected government officials were expected to obey the elected president of the United States, even when we did not agree with him. So we saluted and implemented the policy.

Nothing changed.

Nothing, at least in my experience and in the experience of other senior leaders I spoke to. Sure, there were a few news reports of troubling injustices elsewhere, chaplains hassled for not giving homosexuality a thumbs-up and the like, but in general, nothing happened. Military life drummed on as usual.

Now, this was not what I had expected, nor did it fit the narrative of many conservatives. We expected major disciplinary problems that never arose. Of course, this was in the early 2010s, so the evidence we observed changed our views. Today, evidence that challenges one's preconceived notions must be disregarded, those presenting such evidence must be labeled "deniers," and you must double-down on your pre-existing beliefs. But back then, in the hazy past, many of us conservatives realized that some of our concerns were unfounded and changed our minds.

That's not to say there was not an adjustment period. I recall standing at a change of command ceremony for a battalion with another full bird as the incoming battalion commander introduced her female life partner. The other colonel remarked, "Well, it's a new Army." It was, but for many, many reasons besides the incoming commanding officer's main squeeze.

The conservative experience with gays in the military and with gay conservatives in civilian life changed the paradigm within which many of us viewed gays. Now, gays are not merely tolerated but welcomed. The excesses of gay leftist activists—like the attacks on religious folks and the bizarre nonsense some activists seek to inject into school curricula—has come to be understood not as essentially gay but as essentially leftist. We've come to realize that the "leftist" part trumps the "gay" part. If you take a gay leftist activist and a feminist leftist activist, you will not find an iota of policy difference between them. That's why gay conservatives and feminist conservatives are, in the eyes of the left, simply conservatives, and therefore the enemy.

And now conservatives see that. They see conservative lesbians and gays as allies, and conservative lesbians and gays see conservatives as their only friends since the left considers them enemies.

Now, back to the acronym.

"B" is for "bi," and the notion that bisexuals come in for any conservative calumny is ridiculous. Trump certainly doesn't care. If he is not anti-lesbian or anti-gay, he is certainly not anti–folks-who-demonstrate-sexual-flexibility. Nor are the conservative Americans who support him.

Of course, Katie Hill, the kinky former congresswoman from California, claimed that she was a victim of discrimination when her cannabis-friendly, San Fernando Valley freaknik lifestyle blew up in her face less than a year into her term thanks to RedState reporter Jennifer Van Laar. For those who somehow missed the story: various photos came out depicting the congresswoman's multi-faceted relationships with men and women, some of whom she employed, and some of whom were apparently enlisted in a "throuple" with her erstwhile hubby. Together, in a display of the good judgment that made her appointment to the House Armed Services Committee a chef's kiss to Democrat seriousness about classified information security, she and her hubby allegedly posted her nudie pics on the web in forums with titles like "Wifesharing" and "WouldYouF**kMyWife." Nancy Pelosi quickly arm-twisted her resignation in order to avoid a Republican victory in the next election, as Hill occupied a—if you would pardon the expression—swing seat.

Hill was not the victim of a giant anti-bi conspiracy, but of her own tawdry couplings with employees. The "B" in "LGBT" is simply not a basis for the bigotry the left imagines infects Trump and his supporters.

The case of the "Ts" is more nuanced.

The "T" is "trans" or "transgender," and this letter is not like the others. The "LGB" in "LGBT" refer to matters of sexual attraction: gay men are gay because they are attracted to men, just as lesbians are lesbians because they're attracted to women. The "T," in contrast, refers to what someone believes him-, her-, or xis-self to be. Being transgender isn't a matter of your objective sexual attraction to someone, but your subjective experience of yourself—even when that experience is completely delusional.

If you are lesbian, gay, or bisexual, that's what you are. You really are lesbian, gay, or bisexual. (Unless you're an upper middle-class girl in a prestigious college trying to freak out daddy—then it's probably temporary.) But if you are a woman who believes she is a man, well, you're not, and you never will be.

So what do the militant transsexuals and their backers among the ruling elite want? They want you to affirm something that is factually false, and that everyone knows damn well is factually false, as a loyalty oath to the leftist cultural narrative.

When leftists insist that men can have periods and women can be fathers, they show the world how far they've departed from reality. But it's also brilliant in the way it makes those who agree complicit.

Trump bears no ill will towards transgender Americans, nor do his supporters. Indeed, conservatives generally feel compassion for them. Again, you can pan for defamatory gold in his tweets, but you will not come up with a single nugget of transphobia. It's clear from decades in the public eye, followed by the microscopic-level scrutiny that followed his descent down the escalator to announce his candidacy in 2015, that Trump is not and has never been some sort of bigot who despises the gender-shifting citizenry. Nor are his supporters.

Why would they be?

The classic drag queens of the past were sassy and campy, and they were less about sexual identity than celebrating exaggerated female attributes. They were always divas, not librarians. And it was not clear that they wanted to, or did, live their lives as women out of the spotlight. The militant trans folks of today, the ones driving the trans train, are a different phenomenon entirely.

The general feeling of conservatives toward these people is compassion. While we may not believe that it's possible to be a man trapped in a woman's body or vice-versa, we can all see that trans people are in distress and want to help them. Feeding people with "gender dysphoria" lies ripped from an ideological playbook fails to recognize the pain and confusion of people suffering under a delusion. It encourages people to drastically and irreversibly alter their bodies through chemical and surgical procedures, which often leave the "patient" just as alienated as before. That's not helping anybody.

Bruce Jenner, now Kaitlin Jenner, was a legendary athlete. He was not going to do the radical and irrevocable things he felt necessary to try to conform himself into being a herself without real mental and emotional pain driving him to do so. And Trump supporters see that. It's not a joke to them—it's sad, because he can never truly be a she.

So, the conservative position is that transgender people don't need any more pain in their lives, and we have no desire to add to it. No one wants to increase the weight they carry. Conservatives offer compassion and support. But to some on the cultural left, that's not enough.

The left demands validation, the affirmation that a man who wishes he were a woman, or a woman who wishes she were a man, can become one. They're trying to force people to concede that $2 + 2 = 5$, just as Orwell predicted. Among themselves, affirming lies is an act of solidarity to reject objective reality in favor of their constructed utopias. When demanded of others, it's a power move, a test of wills.

They exert power over you by forcing you to admit what everyone knows is a lie. A man can never become a woman, no matter how much he may want it to happen. The leftists know it, but again, the lie is an act of solidarity, a confession of loyalty that transcends the surly bonds of objective reality. And you know it too, which makes your concession an act of submission.

The trans craze of the last few years isn't the civil rights frontier it's made out to be. It's a full-blown assault on the meaning of human experience. By tearing down our commonsense experience, the liars can pave the way for the New Man (or New Woman, or New Non-Binary Entity, or whatever) that the leftists have always tried to create. They tried to remake human nature in the French Revolution, in the USSR, and in Red China. Here, they started their campaign to remake us on college campuses, which are the only places with enough dumb people per square foot to give this kind of insanity a foothold to fester and spread.

In the eyes of the gender activists, sex underlies everything—and they have a point. The nuclear family is both a rigidly gendered institution and the elemental building block of Western civilization. It is a powerful counter-institution resistant to collective control. Undermining the family has been the left's end goal for decades, and woke gender ideology is just another wave of the attack. If you deny the reality of gender, then the family unit collapses. It's like pulling the foundation out from under a building and expecting the façade to keep standing.

And what do you think will fill the power vacuum in society after the family collapses? Government. And guess whom the leftists intend to run that government? Hint: it ain't you, or anyone like you, or anyone you might vote for…

Is it all starting to make sense?

The ritual repetition of the official lie that men are women and women are men serves a purpose. Mass indoctrination always starts with little things. Remember the bathroom and locker room intrusions? That was only the start. Today, they're exposing children to "drag queen story hours." And, of course, there is also the de-gendering of children by Mommy Munchausens-by-proxy, delighted to learn that they are now interesting because their little Zander is really little McKenna.

And we get slandered because we don't want to participate in their little games. Newsflash: refusing to play along is not bigotry, it's resisting an unprovoked cultural assault. We have no intention of morphing America into a sexless collective of gender-neutral Eloi until the Morlocks, who don't play these silly games, come along and ring the dinner bell.

Our enemies, like the Red Chinese, the Norks, and those jihadi freaks have a lot of faults, but they all know which restroom to use. How long will we?

And the pronoun thing—really?

Just when you think Democrats like Elizabeth Warren can't out-pander their last pander, they drop the performative "My pronouns are…" like they are a Collectivist Mime major meeting someone for the first time at a Wellesley mixer.

Part of me thinks that all the left's crazy gender talk would be fine if they just kept it to themselves. But they can't do that, can they? No, instead they tell us that we have an obligation to address some twenty-year-old "Olivia" from Connecticut with "ze," "zir" or "zirs," because ze now wants to be called "Oliver."

No.

Normal people go along to get along. We don't offend others because we want to be polite. That's a good thing and a sign of a healthy people. But the liars want to take advantage of our good manners and drop us into their vortex of crazy.

Americans truly are nice people. Aside from New Yorkers, most of us want to be kind, friendly, and inoffensive. And the liars use that default kindness to get around the obvious response to their collective insanity, which is, "Nah, that's stupid, and I'm not doing that because it's stupid."

So, if someone you know is transitioning and sincerely asks you to use his new name "Belinda," you can do it if you want. But you don't have to. You don't have to assure the world that you are a good little drone who sees the emperor's new clothes, and you don't have to believe it.

This might be a kindness to your friend, but a kindness to your friend does not include an obligation to lie and concede that your friend is now a girl, because he will never be a girl. The cause of his pain is not your refusal to embrace a lie. The culprit is biology. Don't accept that your telling the truth is the problem, instead of the gender dysphoria your friend suffers from.

Where does all this lead? Will we become some sort of Sweden, which has fallen far from its Viking days of glory and now leads the world in the sexual homogenization of its children? Probably not. Instead, we may well be saved by soccer moms. These rosé-sipping hausfraus in the suburbs are going to notice that their daughters aren't winning races and swim meets anymore because they're losing to gals who used to be guys. When they were guys and playing on guys' teams, they weren't winners, but now that they're girls, they are cleaning up trophy-wise.

You never see girls who are now boys hopping onto the varsity roster. Wonder why that is if gender is truly just a construct?

Moms are not going to like this, not one little bit. It's one thing to posture as caring and compassionate about our trans population in theory, but it's a whole 'nother story when Ashleigh gets shoulder-checked into the dirt during lacrosse practice by six-foot-two, 190-pound "Carla" who was named "Carl" last semester.

It's simply a matter of time until people start getting fed up with this nonsense. And this nonsense includes all the other letters and symbols that sometimes follow "LTBTQ." You've got "neutrois," "demigender," "intergender," "greygender," (it's not being into old people but something far less interesting), "aporagender," and whatever "maverique" is (it sounds like a new fragrance from Calvin Klein). There's also "gender apathetic," which at this point seems like something we can all sign onto.

All these bizarre labels insist that we care enough about a wacky ideology to ascertain the correct nomenclature and use it correctly in any interaction with another human being.

No.

No, we're not going to do that.

No, we're not going to spend our lives tiptoeing through a veritable minefield of esoteric terms, terrified that we might step on the wrong one by calling a person "gender fluid" when he actually identifies as "androgyne." Why should we live in quiet desperation that we may inadvertently mistake the self-proclaimed gender identity of someone who doesn't have the good manners to give us the benefit of the doubt?

Trump is not bigoted against LGBT people, and his supporters are not either. Our refusal to cater to the taxonomical demands of the left does not make us bigots.

My pronouns are "he/his." Yours are either that, or "she/hers." Period. Which is something only a woman can have.

CHAPTER 4

Trump Is Putin's Pet...
and So Are You Russia-Loving Traitors!

Here's a question I often have when I think about the lies surrounding President Trump: Are the people spewing them cynical frauds, or are they impenetrably stupid real believers in the nonsense they regurgitate? Or has their Trump Derangement Syndrome reached the point where they're certifiably insane, unable to differentiate the figments of their imagination from reality?

Nothing provokes these questions more than the lies about President Trump's purported ties to the Russians.

"Russian ties," of course, would be generous. The liars tend to phrase their accusations in more loaded terms. Sometimes, they say that Trump is "Putin's pet." Most of the time, they say that he's guilty of treason or accuse him of selling the office of the presidency to the highest bidder. We've all seen it live on CNN or MSNBC: some elitist jerk blurts out a Russian slur with quivering lips, a red face, and a shotgun blast of spittle. Even if they are lying, dumb, or crazy, you have to hand it to them—they're truly committed to the bit.

Why is this lie particularly irksome? Because it's been proven false time and time again. And to this day, cosmopolitan liberals in New York or Los

Angeles still think that Trump supporters are witting or unwitting agents of Moscow because they like the Bad Orange Man. It's infuriating.

The most effective lies contain a grain of truth, or so the saying goes. If that's true, then this lie must be the exception that proves the rule because the Russia lies have dominated our political discourse for over three years now without a single piece of supporting evidence.

The only fact the liars can point to is that President Trump campaigned on improving our relationship with Putin's Russia. Is that some treasonous offence? Hillary Clinton tried to do the same thing under Barack Obama. Remember that humiliating "reset button" embarrassment, when Hillary proved her incompetence by presenting Russian Foreign Minister Sergei Lavrov with a token announcing she would "overcharge" Russian relations? Boy, did that prove true. And Obama was never accused of Russian sabotage even though he begged Vlad for "more space" to weaken our military. He practically invited Putin to invade the Crimea while giving us hackneyed clichés about peace, love, and flowers.

Trump saw potential for a relationship with Russia that would serve American interests. That's not crazy. Bringing Russia into our orbit could make for an important counterbalance in our confrontation with Red China. (Kissinger did the same thing with China against the USSR in the seventies.) There is no downside to a better relationship with Russia. The fact that Trump was not foaming at the mouth for conflict with The Bear doesn't mean he wants to jump in bed with it.

Yet the lie continues to be repeated by the true believers and the deranged.

Remember, the elites' narrative is utterly immune to facts. So despite the mountains of exculpatory evidence, the liars still shamelessly accuse President Trump of corrupt dealings with Vladimir Putin and other Russian oligarchs. But whether they feel shame is irrelevant to the truth of the matter. This is a concrete, binary question. It's either true or false, and it can be disproved with compelling evidence.

Is Donald Trump collaborating with Russia? No. That's an objective fact.

Those of us with a few years on this big blue space rock remember the Cold War. Younger folks, who make up a large proportion of the Russophobes on cable TV, were born or became politically aware after America had already won that conflict. They certainly never learned about the Cold War in college, since the only history now considered worth studying is that of America's alleged evil. Plus, describing Marxists as the bad guys would probably leave them *literally* shaking.

But there was a Cold War, and Russia was on the other side, as were most of the older people now getting huffy about The Bear today. During the eighties, it was quite fashionable among the smart set to view the United States under Ronald Reagan as the villain in this struggle. The USSR's intelligence outfit, the KGB—it was kind of like the CIA, but good at its job—was all too happy to indulge the useful idiots in the West, and the useful idiots were only too happy to be indulged. They courted the American intelligentsia, who responded by advocating for a "nuclear freeze." Thank God President Reagan and the conservatives didn't play along. You had the USSR and America's best and brightest lined up on one side backing scams like the "nuclear freeze" movement, with conservatives on the other side pushing to match the enemy via the Reagan arms build-up.

Much of our elite thought Russian communists were better people than ordinary American citizens. Even popular culture was in on it. Remember "Russians," that ear-gouging atrocity by Sting about how Russians love their children too? According to the liberals, the Cold War was a product of President Reagan's cowboy adventurism. The Russkies were swell people; they were just willfully misunderstood by Cro-Magnon Americans.

Lefties loved the Russians long before the eighties. Every liberal has dreamed of leading his own Bolshevik Revolution since 1917. Our American communists—and we had quite a few—were enamored with Lenin and Stalin, and they were willing to overlook the few million broken eggs it takes to make a collectivist omelet.

While there were plenty of active Communist Party members who took direct orders from the Kremlin, there were more soft supporters who didn't want a Party membership card, but were friends and well-wishers.

Lots of those soft supporters occupied our cultural institutions. In 1931, Walter Duranty of the *New York Times* reported of the Soviet Union, "Conditions are bad, but there is no famine." That was news to the millions of starving people Stalin liquidated as he collectivized agricultural production. Duranty literally used the "eggs" metaphor, writing, "But—to put it brutally—you can't make an omelet without breaking eggs." That earned Duranty a Pulitzer Prize.

Yay journalism.

During World War II, the American commies had to endure some head-spinning 180s. First, they followed the Party line on Nazis' being bad, and then did a U-turn when Uncle Joe decided to sign a non-aggression pact with Adolph Hitler. This gave a portion of their cheesy movement whiplash, but it didn't last long. When Hitler invaded Russia, it was back to hating Nazis for our Russia-adoring left.

Hollywood leftists were eager to play up the propaganda about sturdy Russian peasants from the Union of Soviet Socialist Republics resisting the invaders from the National Socialist Workers Party. After the war ended and the Iron Curtain descended on Europe, the left was happy to decry the West's aggression in the form of its not surrendering to the Russians' attempts to destabilize it.

When Joseph McCarthy claimed that the Soviets were seeking to undermine the United States, he was right. But at that time, claiming that the Russians were seeking to influence American citizens was considered wrong-think. This rule lasted until late 2016, when claiming that the Russians were influencing certain Americans became a moral imperative.

Russia's influence on American politics came to a halt when the Berlin Wall fell. After the collapse of the Soviet Union, Russia was no longer the darling of leftists around the world. It was the Wild East. Many of the American smart set went over to help reorganize it into a modern capitalist nation and make their fortunes. The dream of turning Russia into a liberal democracy failed, and Russia did what anyone with even the most cursory understanding of Russian history could have predicted: it reverted to the strongman model of governance.

In Russia, they say that there's no such thing as a former KGB agent. That's why conservatives in the United States started to worry when ex-KGB officer Vladimir Putin rose to power.

At that time, Russia was dealing with the residual problems caused by the USSR's forced assimilation of various ethnic and national groups under one red banner. While the USSR and Russia were not exactly interchangeable, Russians dominated the USSR. When the Soviet Union broke up, a bunch of those republics embraced their inner Fleetwood Mac and tried to go their own way. That's why today, the map of several regions once dominated by the Soviet Union remains a patchwork of miscellaneous-stans and other bizarre little nations.

That would all be well and good if substantial numbers of Russians hadn't migrated to those countries when they were still good comrades. To this day, many of the now independent nation-states which once made up the Soviet Union have large Russian populations who identify with their homeland. Russia views those ethnic minorities as citizens it has a duty to protect and often intervenes militarily to protect its ethnic brothers and sisters. After the fall of the Soviet Union, Russia got into bloody brawls in Chechnya, Georgia, and Ukraine to name just a few.

Conservatives here in the U.S.A. were concerned. Russia often appeared unpredictable, and its massive nuclear arsenal was a cause for worry. Plus, old habits die hard, and the establishment had grown up thinking that the Russians were their mortal enemies. Putin appeared to be assessing turf in Latvia, Lithuania, Estonia, and elsewhere, perhaps with an eye toward restoring the empire the USSR had inherited. He also started pumping money into the Russian military again. But only the conservatives cared.

In any case, by 2012, when the insufferable Mitt Romney was losing to Barack Obama, there was a famous moment that summed up the divide. Romney had stated in an interview that Russia is "without question, our number one geopolitical foe." Later, in 2012, in the second presidential debate, Obama used the quote to clock Romney hard:

> Governor Romney, I'm glad you recognize al-Qaida is a threat, because a few months ago when you were asked what is the biggest geopolitical group facing America, you said Russia, not al-Qaida. You said Russia. And the 1980s are now calling to ask for their foreign policy back. Because the Cold War has been over for twenty years.

As Mistress Candy Crowley can testify, punishing Mitt Romney is not exactly hard. But even Barack Obama knew that Russia was a sideshow, an afterthought, a feeble giant with a birthrate approaching zero and an average life expectancy in free fall. Russia was hardly a geopolitical threat: its whole national character was consumed by vodka and ennui.

Yet just four years later—that's four years under Obama's watch—liberals want you to believe that Russia has reemerged as the greatest peril in America's long history of perils. And that peril consists of a few computer geekskis in some St. Petersburg basement running ads on Facebook about how Hillary is bad.

Now, in order to understand this reversal, you have to understand how liberals think. When the smartest, most talented, and healthiest woman in the whole wide world gets broken and humiliated by a reality TV–star real estate developer from Queens, liberals just assumed that there was foul play. That Hillary Clinton, the woman whom so many elites aspire to be, lost to Donald Trump is a thought they cannot bear.

In their minds, Hillary Clinton lost because a foreign power interfered in our electoral process, not because the elites she represents failed to provide peace and prosperity for several decades. The elites don't understand that ordinary Americans were fed up with their Hillary Clintons—that we were fed up with them. Regular people believed the ruling caste when they said they were coming for our guns, our religion, and our single-sex toilets. Voting for Trump was a way to protect ourselves. That's to say nothing of Hillary herself, who is so unlikable that the thought of her grating hiss emanating from the White House until January 2021 would drive otherwise moderate men to desperate measures.

No, instead of any of those flaws, it had to be Russians—Russians and some Facebook ads that tricked rubes in Wisconsin out of voting for the woman who couldn't place Wisconsin on a map.

It's an interesting theory, that the Russians stole the election by convincing the dense, easily-manipulated nitwits who Hillary felt belonged to her to vote for her opponent.

But it didn't stop there. You watched three years of Russiagate, a manufactured scandal based on the bizarre notion that Donald Trump somehow received secret instructions from Vladimir Putin. Our intelligence agencies and the FBI fell for it, which is no surprise. They may have even circulated it. I would call their recent record "checkered" if there were any successes to break up the failures. If taking ten years to hunt down the most wanted man in the world counts as a "success," perhaps the CIA's success criteria need some revamping.

You see, the elites were desperate to believe that Russia was somehow involved with the Trump campaign. It *needed* to be true, regardless of whether there was evidence. Now, they had evidence that Bill Clinton pocketed $500,000 in Kremlin cash for a Moscow speaking gig, but that was no biggie. They were not "investigating" foreign interference in any meaningful sense of the word; they were using unverified gossip as a pretext to spy on the political campaign of the presidential candidate they wanted to destroy.

That's how the FBI got their hands on the infamous Steele dossier, which contained all of the salacious and unverified dirt they wanted. There was one problem: the dossier was paid for by Hillary Clinton and her friends. But that little credibility strike didn't present an insurmountable obstacle. Instead of being honest with their sources, they obscured the document's provenance to those who might be interested, such as the media, the FISA courts, and even President-elect Trump.

What a document it was! Sure, the dossier contained allegations of corruption, but who cares about mundane influence peddling when you have reports about a couple of Moscow trollops taking leaks on the guy who was going into the White House?

It was a golden shower of defamation, everything they desperately wanted to hear. No wonder they fell for it hook, line, and sinker.

Of course, the dossier was a lie—all of it, top to bottom, as the Intelligence Community Inspector General Michael Horowitz finally confirmed in late 2019. Meanwhile, establishment golem Robert Mueller, who spent years and millions of dollars investigating all this terrible Trump–Russia collusion, never saw the dossier's fraud fit to mention.

Mueller found what corrupt FBI agents knew from the very beginning: there was no *there* there. It only took him an investigation lasting approximately forever and conducted by a bunch of Hillary donors to come to that conclusion. Mueller's whole team would have sacrificed their left testicles to find any dirt on the president. What did they get? Nothing, nada, zip.

But that didn't stop the defamation. It barely even slowed it down.

Trump hasn't just been cleared by a massive investigation run by his political enemies; he's also been harder on the Russians than any other president in decades.

When Obama was president, Putin invaded Ukraine, and Barry shrugged. The Ukrainians asked America for help, meaning guns and bullets and stuff useful for killing invading Russians. Obama sent them blankets and platitudes.

Trump sent them Javelin missiles, as well as other weapons and ammo to help the Ukrainians kill Russians. But perhaps this was all part of some cunning plan, some sort of secret accord with Putin to throw the bloodhounds off the trail of their covert connection.

And what about the Russians that President Trump killed in Syria?

When Bashar al-Assad's government began to totter, a lot of Russian "mercenaries" started operating in Syria. Only a fool would think that a bunch of Russian soldiers of fortune went to Syria without a big thumbs-up from old Vlad. Everyone knows they were agents of the Russian state sent to Syria to project Russian power in the Middle East.

In any case, a unit of them got a bit uppity and started moving on an American outpost. At the time, American forces in Syria were light, so there were only a few of our boys manning the outpost. But the way Americans go to war is that they try not to engage with rifles and such because this tends to give the enemy a fair chance. You get guys blazing at each other, M4s on our side and AKs on theirs, and that's pretty even. So, we don't do that in the U.S. Army when we can avoid it. Instead, we integrate fires from mortars, artillery, missiles, helicopter gunships, drones, fighter jets, and bombers so that we can literally blow the living shit out of anyone stupid enough to come at us.

The Russian mercs were stupid enough to come at us. Now they're dead. That's dozens, maybe hundreds, of Russians killed under President Trump's watch. Just to repeat: he *killed* them. Does that sound like something a pal, buddy, or covert Russian operative would do?

And Trump has slapped sanctions on the Russians. He even slapped sanctions on the company building the Nord Stream 2 gas pipeline, a major Russian infrastructure project designed to bring petroleum to Germany through the Baltic Sea.

Again, not the acts of a chum, amigo, or bro.

President Trump's actions have vindicated him from the ridiculous defamations the liars continue to circulate. A major investigation conducted by people itching for Trump's distinctive scalp found no collusion. A separate investigation found the dossier, on which the liars relied for several years of anti-Trump material, completely fabricated. On top of that, President Trump armed Russia's enemy on one side of the world while literally killing Russians on the other. At the same time, he's strangled Russia's economy with sanctions.

If Trump is colluding with Vladimir Putin, he is doing it all wrong. In fact, he's the worst colluder in the history of collusion. And if Vladimir Putin interfered in our election to help Donald Trump, he got a raw deal.

But how do the liars respond to facts disproving their fever dreams? They double down and lie some more.

Now, it's not easy to maintain a lie in the face of plain evidence. In order to even try it, you need someone who really makes you wonder whether they are dishonest, dumb, or deranged.

You need Representative Maxine Waters.

The Democrats called on Representative Waters in their hour of need, and Mad Maxine did not disappoint. Ever since President Trump took office, she has been a font of inspiration to the #Resistance and anti-Trump brigades. But even after the Russian collusion music came to a close, she still kept the dance alive. On December 20, 2019, she tweeted:

> Revelation by former WH officials proves what we've known all along: Trump is #PutinsPuppet. Trump repeated Putin's talking point that Ukraine, not Russia, interfered in the '16 election. Mark my words. If the Senate doesn't remove him, Trump will invite Putin to the WH next yr.

No, that's not at all insane and stupid. Is the troubled Representative Maxine too stupid to see evidence that disagreed with her foregone conclusion that President Trump is an agent of the KGB? Or is she simply willing to say anything to keep her five minutes of fame in the #Resistance spotlight going?

As we've said repeatedly, the lies about President Trump target you more than they target him. By siding with a president who will advocate for your interests, you are really—so the narrative goes—siding with some foreign potentate. And though being defamed is always frustrating, this lie especially bothers so many Trump supporters because of our history. While America's ruling elite canoodled with the Soviets during the Cold War, we shipped off around the world in uniform to confront the Russians. And now, those same Champagne Socialists have the nerve to call us Russian agents.

I served in the then-Federal Republic of Germany preparing to fight an army of Ivans while the red-faced Putin Truthers now infesting MSNBC were kissing KGB keister over the nuclear freeze. And there were a lot of Ivans, a lot more Ivans than GI Joes, making our orders pretty simple: hold out and try not to die before we can ship the rest of the army over from the continental U.S. If combat arose, we did not expect to make it out alive. Our job was to die at our posts stopping the Russians who decided to come over the border at the Fulda Gap.

Later, after we won the Cold War with no real help from the left in America, I went to Ukraine four times to train their soldiers. And in Kosovo, I worked with a battalion of Ukrainian soldiers. If I am a Putin puppet, I'm doing it wrong. And so are the rest of the folks who get tarred with this slime.

My story isn't unique. Millions of Americans put their asses (or supported the asses of loved ones) on the line against the Russians. Our credentials *vis a vis* The Bear are pretty damned solid, a lot more solid than those of the *Vox*-scribbling hipsters and Never Trump grifters whose newfound Russophobia will be forgotten the second it stops being useful for ginning up their dumb friends.

But then we get back on social media, and soon some neck-bearded liberal blue-check veteran of a thousand games of *Call of Duty* will be at it again with hashtag "#PutinsPet" or some other idiocy. Ugh. You know, Russia remains our enemy, and Putin's a thug, and but at least Vlad's not an insufferable sissy.

CHAPTER 5

Trump Is Literally a Nazi...
and So Are You Goose-Stepping Stormtroopers!

Of all the lies about Donald Trump, the charge that the president of the United States is a "Nazi" ranks among the most dishonest. President Trump is not some jack-booted tyrant dispatching storm-troopers to imprison his political opponents. The man can hardly control the leakers in his own administration. When one thinks of a disciplined ideologue willing to die for the glory of the Thousand-Year Reich, yeah, you think of Donald Trump. And of your next bong hit.

It would be silly if it were not such a vicious blood libel.

When the liars call Trump a "Nazi," they don't mean that he is a latter-day devotee of the National Socialist Workers' Party. In their usage, "Nazi" isn't a specific political ideology or concrete historical phenom-enon; it's liberal shorthand for everything that stands between them and their hippie utopia. They want to call everything that they disagree with evil, and the Nazis just happen to be the paragon of evil in our time.

A look at the real Nazis would quickly make liberals rethink whether it's wise to bring up the Third Reich so often. If you ever want to give a liberal a history lesson, remind them about the "socialist" part of the

National Socialist Workers' Party. That will teach them something about the Nazis that they didn't pick up in *Raiders of the Lost Ark*.

The Nazis were collectivists who most differed from their international socialist brethren in their efficient organization of military operations and murder. Violence and bloodshed were a central part of the Nazis' ideological platform. But that's only a difference of appearance. While socialism may be all peace and love in its advertising, that's not how it looks in practice. When you elevate the state over the rights of the individual, it's only a matter of time until you're ruled by blood-fueled tyrants.

In fact, in the end, the Nazi brand of socialism and the standard form of socialism both end up in the same place: a mass grave outside of a camp for the enemies of the dictator who inevitably runs the show.

Nazism is a subspecies of the socialist pathogen, and Trump is a lot of things, but he is certainly not a socialist.

"Trump totally is a Nazi for real" is perhaps the ultimate instance of, "It's bad, so Trump has to be it." We can even break this reasoning down into a simple formula:

Trump = Bad
Nazi = Bad
Trump = Nazi

Basically, if you don't agree that Donald Trump is a Nazi, the direct heir of Herr Hitler, you hate science. Or, at least, you hate mathematics. You probably hate science too, though. President Trump has done more to revive the power of the American individual than any president in recent memory. He is taking on socialism at home and abroad, while making sure that American capitalism works for everyone. Free elections, free speech, and freedom of religion are stronger in Trump's America than under his predecessors, which is difficult to square with the state monopoly over the economy and culture that defined Nazi rule.

Do we really need to break down the lie? Why not? How is Trump not a Nazi?

Well, because he possesses none of the telltale attributes of a National Socialist leader.

Trump has not claimed absolute power, nor has he created his own secret police. In fact, our closest equivalent to the secret police actively works to undermine him every day. He hasn't demanded that people greet him with a mock Roman salute. No one is shouting "Heil Trump!" from the rooftops. His chaotic rallies are hardly reruns of *Triumph of the Will*, Brad Parscale is no Leni Riefenstahl, and Fox News is not *Der Stürmer*.

Trump has not ordered the murder of "defectives" who fail to meet the standards of his eugenics policies. There is no Department of Phrenology obsessed with collecting data on the skull sizes of various ethnic groups. There are no mandatory Trump Youth reading groups discussing *The Art of the Deal* despite the fact that it's eminently more readable than *Mein Kampf*. And President Trump isn't trying to burn the books. The only book-burnings under Trump's watch are by the purple-haired outrage mobs on college campuses.

President Trump hasn't conscripted millions of American youth into his war machine; he's tried to bring the troops home. He hasn't forced our corporations to go into war production mode; he's taken on the Military Industrial Complex. Our army is not blitzkrieging its way through Belgium on the way to Paris (though if Trump shouted at them, the French would probably surrender). Rather, President Trump is bringing our endless wars to a close.

Hitler killed millions of innocent people in concentration camps that were worthy of the name. Today, Trump haters insist that the short-term detention of illegal aliens arrested at the border are somehow comparable. That's how desperate they are to stretch the Trump–Hitler comparison. They ignore the fact that those detention centers existed under Obama, who put children in cages and then had his lackeys in the media blame President Trump for trying to alleviate the conditions of detainees.

Hitler's German critics were brave figures who defied their society and their government to stand up for humanity. Many died lonely, anonymous deaths in Gestapo prisons. Trump's critics, meanwhile, ape the prejudices of society's elite against his benighted supporters to great applause. None of them end up guillotined in dank dungeons. They get shows on Netflix, million-dollar book deals, and hundreds of thousands of Twitter followers.

President Trump is not only miles ideologically from Hitler's National Socialism, but he also bears no personal resemblance to Hitler as a man. The uni-testicled Austrian housepainter and the all-man Queens real estate developer have nothing in common. Hitler was a pill-popping vegetarian who loved his dog. Trump is a teetotaling food junkie who, for some unfathomable reason, is not a dog person. I'll be the first to admit that not liking dogs is a strike against the president, but it hardly makes him Hitler. Plus, Hitler killed his dog moments before he killed himself, like a coward.

Unlike Hitler, Trump has never killed a dog. And unlike Barack Obama, he has never eaten one.

There are undeniable similarities between the two men, however, that we cannot gloss over: both are featherless bipeds, and both breathe oxygen. That's pretty much it.

All this would, in a sane world, cause those babbling about a fanciful Trump–Hitler nexus to slink away ashamed. But as we have seen, bourgeois conceits like "facts" do not matter, and shame is no longer a thing. What matters is that Nazis are really bad, and Hitler was really bad, and so Trump has to be a Nazi, if not actually Hitler, because he is really, really bad.

Except Trump is not a Nazi, and he is not Hitler, and normal people— those without an agenda and/or those who aren't staggeringly dumb—get that. Trump's America as the Fourth Reich? That's, if you'll pardon the expression, a bridge too far.

While some of the liars concede that Trump isn't a Nazi, they insist that he's close enough. That's why they call him a "white nationalist" or "white supremacist": not quite a Nazi in the finer points, but of the same family tree. Those terms often end up being used interchangeably with "Nazi," but the Nazis were organized—*really* organized—and the "white power" idiots can't plan or organize beyond, "It's Fred's turn to bring a sixer of Old English 800 to my mom's house, where we'll sit in the basement and blame black people because girls won't talk to us."

Now, we don't dispute that some people draw their *raison d'être* from their dermatological pallor. But in recent years, liberals have called so many people white nationalists and white supremacists that the terms have lost precise meanings. Today, you're a "white supremacist" if you hold views that aren't in vogue among the elite, not if you're someone who believes white people are biologically superior to others.

Old-school white supremacists, the kind who draw their entire identity from the fact that their great-great-grandfathers came from Norway, are vanishingly rare. And while most of us hardly ever encounter the old-fashioned kind of white supremacist, the liars would have you believe that we're in the midst of a white supremacy epidemic.

That, of course, is demonstrably false. The Southern Poverty Law Center, that pack of leftist bullies that's been fundraising off these marginal cretins' loser antics for decades, estimates the Ku Klux Klan consists of just 5,000 to 8,000 robe-clad dummies nationwide. A century ago, when the Democrat-founded, Democrat-supporting flock of fools was at its peak, membership numbered nearly four million. There just are not that many of them today. The total number of organized white supremacists is roughly equivalent to the population of an anonymous town you speed through on the interstate in thirty seconds. That means that in a country of well over 300 million people, white supremacists are as much a rounding error as a parenting error.

And yet, the liars want you to think that President Trump is the leader of this tiny band of misfits, that he's their champion in Washington, D.C. Yeah, Trump is going to ditch his gorgeous wife to cruise out to some field and light up a cross with his pals from the local klavern. If he's lucky, he'll be the next Exalted Cyclops!

This is not a thing.

But the inherent implausibility of this notion did not stop Bernie Sanders from calling him a white supremacist:

> Look, and it gives me no pleasure to say this, but I think all of the evidence out there suggests that we have a president who is a racist, who is a xenophobe, who appeals and is trying to appeal to white nationalism. And, you know, it breaks my heart to have to say that this is the person we have who is president of the United States.

Gosh, you would think a fellow socialist would show the Nazis a little love, if only out of professional courtesy.

And Sitting Bolshevik, sometimes known as Elizabeth Warren, jumped in too. Every Democrat presidential candidate in the primary inundated the American public with accusations that Trump is racist. Joe Biden built his campaign on linking Trump to the Charlottesville rally, claiming that Charlottesville, not his hope to keep lining his family's pockets, was the reason behind his most recent run at our nation's highest office. Warren publicly called Trump a white supremacist countless times. "He has given aid and comfort to white supremacists," Warren once told the *New York Times*. "He's done the wink and a nod. He has talked about white supremacists as fine people. He's done everything he can to stir up racial conflict and hatred in this country." ("Everything" does not include pretending to be a minority to get a cushy academic post in the People's Republic of Cambridge.)

Notice how the liars never specify Trump's white supremacist actions. They say that Trump "is trying to appeal to white nationalism" or that he's "done the wink and a nod" or that he's "dog whistling" to racists. They pretend that they can read President Trump's mind, uncovering all sorts of secret motivations that divulge his closet Nazism. But don't be fooled: it's just more projection by race-hustling liars.

They need to read so much into Trump's words because he has never actually said or done anything untoward. It would be one thing if Trump was on record saying "I think white people are better than everyone else." That would clarify things. But instead, the liars assume what they want to prove. They assume that Trump is racist and twist his every word to confirm their assumption. They even use his denouncements of racism as proof. It's always weird how often what people can't prove but just sort of know fits their preexisting prejudices perfectly.

So is President Trump a covert white supremacist? To believe that hodgepodge, you'd have to overlook Trump's decades of close friendship with minorities without a whiff of suspected prejudice. Yeah, sure if there's anything Trump is all about, if there is anything that he cares about, it's his racial identity. Not money. Not family. Not women. No, it's his skin tone. Russell Simmons, Don King, Mike Tyson, and even Al Sharpton have all boasted close personal relationships with Donald Trump. Not one of them ever said he thought Trump was racist when they were buddying up with him on his private jet.

Some of the real race-obsessed goofs have repackaged their nonsense in recent years. Some call themselves "alt-right," another term that is nearly meaningless due to its lack of specificity. Now in declining use, the term "alt-right" was often stretched to include people who found Jeb! Bush annoying because he is a human puffball who is fawningly obedient to the bipartisan elites. Basically, if Jeb! begged you to "Please clap," and you didn't, the liars could call you "alt-right."

A few real jerks tried to infiltrate mainstream movements, like the resistance to the statue-removal craze. Opposing revisionist leftists who wanted to wipe away history was not a "white supremacist" position. It was a "history supremacist" position, which held that the truth about the past should not be rewritten to satisfy the bizarre obsessions of people who subscribe to *Mother Jones* and intentionally read Vox.com.

This came to a head in Virginia, where a backlash against the removal of Confederate memorials was exploited by both white supremacist jerks and radical leftist jerks. The march of the morons at

Charlottesville in 2017 did not start the ridiculous cycle of "Trump is a Nazi white supremacist who is pretty much Hitler!" lies. It just gave the liars something to try to hang their knit caps on. When it happened, Trump was pressured to "repudiate" the people he had nothing to do with. He then talked to the press, and the Big Lie—ironically, a Nazi propaganda technique—that Trump supported these tiki torch-wielding weirdos was born.

Everyone should read the full statement that Trump gave the reporter, not just the cherry-picked outtakes the mainstream media and Democratic politicians twisted to push the lie. Reading the exchange in full proves that Trump never said the white dudes shouting racial slogans were "very fine people." Many others have debunked this skeevy lie in much greater detail, among them *Dilbert* creator, Scott Adams. But you don't need to read any analysis to learn the truth, you just need to read the statement for yourself. Trump clearly said that there were "rough, bad people—neo-Nazis, white nationalists, whatever you want to call them."

Why would Trump tongue-bathe the same folks he called "bad people"? There's no need to worry about that. Instead, to protect their narrative, the media pretends it never happened. The narrative says that Trump is a secret white nationalist, and so the facts supporting the narrative were born. And if the facts get in the way, well, just ignore them. Plus, what's the risk? It's not like some other mainstream media journalist is going to come along and correct you.

The elites call Trump a Nazi, a white nationalist, and a white supremacist in order to void his legitimacy and render him so radioactive that no decent person would have anything to do with him. But in order for that to work, decent people have to be stupid enough to believe their lies. A growing number of Americans are shrugging off this particular calumny. If, as the end of his first term in office approaches, there are still no swastika banners hanging off the faces of our public buildings nor formations goose-stepping up Broadway, the Fourth Reich is probably not in the cards. And people are going to see that.

The lie will live on, no matter how manifestly ridiculous it becomes. While calling Trump a Nazi may delegitimize Trump's presidency, it also legitimizes leftists to fight Trump supporters by any means necessary. If Trump is an evil white nationalist overlord, leftists can paint his supporters with the same brush. They can take authoritarian measures to fight for "our democracy" against the unwashed Jesus gun people who voted for Trump. You backwoods cattle molesters pose a threat that only the liberals can understand, so they're justified in using all the levers of power to silence your voice and remove your president from office.

And it's always "our democracy," even though this is a republic, because precision in language just gets in the way of the narrative. "Democracy" sounds better than "republic" to dumb people.

But maybe it's not a lie. Maybe we are on the verge of *Hitler 2: Heil Donald*. To believe that, you'd have to think that the half of America that fell for the Evil Orange Dictator is waiting for the chance to form an Aryan police state, to racially "purify" the population, and want a *Führer* to call their own.

You'd have to think that millions of American patriots watched *Saving Private Ryan* and rooted against Tom Hanks. Or that millions more felt *Hogan's Heroes* was really unfair to Colonel Klink. Because Americans are secretly Nazis, see?

Think back through your life. Carefully scour your memory banks. Have you once, in your entire life, met anyone who said anything remotely like, "You know what'd be cool? An American Hitler. I'd really like to ditch this whole Constitution thing and become a Nazi state. How about you?"

If you have had this happen, you probably got cornered by a creepy loner at the world's crummiest party. Or you spent time in a nuthouse or a jail, hopefully on the staff. Maybe you were that unlucky Uber driver who found a chatty, aspiring *übermensch* riding in your Camry down to the local beer hall. But on the off chance you have encountered such a person, it was almost certainly a one-off, a uniquely troubling interaction that you have tried hard to suppress until this chapter brought it all back to the surface. Sorry.

And if it was not unique, if it happens a lot, do a personal inventory.

There is no significant constituency who supported Donald Trump because they dreamed of installing a totalitarian regime in the United States. The notion that half of America covertly yearns to resurrect the swastika is a fever dream of people who are stupid, insane, or some combination of the two.

Or are the liars just projecting their own fascist fantasies?

Think about it. Which side embraces policies that resemble those of the Nazis? The Democrats are trifling with socialism, not Donald Trump, and Nazis are just another breed of that noxious species. The Democrats, not Donald Trump, are the ones who tried to suppress political speech with a constitutional amendment to undo the *Citizens United* Supreme Court decision, not Donald Trump. That barred the government from prosecuting people for showing a film critical of Hillary Clinton under the auspices of "campaign finance laws." That sounds a lot more totalitarian than defending the absolute freedom of political speech. They even support the use of governmental agencies—the IRS, the FBI and so forth—to suppress political opponents. How much more totalitarian can you get?

Democrats want to disarm the citizenry, something the Nazis did as soon as they took power. They also have a hierarchy of approved and disapproved races, and they eagerly support discriminating against certain races in hiring, in the courts, and elsewhere. And we know that the Democrats approve of terminating unwanted, "unworthy" lives. Abortion is practically a sacrament. The Nazis were all in on that.

So maybe when Trump and his supporters are being called "Nazis," it's something more than just a lame epithet that no one with an IQ hovering above room temperature takes seriously. Maybe it's a peek into the red, white, and black dreams of the liars pushing that slander.

And as for Trump's being a Nazi, call us when he invades Poland.

CHAPTER 6

Trump Is Totally Corrupt...
and You Don't Care!

Do you ever wonder what the presidency has cost Donald Trump? And I don't mean in social capital, though that must be considerable. The man went from the toast of New York high society to an outcast from the social circles he used to frequent. I mean in terms of money, cash, moolah, ducats, the stuff that makes the world go 'round.

How much has being the president cost Trump in dollars and cents?

We know he does not take a government paycheck. The White House issues a press release every quarter announcing where a three-month portion of President Trump's forgone salary of $400,000 per year went. We also know that he had to divest himself of his considerable business holdings. While he's still schooling his foes in the art of the deal, he's not taking home a cash reward for his efforts anymore. How much money do you think Trump is passing up to serve his country?

It's an interesting, if relatively unimportant question. But you'd have to be a freaking moron to wonder how much *more* money Trump makes as president. Yet the liars act like Trump is cashing in on the presidency.

Yeah, he's going to turn a profit off this White House scam by convincing Qatari diplomats to rent out the presidential suite at the Trump Hotel. Sounds legit.

The "Trump is corrupt" lie is absurd, but that has not stopped it from doing the rounds again and again. Every time Trump makes a foreign policy decision, we're told that some Trump property in or near the region in question is his real concern. He's constantly receiving those sweet, sweet emoluments, and he spends his nights in the White House checking the occupancy in his hotels before he goes downstairs to the secret money pool he had installed by the Secret Service to bathe nude in a pond of $100 bills. Give me a break.

But the liars are half-right: we rubes don't care. We don't care about whatever particular allegation they've cooked up this week because the whole notion that Trump is corrupt is transparently ridiculous. As we have seen, the liars seem to be unable to resist the temptation to assert that Trump must be every single bad thing it is possible to be.

Corruption bad, Trump bad, so Trump corrupt. Simple and dumb.

Perhaps some of it comes from his background. He was a New York real estate developer, a line of work that requires quite a bit of wheeling and dealing. He's no doubt made some sharp deals and done business with some sketchy dudes, but does that indicate "corruption"? Doesn't "corruption" involve the bending or breaking of laws and the ill-gotten gain of cash? Okay, then what was his corruption?

Didn't Robert Mueller spend a couple years and tens of millions of bucks chasing down every possible lead that might help get this interloper out of the Oval Office? Couldn't these legendary corruption bloodhounds sniff out Trump's secret hidden wrongdoing? The media told us they were the best of the best, right?

Nope.

Sure, they nicked Paul Manafort, but Manafort's corrupt business dealings had nothing to do with his work on the Trump campaign. In fact, they predate his acquaintance with Donald Trump by more than half a decade. If knowing someone who did corrupt things a long time ago is just cause for removal, most members of Congress should start getting nervous.

And what about Trump's tax returns? Obviously, he doesn't want to release them because he's hiding something criminal, right?

We've already demonstrated how the liars turn a lack of evidence for their baseless claims into proof of Trump's wrongdoing. It's the same thing here: they have no evidence that President Trump did anything wrong, but they defame him anyway.

Look at how they've treated Trump over his tax returns. They accused him of corruption and demanded he prove himself innocent by providing them with his complete financial records. Then, when he refused to do so, they argued that his refusal was proof that Trump is indeed corrupt. Why wouldn't he turn over his financial records if he had nothing to hide?

We should praise Trump's decision to hold firm against their demands for his financial records. Resisting their ludicrous harassment protects the institution of the presidency. Imagine if every president had the entirety of his financial records subpoenaed by Congress. It would be a disaster, especially because it would be yet another new rule that only gets enforced against Republicans. With a Democrat in the Oval Office, can you imagine how much spin the media would cook up to demand privacy for the papers and effects of their candidate in power?

They're so desperate to find corruption that they'll turn anything into a headline. Remember the Air Force junket scandal that arose and disappeared in about thirty seconds? U.S. Air Force jet crews stuck over in the British Isles were allegedly ordered to travel out of their way to stay at Trump properties. In order for the corruption accusation to make any sense, you have to believe that Trump was monitoring the temporary duty lodging choices of individual C-17 crews and decided that he wanted his chunk of those government hotel rates. He then personally directed the Secretary of the Air Force to make sure his property could wring every pound out of those layovers. It sounds as plausible as unicorns.

The Air Force had to take time away from defending America to explain the obvious to our intrepid journalists.

The media tried to pull the same stunt in the Trump National Doral Miami G7 summit imbroglio, when Trump volunteered that property to host our ungrateful and surly allies under the Florida sun. According to our elites, that was another crime, and they even got some weak Republican to chime in instead of responding with the only rational response—"Oh, shut up."

Of course, the property was offered up for the summit at cost, and the resort probably would have taken a hit in the end. But according to the powers that be, it "looked bad." Yeah, to the idiots who hate Trump no matter what he does. Not needing the hassle, Trump withdrew the offer. Fine. Next time, put the euroweenies up in a Motel 6 and feed them at Applebee's. The press can sleep in their rented Kias out in the parking lot.

The idea that Donald Trump became president so he could chisel away what amounts to a rounding error of the rounding errors in his previous income by leveraging the office is silly. But perhaps the corruption lies aren't meant to take down Trump. Maybe they are deployed to obscure actual corruption.

How did the Clintons get so rich? Hillary always talks about how impoverished the Clintons were while in the White House. Well, that was then, and this is now. Today they are set, loaded, and full to the gills with cash. The cash river isn't flowing quite like it was in the past, when Hillary had a future stint in the Oval Office to market, before she had the bad luck of not facing Jeb! Bush and losing the election, but the money is still coming in. Hillary has got her unreadable books and her unlistenable speaking gigs. Plus, Hillary was always able to monetize her or her hubby's offices. Remember her cattle futures investments while she was the first lady of Arkansas?

There are also her even less savory influence-peddling schemes. But the less that is said about the Clinton Foundation the better. Especially if you don't want to wake up having killed yourself.

And what about the Obamas, who recently bought a seaside mansion in Martha's Vineyard? They, of course, signed mega-million book deals and a deal with Netflix once they left office. Never in the field of human endeavor was so much made by so few for doing so shitty a job.

Is that "corruption?" Maybe not entirely from a purely legal point of view, but this post-presidential money-grubbing is dirty and wrong. Nobody complains because the establishment darlings and media lackies are the culprits. Nothing to see here, just move along.

But there's plenty of hard corruption to write home about, especially from places like Ukraine. Look at Joe Biden, who proudly calls himself one of the poorest members of the political elite. By poorest, Biden means "has little money," not "has been consistently terrible at his job since before *Happy Days* went on the air."

His financial disclosures reflect that he does not have oodles of cash, but he's not hurting. His net worth excludes his actual net. What are the chances that Joe Biden has paid for his own dinner once in the last forty years? About the same as the odds his loser son Hunter got his gig with a Ukrainian oligarch for upwards of $50,000 a month for being competent, capable, and totally not more interested in huffing rails off the tush of a hooker named Svetlana in some Kiev hotel room.

Hunter's talents appear limited to smoking crack and banging strippers, if the reports and paternity suits are anything to go by. He got with his dead brother's wife—the best we can hope for is that he liberally interpreted his Old Testament obligations—and he got kicked out of the Navy for peeing hot on a dope test during his first reserve drill. With that CV, plus his total lack of gas industry experience or basic familiarity with Ukraine, Hunter was a natural for a no-show seat on the board of a corrupt company in a country his pa was overseeing as veep.

You might call that "corruption," but to establishment politicians and the mainstream media, it's "a cruel attack on Joe Biden's only surviving son."

Isn't it weird that the media accuses the Trumps of wallowing in corruption without any evidence while they willfully ignore the heaps of evidence demonstrating Hunter Biden's manifest corruption?

In order to believe that Donald Trump is corrupt, you have to first believe that Donald Trump only cares about money, that he's Scrooge McDuck with orange hair. He's not. He's given up more money to do this job than most of us could ever imagine, and we know it. In truth, Trump supporters aren't happy with corruption; we're disgusted by it. That's why we elected Donald Trump. We knew he was a patriot who could not be bought by the special interests that own the swamp creatures. So when those same swamp creatures screech that he is corrupt, it's hard for us to take them seriously.

CHAPTER 7

Trump Is a Warmonger...
and So Are All You
Bloodthirsty Monsters!

Donald Trump mongers a lot of things, but war is not one of them. President Trump is the first president committed to peace that we've had in a generation. Nevertheless, the establishment likes to say he is some sort of reckless, six-gun nut intent on ramping up conflict and violence around the world. It's objectively, demonstrably false, but the defamers either don't care or can't get their heads around the fact that Trump has out-peaceniked their heroes.

Libya anyone?

Syria?

Hello?

They're not listening. You see, much like Trump must be a racist, or a Nazi, or a homophobe, Trump *has* to be a warmonger because warmongers are bad. Being anti-war is *their* thing, and they can't let Trump take it from them. They're the ones who bring the peace, love, and flowers, even if their heroes bring drones, JDAMs, and Hellfires.

When it comes to foreign policy, Trump has turned their world upside down, and it freaks them out.

Trump is as far from a warmonger as you can get. If anything, he's a peacemonger, consistently disappointing and frustrating the hawks who want him to get into new wars and stay in the wars we're currently fighting. And the liars don't understand that you support him in that endeavor.

Trump was elected, expressly and explicitly, to clean up the military mess that the permanent bipartisan fusion party (thank you, writer and pal Michael Walsh) had made in the decades following the Gulf War. The war to expel Saddam Hussein from Kuwait was America's first real war in a long time. And America's spectacular, unequivocal victory—in terms of the combat, if not in establishing long-term peace and stability—made American elites much less reticent about going to war. It made longer wars a viable American foreign policy option again.

Today, a lot of people don't remember the Gulf War. I do because I was there. It came about twenty years after our ignominious retreat from Vietnam, followed by a prolonged period of general peace that stemmed in large part from the ass-kicking our best and the brightest got in Southeast Asia.

The hesitation foreign policy planners felt towards engagement even had a name, the "Vietnam Syndrome," and during that time, our military adventures were, if not completely nonexistent, limited in a way that Americans would not recognize today. The only engagement of note was Jimmy Carter's clusterfark of a hostage rescue that ended with the mullahs putting out video of charred American warriors at the Desert One crash site in 1980.

It took Ronald Reagan several years to even think about adopting a more muscular policy. In 1983, an American battleship shelled Syrian targets in Lebanon after a suicide bomber attacked a Marine barracks. Almost simultaneously, an American force crushed the Cubans and their puppets in Grenada. In 1986, we shot down a couple Libyan fighters over the Gulf of Sidra. In 1988, we converted most of the Iranian Navy's capital ships to submarines, involuntarily. Then, in 1989, we tossed Manuel Noriega out of power in Panama.

Notice the trend line? America's toe-dips back into the war pond started off ugly, but as time went on, the results got better and better. We started winning, and we liked it. We grabbed a nice tropical island from the commies, shot down some jerks' planes, sank some other jerks' boats, then busted a pock-marked, drug-dealing thug and stuck him in the pokey. Uncle Sam was getting his groove back.

Then came the Gulf War, where we defeated the Vietnam Syndrome as decisively as we defeated the Iraqi forces. America left her reticence to use her considerable military might in a smoking heap in the desert.

By the 1990s, war was once again a viable foreign policy option. We went into Haiti to make it stop being Haiti, and we went into Somalia to make it stop being Somalia. The former led to the death of nearly two dozen Americans during the battle immortalized in the book and movie *Black Hawk Down*. We killed about a thousand of them.

Later in the decade, Bill Clinton—an actual draft dodger, as opposed to Trump, whose deferments were legitimate—sent American forces into Bosnia and allegedly gave the order to do so over the telephone while Monica Lewinsky gave him something herself. Clinton went on to launch an air war against Serbia over Kosovo, where American soldiers remain stationed today. He also flattened an aspirin factory in Sudan after some al-Qaeda terrorist bombings, which kept happening, but he famously declined to smoke Osama bin Laden when the opportunity presented itself.

That was the state of play in American foreign policy when a bunch of seventh century cultists decided to fly four airplanes into American buildings on September 11, 2001. Our military was locked and loaded, but more importantly, our government was blooded and ready. There was some initial talk about Vietnam, but it was drowned out by the overwhelming sentiment that these sons of bitches and their friends all had to die. Only one person in Congress, a buffoon who represented the area around Berkeley, voted against killing those responsible for the attacks where they lived. We did that in a few weeks. Then we expanded the mission and sought to make the Afghans stop being Afghans. Big mistake.

We're still there, all these years later, still trying to do the same thing.

And then we invaded Iraq, another George W. Bush brainchild. But he was not alone. Most of the establishment was down with the fight. It seemed like a good idea at the time to many people, not least of all Hillary Clinton and Joe Biden. (That Biden supported it should have caused everyone else to rethink it.) There were some people who weren't on the bandwagon, but the establishment had made its decision. War it was. In retrospect, many of the war's cheerleaders later blamed those awful neo-cons and their ideas about nation-building, conveniently forgetting that this kind of mushy foreign policy goo started with Woodrow Wilson and that those same ideas had propelled us to engage in Africa and the Balkans during the 1990s. Disregard the revisionists: Iraq was always as much about the liberal notion of Iraqis yearning to be just like Americans as it was about stockpiles of WMDs, and it was not just the neo-cons who advocated for the war.

We crushed the army in weeks and occupied the country—a magnificent military achievement. Then we expanded the mission to make the Iraqis stop being Iraqi. Another big mistake.

We're still there too.

Is anyone noticing a theme?

Later, Libya happened. Hillary Clinton, ensconced as the secretary of state, and Barack Obama decided it was not enough to have Muammar Gaddafi trapped in a figurative box. No, he had to go for some reason, despite the fact that he posed no threat to American citizens or American interests. They wanted to liberate the Libyan people, just like their predecessors had tried to "liberate" the Somalis, Bosnians, Afghans, and Iraqis. They made sure Gaddafi met his maker in a very ugly way (it's on video), and I doubt many Libyans have since felt liberated. Today, they're running slave markets in Tripoli, something that certainly didn't exist before Gaddafi met his dismal end. That doesn't sound like progress to me.

Later, there was the Benghazi terrorist attack, a rare instance in recent history where we Americans did not fight enough. The elites tried to pass off the laughable lie that American forces could not have aided our besieged consulate. For a guy so eager to pull the trigger—Obama authorized hundreds of drone strikes—his failure to do so on September 11, 2012, in support of the Americans fighting for their lives is incomprehensible. That is, unless you understand progressives.

And our guys were also fighting in Yemen, Niger, Syria, Somalia (again), and who knows where else. That's not to say we don't have enemies in those places, enemies richly deserving of the righteous hot-lead death our amazing warriors deliver to them. It just demonstrates that American soldiers are fighting in a whole lot of places, and most of us have no clear understanding of why or to what end. War has gone from our last option to our first option, and we're chasing demons across the world without a clear understanding of what we want.

Permanent war is now considered normal. Remember, if you are an American who is under twenty-five, then your country has been at war for your entire conscious life. If you are an American who was born in 1983 or later, you've spent your entire adult life in a country at war.

So, here comes Trump, a Republican who did not hesitate to call W a fool for bumbling us into Iraq. It was mind-boggling—well, a lot of things he said were mind-boggling, but this was not some funny mind-screw like saying Ted Cruz's pa offed JFK. This was, holy crap, what was this? Republican candidates just did not trash the last Republican president, especially for going to war!

That's true, but Donald Trump was not a "Republican" in the sense the other Republicans were Republicans. He wasn't an establishment drone repeating the same warmed-over talking points. He was something else, unique, *sui generis* among Republican candidates. He was the hawk who was not like other hawks, while being the dove who was not like other doves.

There's a word for Donald Trump's foreign policy impulses, imperfect though it may be: Donald Trump is a Jacksonian.

Andrew Jackson was a Democrat in the sense that the party has long abandoned. Today, Democrats consider Andrew Jackson and the working man inveterate racists, like the rest of the historical Democrats.

Jackson appealed to the working man, the common man, the rough and plain man who did the dirty work of building this country. And that kind of man also did most of the work defending this country.

Those folks still do. The word "populist" gets attached to them a lot; it is not clear exactly what the word means, but from the way the elite deploys it, it cannot be anything good. "Populist" isn't descriptive, it's a slur which signals that the Jacksonians are not in with the right-thinkers. They tend to be working class or middle class, and they tend to speak their mind and operate less from ideology than gut instinct and common sense.

The elites find Jacksonians frightening and think they should shut up, work, pay taxes, enlist, and obey their betters. You do not meet a lot of Jacksonian performance artists or newspaper editors. You do meet a lot of Jacksonians at truck stops, on farms, in the barracks, and at construction sites.

Gee, did any prominent political figure that you know of grow up around construction sites?

Jacksonians are certainly not pacifists, and few of them were raised with their Montessori teachers telling them to use their words rather than fight. A Jacksonian has probably been in his fair share of bar fights, while an elitist has been in many Twitter fights with, well, Jacksonians who say crazy, bigoted things like, "Dudes can't get pregnant" and, "If you got a frank 'n' beans, you're a guy."

Jackson himself was certainly no pacifist. They called him "Old Hickory" for a reason. He was a pretty nasty general who believed that the best kind of war is the kind that you have won. This is the kind of thinking about war you get when you take policy advice from the guys who get stuck fighting them. It's the eggheads and theorists, often tiresome wannabes in stupid fedoras, who imagine that there are other laudable outcomes in war besides victory. Thanks to those folks, we're still guarding the demilitarized zone between the Koreas. They're the ones who thought we could prevail in Vietnam while taking everything that might have led to something like victory off the table. "Bomb Hanoi?

We can't do that!" they howled. Nixon finally sent in the B-52s and the commies went right back to the Paris peace table.

Jacksonians do not understand why you would fight a war, spill our blood, and squander our treasure if you are unwilling to do what it takes to win. Again, they are not pacifists—they are perfectly happy to fight—they just need a good reason.

A good reason can come in many forms. It can be the enemy's bombing Pearl Harbor or flying jets into the World Trade Center or just being an unmitigated asshole like Saddam Hussein. If you can come up with a sensible rationale for fighting, Jacksonians will often go along with it. But this does not extend to silly rationales, like some newly invented moral duty to referee between two groups of Third World savages. The reason for conflict has to be grounded in concrete American interests or direct threats to American safety. Jacksonians don't go to war to protect the abstract rights of people who are likely to turn on our boys for interfering with their fun.

This is what many people misunderstand about Jacksonians. They are not anti-war *per se*. They are anti-stupid war.

And that understanding leads to the second requirement. If you propose to fight, then you must have the will to win. And you cannot drag it out forever, dithering and handling the enemy with kid gloves while American kids come back in full metal gloves.

If a war is worth fighting, that means it is worth winning, and winning may mean doing very mean and ugly things to the enemy. That includes bombing its cities, including with hot rocks if that's what it takes to win. The Hiroshima and Nagasaki issue is a terrific test for Jacksonian inclinations. A Jacksonian's response to the question of whether America was morally right to nuke the Nipponese is "Oh, hell yeah." Remember, several million Americans, having fought their way through Europe and across the Pacific, were about to invade the home islands of Japan. That would have meant millions of American troops dead or wounded. Oh, and a lot more Japanese soldiers and civilians, not that that mattered too much. Plus, the Japanese had started it, and we had a right to finish it however we needed to. Screw them.

That's the quintessential Jacksonian mindset: just win, baby. And if you don't want none, don't start none.

That's also the mindset of Donald Trump.

Donald Trump rejected the elite foreign policy consensus that dominated Washington since the end of the Cold War. Republicans, with the exception of kooky uncles Rand and Ron Paul, wanted to go at anyone who looked at America cross-eyed. They called it peace through strength, but "peace" proved the least important part of the formula.

And, as we have seen, Democrats realized that they can do war too, with one caveat: for the liberal warmongers, the war cannot support any vital American interest. If the war might ensure American access to oil, for example, then it is morally bankrupt and cannot be tolerated. If it means getting in between warring factions to protect people whose suffering made people in Santa Monica sad when they saw it on their Facebook feeds, then we have to do it.

So, basically, the establishment is composed of hawks and self-hating hawks.

There were also a few peaceniks whining about how America sucks. The peaceniks liked war too, by the way, but only when their commie heroes were waging them. Remember, the people out there protesting Vietnam and later Iraq generally did not want peace; they just wanted America to lose.

So, there was a general bipartisan fusion consensus that America should be involved in all sorts of military conflicts around the world. And Trump declared war on that consensus.

Now, understand that like a good Jacksonian, Trump loves the military. In fact, one of the go-to outrages cited by the Trump-is-a-warmonger brigade is his desire for big, beautiful military parades to honor our troops.

A fervent pro-military bent is essential to Jacksonianism. Jacksonians love the Army, Marines, Navy, Air Force and, when they remember it, the Coast Guard. Hell, they already love the Space Force without knowing what it does. And they're right to love our armed forces. After all, it's their sons and daughters who make up the military.

The Jacksonians made those countless *NCIS* spinoffs ratings hits when no one in the elite ever watched an episode. While Jacksonians went out to see *American Sniper* after getting some pizza and brews, the elite took their little boys to see *Frozen* again after stopping for kale salad and kombucha.

Trump loves the military and our soldiers, as do his Jacksonian supporters. That's why has he no intention of wasting American lives on useless conflicts halfway across the planet. Moreover, he thinks of existing commitments with common sense. He asks if we are willing to win, and whether it's worth it. In Afghanistan, winning would mean more soldiers deployed and a lot of dead Afghans. Trump has correctly assessed that we are unwilling to do what's needed to secure victory in that theater, so he wants to get out.

As for Syria and Iraq, we've completed our mission. Then we completed the next mission that crept along in the region. And the next one. It seems like every time we're finished with one mission, our armchair generals find something else to do. No thanks. It's time to get off the mission creep rat wheel. It's time to go.

But the elites resist. Part of the reason for their resistance is that they think that everything Trump wants must be wrong. Another part is the power of bureaucratic inertia. After all, the Pentagon is the largest bureaucracy on Earth.

The sunk cost fallacy is also to blame, which is especially true in the military. When your buddies have been dying somewhere for the last two decades, you may come to think that leaving without victory makes their sacrifice meaningless. Though understandable, it's the wrong way to think about the death of servicemen. Their sacrifices were not meaningless. The lost are heroes. There was nothing immoral about those wars, nothing to be ashamed of, and good riddance to the sons of bitches our troops sent to hell. Even if you disagreed, further sacrifices to a useless cause could never validate past ones.

Plus, there is the fact that some people like the endless wars. For some in the government, endless war provides opportunities. For some corporations, they provide a spigot to drain cash from Uncle Sam. Others just never seem to meet a war they don't want someone else to fight. But enough about Bill Kristol.

Every time Trump trial-balloons shutting down one of these lost causes, those factors combine to spark a veritable firestorm.

Take the October 2019 Syria pullout as an example. The Turkish dictator Recep Tayyip Erdogan called Trump to inform him that Turkish forces would enter a wide swath of northern Syria to clear out some communist Kurdish terrorists based in the region. Trump, unwilling to get our forces caught in the middle, directed that we pull our Special Forces units out of the area.

A firestorm was ignited. If you were to judge by the reaction of the foreign policy establishment, you'd think Erdogan had committed a greater atrocity than the Turks' Armenian genocide. Meanwhile, the same experts cried out that we were betraying "the Kurds," who were invariably referred to as a monolithic group, another lie. The Kurds are composed of many different factions who share a general ethnic heritage (including those aforementioned communist terrorists). Why should we put American lives on the line to defend them? The Kurds were never our ally against Turkey. We have no treaty ratified by the Senate obligating America to fight beside the Kurds in order to secure the Syrian border against...well, a NATO ally with whom we have a mutual defense treaty.

Many of Trump's supporters, not all of whom supported this decision (many worried about the Kurds, who ended up just fine), noted bitterly that the establishment considered the defense of Syria's border a moral imperative while simultaneously insisting that it's a moral imperative *not* to defend our own.

That's not an easy sell to Team Andrew J.

Jacksonians applaud the Syria decision because they see it in much simpler terms: Trump avoided war and pulled American forces out of a combat zone that served no strategic interest. And yet, the same people who insist that Trump is a warmonger thought this was bad.

Trump again proved that he is not a warmonger when he defused mounting tensions with Iran in January 2020. You could almost hear the establishment's collective groan when Trump declined to retaliate against the inept Iranian missile barrage that followed the hellfiring of Qasem Soleimani. The media and Democrats had spent the previous days demanding that Trump not launch a war against Iran, and when Trump did exactly that, they criticized him again.

The monster.

Trump understands that war may be good for businesses tied to the arms industry. That's not his concern. He knows it's bad for the overall economy, it's bad for the country, and it's bad politics. He knows that a major new war would distract him from keeping the promises that got him elected. So do his opponents. For all their moaning and groaning about Trump's bluster with the mullahs, his political enemies really hoped he'd start a new war in the Persian Gulf.

Nope.

Trump is not a pointy-headed intellectual, and he has no interest in summing up his foreign policy thoughts in some tome. He has eggheads to do that for him, like Secretary of State Mike Pompeo, who articulated the Trump Doctrine to a Claremont Institute gathering in May 2019. This speech, in front of the conservative movement's premier intellectual body, was the first intellectual articulation of the way of thinking that Trump single-handedly brought to our foreign relations. It's a common-sense approach that eschews the jargon and sclerosis of political science theories in favor of practical experience, the opposite of what they teach to aspiring Ivy League elitists. Trump might not be able to quote Clausewitz, but he knows that after twenty years, sticking around Kabul doesn't make a lick of sense.

The Trump Doctrine is simple: America's interests come first, and if you hurt an American, we'll kill you. If you don't want to do business with us—and we *love* doing business—then just leave us alone and do your seventh century thing. We'll return the favor.

Simple. Commonsense. Realistic.

For decades, the foreign policy elite insisted on conducting failed crusades for causes Americans just don't care about. Moreover, that same elite managed to bungle the few missions Americans did care about, creating morass after morass of conflict zones that the American military could not get out of. In response, the voters decided to replace the establishment not with something new, but with something old, Old Hickoryism. They voted for a guy who wanted peace, but peace from strength, not weakness. Just ask Soleimani what that means, if you can find one of his ears.

Compared to Hillary, Obama, and the rest of the peace-sign posse, Trump is practically Gandhi. True to form, the liars still trash him as a threat to peace, even as he steers us clear of wars they desperately want to start. How do they rationalize their own hypocrisy? Well, to the liars, all is fair in love and war, and they declared war against Trump a long time ago.

CHAPTER 8

Trump Hates Immigrants...
and You Hate Them Too!

The "Trump and you rube bigots from flyover-land hate immigrants" lie is a ham-fisted ploy designed to stop you from talking about a problem that the liars do not want to solve. Immigration has caused real problems for millions of American citizens. But instead of addressing those problems, the liars and the elites want to keep importing people for their own purposes.

As we've seen, when faced with the option of changing their policy or defaming those who disagree them, the liars will always choose the latter. Instead of openly defending their position, they prefer to turn legitimate opposing views into hate crimes. That way, they can silence dissent while they continue business as usual.

No one will talk about the costs, except Donald Trump, that is.

He must have missed the memo saying that an immigration system that weighs the costs and benefits of immigration against the interests of regular American citizens is xenophobic and bigoted. Maybe his immigrant wife hid that memo from him. Which is weird to say because, you know, he hates immigrants.

Throughout this chapter, there will be some overlap between legal and illegal immigrants. The pro-illegal immigrant faction loves to obscure the distinction between legal and illegal immigration because it allows them to conflate the lawful newcomer who waited patiently for a visa with some MS-13 slug who waded across the Rio Grande after being sent back three times previously for committing crimes in the U.S.A. While legal and illegal immigration are different issues, the establishment wanted the entire question of how many foreigners should come to America taken off the table. All the best and brightest agree with that.

But Trump refuses to recognize the open borders "consensus" that he and his supporters were never consulted about. The fact that he was willing to reject that consensus was one of the key reasons his presidential campaign took off like a rocket as soon as he announced his candidacy. The elites wanted to keep inching America towards their hemispheric common market dream, while Trump stood with the American people in opposition.

Immigration is an immense political and cultural issue, and the idea that it can be placed off limits is a dagger aimed at the heart of our republic. Debate, which necessarily includes both sides of a given issue, is central to the whole idea of self-government. Placing an entire side of any given debate outside the bounds of discussion is tyrannical and wrong. But the liars don't want a debate, they want to fix the results in their favor. Real debate offers the possibility that one side doesn't get what it wants. And the ruling class can't accept that possibility, not when the stakes are so high.

It's profoundly dictatorial. You can't have a free society when one faction wills its preferred policies into existence over and against the protestations of electoral majorities. Yet that's exactly what is happening with immigration. Immigration advocates are advancing their agenda in unconstitutional ways. And when it comes to illegal immigration, those invaders are, well, illegal. The laws forbidding unlawful entry (and the visa overstays of legal visitors) were passed by our Congress and signed by past presidents. Those laws forbid the current ad hoc policy of non-enforcement. Refusing to enforce the agreed-upon laws isn't democratic, it's the *opposite* of democratic—it's tyrannical!

But the elite doesn't want to resolve immigration democratically because they know regular people don't want to invite in a huge chunk of the Third World, much less fork over their cash to pay for the newcomers' doctors. Their resistance is not arbitrary contempt for immigrants. It's not blind hate. Immigration, legal and illegal, has costs and benefits, and the people reaping the benefits don't have to pay the costs. Regular folks—the ones being disenfranchised—do.

Trump speaks for them.

But wait, didn't Trump say that all Mexicans were drug dealers and rapists and all sorts of other horrible things? The media seems to think so. All the smart people on Twitter with blue checks next to their names seem to think so. So, it must be true, right?

Right?

Well, when Trump came down the escalator in June 2015 to announce what most of us (myself included) thought was at best a quixotic campaign for the presidency, he did point to some dangers illegal immigrants pose. That was revolutionary. No one was supposed to do that. We were supposed to pretend that everyone showing up here, whether legally or illegally, is a hard-working, law-abiding asset to our society.

It didn't matter whether you came here because your second cousin won a visa lottery or because you hired a coyote to traffic you across our southern border: no matter your story, we had to pretend that all immigrants were beyond reproach. But some did deserve reproach.

Trump refused to pretend. And sometimes the truth is not mindless bigotry, it's just the truth. In that first campaign speech, Trump declared his willingness to state inconvenient truths about immigration, and the elite will never forgive him for it.

You've heard it a thousand times. "When Mexico sends its people," Trump told the crowd, "they're not sending their best." It's unforgivable because it is objectively true. Mexico doesn't send its "best." Its "best" stay there and exploit the people who run away north. "They're sending people that have lots of problems," he went on, "and they're bringing those problems with [them]." Mexico indisputably sends drugs and criminals to America. Some good people may also come, but that's not the point. The point is that illegal immigration comes at real costs to American lives, and before Trump, no one wanted to talk about them.

Trump violated elite norms by refusing to pretend that anyone coming over the border is an industrious soul whom we ought to welcome. He rejected the ridiculous contention that the only thing preventing illegal immigrants from positively contributing to society is their lack of documentation. He even rejected the disingenuous "undocumented" euphemism that the open borders clique wants to substitute for the accurate description "illegal alien." Not having proper legal documentation is not some aberration that befalls the unlucky. It's the default state for everyone on Earth who is not an American citizen or a legal resident. "Undocumented immigrant" falsely insinuates that criminals who ignore our laws have done nothing wrong and are just the victims of some inexplicable bureaucratic SNAFU.

Illegal immigration is a dangerous drain on American resources. Not everyone coming over illegally is hardworking and not everyone coming here is a net plus to America. According to Steven A. Camarota and Karen Zeigler of the Center for Immigration Studies, writing on November 20, 2018, 35 percent of native households access welfare programs, while 63 percent of non-citizen households do. If immigrants are such a boon to our society, why are so many receiving public assistance? A significant number of the uninvited guests in our great Unmelting Pot are not exactly Horatio Alger-ing their way to the top.

And if immigrants do not take advantage of our public benefits, why do the uncontrolled immigration advocates freak out whenever someone suggests limiting their access to the public trough?

Not all immigrants arrive with palms up. Many of the entrepreneurial success stories the uncontrolled immigration advocates tell are true. Immigrants have long contributed to American society and can bring fresh ideas, energy, and enthusiasm. Every one of us has walked into a store or restaurant run by immigrants whose hard work and commitment made our lives better (and theirs). High tech has gone even higher because foreigners decided to come here and build their dreams in our country. Some of us, such as the president and myself, married immigrants.

Some people who come here illegally are "good," but with an asterisk: they may be good in some cosmic sense, but they are bad in the very real sense that they broke our laws. We do have the right to make our own laws, you know, and we should expect everyone to follow them.

But the benefits of immigration are not what's at issue. We're here to dispel lies and defamations, and there's no informal web of slander designed to keep people from talking about the good things immigrants do.

The liars don't want Trump, or you, to talk about the costs of immigration. And there are costs. There are infrastructure costs, as American citizens are called on to bear the brunt of additional people, legal and illegal, using our schools, streets, and emergency rooms. There are cultural costs, as massive influxes of people from different nations obviously impact a nation's social structure. We have seen it before with Irish and Italian immigrants who took time to assimilate. The new arrivals may well assimilate, but the assimilation process includes conflict and social disruption. Plus, today there is huge pressure *not* to assimilate. In the past, Irish, Italians, and other immigrants were taught to leave behind their former way of life and adopt American habits; today, elites tell immigrants to retain the trappings of their former homes while here in America. No wonder too many immigrants aren't assimilating.

Moreover, there are economic costs, particularly related to jobs and wages. Remember, we are constantly told these foreigners are here to work, but every job an immigrant takes means a job somebody already here can't fill. Supply and demand is a harsh mistress. If you have a limited number of low-skill jobs, the kind that a former *campesino* from Oaxaca might be willing to do for half-price, then American citizens will quickly find themselves out of work when a couple million people from Oaxaca show up. That's basic. And it's not only on the low end. We have all read stories of skilled American workers training their foreign replacements brought over on H-1B visas to work for a fraction of their salaries.

Those are real effects Americans feel thanks to our unfettered immigration policies. Shouldn't we be free to discuss that impact without being called racists?

Apparently not.

Again, this is not to say that we should never invite newcomers to America, but we citizens should be able to discuss the pace and extent of immigration without being showered with epithets or chased out of polite society. After all, it is our country, and it's our right to have a say in what happens inside it.

But not everyone feels that way. Unrestrained immigration is not up for debate. It's something that our elite generally wants off limits.

That means shutting down discussion about the most infamous consequence of immigration, crime. We would not have Angel Moms if we did not have angels, or children murdered by illegal aliens. Alien crime is real, and the demand that we tolerate it in silence is itself intolerable.

As for Trump's pointing out that some illegals are criminals, well, some illegals are criminals. Actually, all of them are—some just have a more varied portfolio than others. And yet, the smart set will throw a hissy fit when you point out that Mexicans have a connection to the dope trade or that World War Tres is going on just south of the border. Don't even think about mentioning the fact that the Mexican Army appears to be losing that war to the violent drug cartels.

There is a significant amount of immigrant crime, and even though mainstream outlets won't cover it, sometimes it's too big to hide. The guys who blew up the Boston Marathon? Immigrants. MS-13? Immigrants? The 9/11 guys? Immigrants (or at least long-term residents). But there is a slew of less infamous crime committed by immigrants. You will not hear about it from the mainstream media—well, maybe down deep in the twenty-third paragraph—but conservative outlets will point it out. The uncontrolled immigration advocates insist that immigrant crime rates are below that of American citizens, but isn't one murder, one rape, too many?

The Department of Justice's "Alien Incarceration Report–Fiscal Year 2018, Quarter 2" sheds some light on the situation. According to the report, 21 percent of folks in federal pokey are immigrants, more than half of whom entered the country illegally. According to a 2017 study, the immigrant portion of the U.S. population was 13.6 percent. Unless math suddenly became racist, which they're probably teaching in math departments on college campuses, 13.6 percent is less than 21 percent.

That means Uncle Sam is locking immigrants up at about 150 percent of the rate of native-born Americans. As the SJWs say, that's problematic. And according to the liars, it's so problematic that we should all close our eyes and pretend the problem doesn't exist.

Trump is not that kind of guy; he simply pointed out something undeniable. Immigrants, illegal and otherwise, commit crimes, sometimes horrific ones. That is a tangible cost of mass immigration. And maybe it's a cost that we are willing to bear. But in the eyes of the establishment, Donald Trump's crime was to raise the issue for discussion after most of the best and brightest had declared the discussion closed.

Why are so many people in our elite committed to uncontrolled immigration? What motivates them to support widespread flaunting of the law, or to tar and feather anyone who raises legitimate concerns? Viewed in the most favorable light, they have an altruistic urge to help the huddled masses yearning to be free. Viewed in a truer light, uncontrolled immigration is a huge boon to various components of the elite, and the virtue signaling opportunities are almost too good to pass up.

Corporations love the idea of unrestrained immigration because they get a nearly endless supply of workers willing to do more work for less money than American workers. Plus, more people inside our borders means more people to buy Chinese-made junk from companies like Walmart. For the corporations, mass immigration is a win-win.

Meanwhile, Democrat politicians love the idea of importing new voters more likely to vote Democrat. Just look at California—massive immigration shifted the Golden State from red to solid blue over the last three decades. But despite the fact that Democrats openly tout their strategy's success, when Republicans point it out, they shriek that the Republicans are pushing a neo-Nazi "Replacement Theory." Just because some tiki-torch losers have stumbled onto the obvious does not change the facts. The Democrat Party wants unrestricted immigration to boost their electoral prospects. The whole party dreams of tearing down whatever barriers exist between the United States and Mexico, and for years they've advocated giving illegal immigrants citizenship. As if that weren't enough, the 2020 Democrat presidential primary candidates sought to offer immigrants even more carrots to cross the border illegally, calling for the funding of illegal alien medical care. And the Democrats want to make those newcomers citizens via amnesty.

If the Democrats thought that newly minted citizens would vote Republican, they would oppose illegal immigration as staunchly as they did a generation ago, back when they were the party of the working class instead of the talking and typing class. Simultaneously, the Party also fights any kind of limits on legal immigration, believing that most immigrant citizens will eventually find their way to the donkeys.

Inexplicably, some Republicans still advocate open borders. While some are just virtue signaling to their Democrat cocktail party clique, others are puppets of the corporate donors. And some may even believe the fantasies of the gentry right who scribbled away in dead or dying conservative journals like the late, unlamented *Weekly Standard* about how the "traditional values" of immigrants, both illegal and legal could be the key to the GOP's earning their electoral loyalty. That has gone about as well as most of the losers' schemes.

One of the best things about Trump is that he will not be shut up. Even though his mouth can sometimes get him in trouble, it's invaluable in fighting the open borders brigade. In 2016 and thereafter, President Trump single-handedly busted open the discussion of a topic that the elite had decided was off limits. They tried to keep it off limits with a flurry of lies about anyone brave enough to challenge the elite consensus. Luckily for us, Trump did not care about their lies. And while the liars still insist that Trump and his supporters hate immigrants, we're all talking about immigration now, lies and defamations be damned.

CHAPTER 9

Trump Hates Women...
and So Do You, Including You Women!

Donald Trump hates women? Oh, come on. He loves women. He loves beautiful women, attractive women, and good-looking women.

Okay, that's a joke, but so is the idea that Trump hates women. It's simply not true. But as we have seen, truth is beside the point. Trump, and you, *have* to hate women—even if you are a woman yourself!

The real issue, besides his being a Republican, is that Trump does not do the modern male schtick. Donald Trump forthrightly owns his cisgendered-ness, and he eagerly embraces traditional concepts of female beauty.

In other words, he's a man and isn't ashamed of it.

The liars want you to think that Trump's gleeful years as a playboy, including dating *Playboy* playmates, masks his deep resentment for the female of the species. Trump didn't chase tail because he likes sex. No, his lifestyle is a lid covering a seething cauldron of misogyny.

Calling Trump a misogynist is more than a clumsy attempt to smear him: it's an integral part of a broader push to denigrate and eliminate traditional masculinity. Remember, neutered, soft males are easier to control. Look at the drones on our college campuses and how eagerly they obey. Trump's in-your-face phallocentrism goes hand in hand with his utter unwillingness to submit to the incessant whining of the left. You're the same way, which is why they try to make you out as a misogynist too.

Think of Trump as the ultimate bad boy, the handsome, sexy mistake most women either make or secretly dream about making. A lot of the liberal feminists disdain Trump because they identify him with the daddy who rejected them, or they compare him to the soft lump of biological male sitting on the couch they picked out together at Pottery Barn and waiting for her to come home from work so he can share his feelings with her. Trump is, simultaneously, the man they desire and despise.

Trump's antics are easy for them to caricature as monstrous. Trump was not a gentleman in his youth, nor even in his late middle age. He was loud, vulgar, and not particularly concerned with the kind of propriety that our liberal friends usually dismiss as bourgeois constraints on their self-actualization. But boy, do they ever miss those gentlemanly attributes when they are gone.

In a curious twist of fate, Trump lived his younger days exactly how the liberal elites have advocated since the sexual revolution. If it felt good, he did it, and he had the cash to ensure that if it felt good and he wanted to do it, he could afford to do it. If anything, Trump was the perfect embodiment of the sixties. He flaunted conventional morality, and for some reason that's why the people who demand you cast off your old, tired morals hate him. The new morality gave men like Trump the opportunity to swing with Playmates, while it gave the liberal feminists the opportunity to get with the kind of men who get with liberal feminists.

No wonder they're miserable.

Trump was one of the winners of the sexual revolution and, true to form, liberal feminist women were the losers. Have you ever seen a happy liberal feminist?

But Trump is happy. He loves being Trump. And that must grate the self-loathing liberal feminists to no end.

Trump does not care about feminism or any of the other ideological fetishes that obsess Wellesley graduates and *Teen Vogue* editors. He does not care about "women" in the abstract—he doesn't think twice about them. Rather, he sees women through the same real estate developer lenses through which he sees everyone else. He thinks about women according to his needs, a purely transactional view that drives the feminists nuts.

Feminists demand that men consider them as valuable, important individuals whose femininity provides a key component of their identity and who deserve to be appreciated and respected for themselves. Trump sees women in terms of what they can do for him, whether that be in business, in politics, or in the sack. But here's the thing—he sees men in much the same way, sack excluded.

It does not help that Trump is pretty much the captain *and* owner of the football team in terms of his place in American culture. The *New York Post* sold zillions of copies chronicling Donald Trump's amorous adventures cutting a swathe through the willing flesh available to a guy with good looks, celebrity, and a bottomless well of dollars. He was the happy-go-lucky—*very happy*—counterpoint to the pointy-headed liberal archetype of the sexually liberated male.

Hugh Hefner made a lot of money selling dirty pics, but he was trying to also push a philosophy, a cool, hip, intellectual sexuality where the mind was on par with the genitals. In reality, all that was so much dross. No one read *Playboy* for the articles. Few guys really wanted to be the smoking jacket–clad swell nattering on about Thelonious Monk. They wanted to be Donald Trump, scoring with pneumatic bimbettes two at a time. And later, when it came time to settle down and get married, they wanted to do so with a gorgeous ex-model who radiated class rather than the kind of neurotic career gal who wore an "I'm with Her" button on November 8, 2016.

Trump represents a visceral male sexuality that alternately terrifies, horrifies, and intrigues the stifled, repressed members of the Liberal Junior Anti-Sex League. As Camille Paglia points out again and again in her *oeuvre*, male sexuality is powerful, dangerous, and uncontrollable.

At some instinctive level, liberal elites know that, which is why they work so hard to tame and shackle masculine impulses.

Trump not only rejects the feminist vision of relations between the sexes as a complex interaction based on guilt, power, privilege, and oppression, his popularity proves that most normal people do too. Such widespread rejection is intolerable to liberal feminists. In their eyes, anyone who isn't as miserable as they are is brainwashed by the patriarchy.

And because Trump is not a miserable, self-loathing man, he must be a seething woman-hater. But all Trump wanted to do was get laid.

That's why it is almost pointless to wonder what is misogynistic in Trump's conduct. Actual misogyny does not matter to the liars any more than actual racism, or homophobia, or any of the other -isms and phobias which allegedly afflict Trump and you. In their eyes, Trump hates women because he refuses to see men and women as the liars demand they be seen. And more importantly, he's a misogynist because he is a Republican.

So do not bother asking when Trump ever opined that women are inferior to men. Has he demanded that women be consigned to their homes? Did he give Ivanka the choice of being a nurse or a teacher? Have he and Mike Pence submitted draft legislation imposing handmaid outfits upon our female populace? You would think so with all the nitwits scuttling about Capitol Hill during the Brett Kavanaugh hearings in their goofy red robes.

Yeah, if there's one thing Donald Trump dreams of, it's a sexually repressed theocracy where females are forced into shapeless, baggy garments that hide their bods.

It's not just Trump who is conspiring against womankind, it's all of you chauvinist pigs out there in Jesusland. There is this odd narrative that women are, for example, victims of an all-encompassing plot to exclude them from entry into various fields. According to the true believers, men in charge just can't bear the thought of women estrogening up their occupations.

But that's preposterous. Most people want to work with people who can get a job done. Donald Trump is the same way. If there is one thing Trump has always been, even in the twilight of his Don Juan days, it's a bottom-line guy. If you can make him money and can perform, you're good to go, genitals be damned.

Plus, can you imagine a group of men conspiring to act against women? It sounds more like kindergarten than the board room. Search your memory banks for a time in your life when you encountered a sexist conspiracy based purely on gender. Chances are, you will come up blank. But when a conspiracy doesn't exist, liberal feminists will just make one up in order to fill their empty lives.

Now, sexual harassment isn't something liberal feminists have made up. And as we recently learned, it's especially prevalent among big Democrat pols and donors. Harvey Weinstein, a close personal friend of Hillary Clinton, Barack Obama, and the rest of the smart set, used his power and position to directly reward or punish women based on their willingness to abase themselves with him. But according to the liberal feminists, that's different from sexism.

Donald Trump's record of sexism is non-existent. He never denied women jobs or opportunities based on their dual XX chromosomes. And so, without any record of real sexism, the liars try to paint the Donald as a sex predator. They know sex predators well, since most of their icons were notorious womanizers and sleazebags. JFK, Mr. Hillary, Badfinger Biden, the aforementioned Harvey—find a popular Democrat, and you'll probably find someone who dismisses his victims with a sneer and a suggestion to put some ice on that.

Or leaves them to drown in an Oldsmobile he drove off a bridge.

We keep hearing about Trump's "War on Women," but where are the casualties? Sure, there are a bunch of accusers good for some MSNBC hits. And there were various ladies whose silence he bought or tried to buy. They ended up not being silent, but no one cared. In the end, Stormy Daniels's lawyer and former resistance hero Michael Avenatti treated her worse than Trump ever did.

There was the Brett Kavanaugh imbroglio, and Trump was labeled a sexist monster for not withdrawing the nomination of a guy baselessly accused of running a teen rape gang. Except no one believed Kavanaugh was Harvey Weinstein in a robe, and Trump looked like a man for not folding under the barrage of lies. Just imagine Mitt Romney in that situation with his binders full of submission.

The *Access Hollywood* tape was supposed to seal Trump's doom in 2016 by showing his burning enmity toward the fairer sex. What it really showed was the utterly transactional nature of his extracurricular relationships. Leaked by NBC, the decade-old tape had Trump and Billy Bush—wait, weren't the Bushes gentlemen?—chatting about Trump's pre-canoodling tactics. There were two particularly juicy paragraphs that were supposed to indict and convict him:

> I moved on her, and I failed. I'll admit it. I did try and fuck her. She was married. And I moved on her very heavily. In fact, I took her out furniture shopping. She wanted to get some furniture. I said, "I'll show you where they have some nice furniture." I took her out furniture—I moved on her like a bitch. But I couldn't get there. And she was married. Then all of a sudden I see her, she's now got the big phony tits and everything. She's totally changed her look.
>
> I better use some Tic Tacs just in case I start kissing her. You know I'm automatically attracted to beautiful—I just start kissing them. It's like a magnet. Just kiss. I don't even wait. And when you're a star, they let you do it. You can do anything. Grab 'em by the pussy. You can do anything.

It's not particularly edifying stuff, nor is it meant to be. It's two guys talking smack, as guys sometimes do in what they believe is a private setting. When the press jumped on it, and they sure did jump on it, it was supposed to destroy Trump's candidacy.

It did not.

The leaked tape couldn't take down Trump because it was nowhere near the Weinsteinian rape monologue that the media made it out to be. Trump's striking out with Nancy O'Dell, the *Access Hollywood* co-host, is hardly sexual assault. And while it's not good to make passes at married women, it's nowhere near the #MeToo revelations that would later embroil many of the elites condemning Trump's remarks. It's actually a bit self-deprecating. He offered her stuff—his attention, furniture—and she blew him off. That's the transactional nature of his world view. He did not close the deal.

The second paragraph is, for Trump's enemies, the money paragraph. Here Trump explains that, in his experience, the women he encounters are often—how to put it?—eager to interact. Trump again fully recognizes the transactional nature of the kind of relationships: "When you're a star, they let you do it." And regular people, though not delighted by this behavior, get it. There are always some women who are ready and willing to engage in a *quid pro quo* with a guy who has something they want.

Gotta watch out for those *quid pro quos*.

Trump's greatest strengths are often his greatest weaknesses. Millions of Americans love the man because he often says the quiet part out loud, and sometimes that gets him into trouble. The *Access Hollywood* tape is an example of such. Does anyone doubt that Bill Clinton thinks exactly the same way, whether around town, in the hot tub with his bouncy, giggly friends while Hillary's out riding her broom, or on Jeffrey Epstein's *Lolita Express*? No. But Big Bubba would never say it; he'd just keep living out his sordid fantasies.

Trump called out the transactional nature of celebrity sexuality, and by doing so, demonstrated that both men and women play the same game for different prizes.

He rejected the notion of the purity of femininity, which is key to the liberal feminist moral argument that somehow masculinity is inferior. Trump, ironically, was sexist for treating men and women the same. They both tend to pursue their objectives. Powerful men want to have sex with beautiful women, while beautiful women want to get things from powerful men. Both want something from the other, and sometimes they come to a deal.

Many young men act the same way. And without defending the young men—many of whom would have been smacked around by older males in the more enlightened past—how should they know any better? Men and women are different, but if commenting on sexual differences puts you in the penalty box, then we shouldn't be shocked when young men treat young ladies like they treat their male friends. And young men do not treat each other gently or considerately.

There was a time when the young Donald Trump and the young men of a similar feather would have been called "cads." But what's a cad once you've erased the differences between the sexes? If gender is a social construct, as our liberal betters so often tell us, then who is to say what is dishonorable and what is patriarchal when men chase women? Is it "oppressive" for men to treat women with traditional forms of deference and respect?

But just because liberals deny the differences between the sexes, that doesn't mean those differences don't exist. Acknowledging those differences is not "sexism," and the unalterable and unyielding differences between men and women will stand the test of time. They can close their eyes to the facts as much as they want, but that won't change a single thing.

Our elites refuse to acknowledge these manifest truths about women in military combat arms positions, or women in other positions where there are concrete facts that make their participation a problem. The rule that facts matter except where they're inconvenient to the narrative just does not fly. The declaration of indisputable truth becomes sexist. But someone like Donald Trump refuses to play by these rules.

The truth is not sexist. It's the truth. And it is the truth no matter how much it undercuts the preferred narrative. To the extent the narrative defies the truth, it itself is a lie.

While the president has, as of this writing, not offered his view of women in the military and the problems inherent with integrating them into all duty positions, this is exactly the kind of situation where alleged sexism is nothing of the sort. In fact, claims of sexism are less a warning label than a bludgeon designed to shut down unapproved thinking and force the speaker back into line.

That's the purpose of the whole "Trump hates women" slander. That's also the purpose of lying about you Trump supporters hating women. As with so many of the other lies, the truth is immaterial. It's simply a ploy, a means to an end. As always, the end is submission to the dominant narrative.

The "Trump hates women" slander will not stop. But then, is it really effective? Does anyone really think that there is some sort of conspiracy against females with Trump as its mastermind? No. And that's a problem—what good is a tired lie that no one believes?

CHAPTER 10

Trump Is Not a Real Conservative...

and Neither Are You, No Matter What You Actually Think!

"Donald Trump is no conservative! And this populist wave infecting our base is itself not conservative! He, and they, have betrayed True Conservatism™! Doom awaits!"

Maybe doom does await, but not because Donald Trump broke the "conservative" establishment's hold on the GOP. The conservative establishment did a pretty remarkable job of dooming itself. And now, it is largely behind the lie that Trump, and you, are somehow not conservative at all.

The conservative establishment is largely made up of people posing as "conservatives," though they are not conservatives in any meaningful sense of the word. They're professional conservatives, always shooting for a slot on the *New York Times* editorial pages or a gig on MSNBC. They play the "conservative balance," providing allegedly conservative input that always happens to reliably support each and every liberal position. It's a role, a mask, a figurative trucker cap reading "CONSERVATIVE," and the professional conservatives are nothing like the conservatives you meet in ordinary life.

They are "conservative" in the sense that they are not actually conservative at all.

After all this time, the professional conservatives still traipse from studio to studio telling liberal talk shows that Donald Trump and the Republican base are no longer "conservative." And liberals love to join in the conservative-shaming. You see, liberals are very, very concerned with the present state of conservatism mostly because it is winning. They prefer the old school conservative, who knew his job was to put up a half-hearted fight, lose gracefully, and then move on to the next failed holding action against the progressive onslaught. These are the same guys who praised George H. W. Bush for lying about "Read my lips—no new taxes" right up until the moment they crucified him for it in 1992.

By saying that Donald Trump isn't a conservative, liberals and the conservative establishment hope to split the Republican Party by peeling off ideological conservatives, leading Trump and his ilk to defeat. The conservative establishment thinks sabotaging Donald Trump will bring them back to power. The Democrats are just in it for the autophagy.

Trump is certainly not like the professional conservatives, which is why he's president and they're one of three nobodies agreeing with Don Lemon. But that doesn't mean Trump isn't conservative in the true sense of the word. In fact, Trump's appeal to American conservatives has forced us to reexamine exactly what American conservatism is today.

Trump was a New York real estate guy of no discernible ideology who had his finger on the pulse of actual voters. As an ideological conservative—I once took a (liberal) date to hear William F. Buckley talk—I did not trust this guy as far as I could throw him. And he's a big dude.

Boy, was I wrong. Trump turned out to be the most conservative president since Ronald Reagan, to the delight of millions of fellow doubters. Look at his unstoppable tsunami of judicial appointments. Every day with Trump in office is conservative Christmas, and he's Santa.

Many of us movement types were skeptical of Trump in 2016 because he lacked ideological moorings. He didn't subscribe to *National Review* or spend much energy expounding the intellectual foundations of conservatism. But while the intellectual component of the movement is important to establish key principles, until Trump came down that famous escalator many of us did not realize just how completely intellectual conservatism had lost its way.

We certainly knew that we'd lost every major fight of the last twenty years. Our movement had been one long series of failures since the Contract with America had brought about some deficit reductions and welfare reform in the mid-nineties. Expanding Medicare under George W. Bush? Perhaps that was a *kind* of success, but just not the *conservative* kind. No Child Left Behind? What could be more conservative than a giant federal government program wresting local control of education from our communities and committing it to the loving care of Washington bureaucrats? Well, pretty much everything would be more conservative than that.

The 2008 financial collapse was the worst of the bunch. A bunch of rich people screwed up betting with our money, so we decided to give them more of our money to help them escape the consequences? If that's "conservative," you can count me out. And leave it to John McCain to exponentially magnify the botched handling of the crisis by panicking and letting Obama roar past him to win election. Why fail a little when you can fail comprehensively?

Even where conservatives did jam down an occasional victory, it was often Pyrrhic to the max. We managed to hold firm and support the Iraq war. Congratulations, conservatism, what an accomplishment that turned out to be. Way to go.

The Bushes were hardly inspirational figures in the political arena. Bush 41 was man enough to dive-bomb the Japanese in World War II, but when it came to disappointing the country club set, the man may as well have had a sponge for a spine. Bush 43 wore his conservatism like a mask at a masquerade ball. Underneath, he was just another moderate with no desire to fight for conservative principles.

His father broke his "Read my lips" no tax increase pledge and W himself unleashed "compassionate conservatism" upon an unwaiting world. HW's tax hike and W's "compassionate conservatism" were hardly any different in substance from what a moderate Democrat would have proposed. It was essentially center-left policy combined with an apology, with a scrap of conservative red meat for the rubes and a wink and a nod to everyone else, letting them know that he really had no truck with this crazy right-wing talk.

The same was true of John McCain, whose entire rationale for his candidacy was his intense and earnest belief that John McCain should be president. McCain would later, after his rejection by Republicans had done the impossible and further embittered him, break his word and save Obamacare, over and against the will of his constituents, his party, and his country. This is the kind of guy the GOP establishment thought was the perfect candidate.

And after McCain's manifest imperfections were manifested, the GOP decided to run a policy duplicate in 2012 who made McCain look like an inspired choice. While McCain spent his twenties locked up in the Hanoi Hilton, Mitt Romney's golden years were filled with avoiding military service and laying off American workers. Mitt Romney was straight outta Massachusetts, the second-place state when it comes to modern presidential candidates. His primary accomplishment, besides creating innovative auto roof torments for dogs, was his own version of Obamacare. He would toss away any chance of success by allowing Candy Crowley to fit him for a vinyl gimp suit on national television when she silenced him with some Obama narrative–supporting baloney during a debate and he just took it like the punk he was and remains.

Our conservative establishment decided this cast of characters was the very best embodiment of conservatism, the best possible standard-bearers for our cause. The establishment and their lackeys had no interest in conserving anything. They just wanted to put up fake resistance while grifting donors.

That was the state of play in the run-up to 2016, when about two dozen Republicans representing all the flavors on the Conservatism, Inc. menu decided to run for president. They ranged from the establishment-loving Jeb! Bush to the establishment-tweaking Ted Cruz. The smart set was all in on Jeb! because they believed that American conservatives were clamoring for yet another colossal failure. Hillary Clinton would have mopped the floor with Jeb!, and he would have thanked her and asked if he may have another. There's a video of Jeb! out there from before the race placing a medal around that creaky harpy's withered neck in recognition of her dedication to our glorious Constitution or some such pap. This is the guy our betters decided should take her on.

Thankfully, we did not obey.

The 2016 candidates were all talking about the same things Beltway conservatives have always talked about: tax cuts, budget cutting, and beefing up the military to go fight foreign wars. But here's the secret—the voters wanted to talk about the issues the establishment wanted to sweep under the rug.

The people were talking about a border in disarray and a deluge of illegal aliens. Well, that was not conservative for some reason ("some reason" being that the GOP's corporate donors wanted an unceasing flow of Third World peasants to silently toil for artificially low wages in their factories and on their farms). Jeb! himself called breaking our immigration laws—you know, the ones that the guy in the job he was half-heartedly running for was supposed to enforce—an "act of love." And when it came to crime, the establishment wanted to ignore atrocities like an illegal alien drinking and driving into a carload of Americans or raping and murdering an American citizen. When the base started clamoring about it, the establishment and their liberal friends called them racist. That wasn't going to last forever.

The people were talking about the consequences of globalization. While establishment donors made millions in a globalized economy, the blue-collar base saw that the costs disproportionately fell on their shoulders. A lot of regular folks were waving *zaijian* to their jobs as their jobs sailed off to China, while politicians across the ideological spectrum told them to "learn to code."

And last but not least, the people were sick and tired of the endless wars. Iraq was back in turmoil as the JV team, ISIS, reconquered the land Bush had barely pried away from the insurgents during the Surge. A slow but steady drumbeat of reported casualties continued month after month from Afghanistan, while the Western world tried to deal with the consequences of two failed states in Libya and Syria. It's one thing to send your kids off to fight—and the GOP base sent its kids off to fight— but it's another to *continue* to send your kids to referee intractable brawls between strange people from unfathomable cultures who, at the end of the day, hate our guts and don't want us around.

None of the conservative candidates were talking about all these things, at least not in depth. But Donald Trump did, and it caused a real scandal. How dare he defy the conservative gospel? *Real* conservatives want tax cuts, budget cuts, and a beefed up military for fighting foreign wars. Who did this vulgar ruffian think he was? And why did his millions of supporters back someone so out of touch with Conservatism, Inc.?

Of course, not being tuned into the conservative ideology echo chamber allowed Trump to avoid GOP indoctrination. Instead of rattling off a list of ideologically informed positions, Trump assessed issues one at a time and went with his gut feeling.

Maybe that gut feeling was what conservatism had been missing all along. Maybe conservative ideology had fallen out of touch with reality, and no longer addressed real peoples' problems anymore. And maybe it was the most unlikely person of all, Donald Trump, who was actually more conservative than the conservatives themselves.

So what is conservatism anyway?

Conservatism is most definitely *not* a set of policy prescriptions. For time immemorial, conservatives have opposed quick, ideological fixes in the name of common sense. Once upon a time, common sense demanded tax cuts, budget cuts, and beefing up the military to fight wars abroad. But that was never the crux of conservatism. Conservatism was the impulse behind those policies, but once the establishment started to focus on the policies and not the impulse, they lost the plot.

Conservatism is a temperament, a world view—something more than slavish adherence to policies that mirror the interests of our ruling class. Conservatism embraces tradition, not mindless reaction. It recognizes the value and incredible wisdom that comes from the past and informs our present. Conservatives look for problems first, not policies, and try to think about how the people who made this country great would have tried to solve them.

Contrary to what the country club clique would have you believe, the populists understand that impulse better than the establishment. Remember the Tea Party? Remember how at every single gathering, the media would focus on the dude in the tri-corner hat LARPing James Madison? It was a big joke to the elite, but at its core the Tea Party demonstrated the commitment of regular folks to what the Founders created. You cannot go to a conservative event without someone trying to hand you a pocket Constitution.

Conserving the republic is the point of conservatism, and that's where the conservative establishment failed actual conservatives most damningly. The establishment acquiesced to turning over greater and greater authority to unaccountable bureaucracies, exporting American industry to countries overseas, and allowing unfettered immigration from the Third World. When people complained, the establishment kept playing its favorite tracks from *The GOP's Greatest Hits of 1984*.

No wonder people stopped listening. When the establishment heard rumblings of discontent, it decided to crank the greatest hits even louder. It took a Donald Trump-sized megaphone for them to hear the base's justified complaints.

When conservatism became a bag of clichés and insider fetishes that only appealed to the think tank and bow tie set, it became indistinguishable from leftism. Conservatism was never a series of slogans and policy prescriptions that required absolute fealty—that's what the left stands for. Instead, conservatives pride themselves on holding ideology in contempt, focusing on the world as it is, and trying to solve problems pragmatically.

Liberalism, like other forms of leftism, assumes the perfectibility of man. It assumes that some future government can resolve all of mankind's problems. But even more dangerously, leftists presume that they have the roadmap to utopia. It doesn't matter whether leftists want to produce the New Soviet Man, the Nazi version of Friedrich Nietzsche's *Übermensch* (remember, National Socialists are socialists, and just because Jonah Goldberg pointed that out does not make it false), or the woke, gender-fluid (locally-sourced) hot chocolate–sipping social justice whiner, the means to that perfect end state is always the wholehearted embrace of leftist ideology. You can become perfect. You just have to submit.

That's why leftism takes on a quasi-religious character. Leftists think they can build heaven on Earth. They want to redeem a fallen humanity. It's no surprise that leftism has all religious fundamentalism's flaws without any of the upside, like belief in a providential God or the possibility of grace. The left cannot tolerate heretics or blasphemers. One must accept the revealed Official Truth without question or dissent in order to make the promise of perfection real. That's why liberals are always placing intentions before results. Results are beside the point, since the point is submission to the dogma.

A given policy—say, giving free money to people who don't want to work—is not measured by its results. Liberals don't care about results, they care about having the right intentions. If they cared about results, we wouldn't have to play hopscotch dodging human waste on the sidewalks of San Francisco. The vague, abstract good of "helping," which is always actually the delicious act of exercising raw power by stealing from Person A to give the fruits of Person A's labor to preferred Person B, trumps what actually happens when the policy is enacted. You see, results are the preserve of political parties, not religious cults, so pointing out failure (like, "the streets are littered with heaps of human dung and discarded syringes") is not merely immaterial, not just irrelevant, but heretical.

Before Donald Trump came on the scene, the conservative establishment was just as much a religious cult as liberalism. Free trade with countries that use slave labor, subsidize their industries, and devalue their currency hurts American workers? Fine with them, as long as you don't question "free" trade. Iraqis aren't waving American flags and holding democratic elections? Doesn't matter, it was the thought that counts.

Conservative policy ideas were no longer measured by their results: they became a creed that you had to believe for admission to the cult. Donald Trump didn't just question the creed, he proudly called it a load of crap. He was a total heretic, and the establishment wanted to burn him at the stake.

But by questioning Conservative, Inc. dogma, Trump brought Republicans back to what matters. He brought conservatives back to pragmatism, gut instinct, and suspicion of ideology. He got us focused on winning, delivering results for the American people, and representing the interests of the American middle class.

That's natural for conservatives, who tend to be the ones who work and produce in occupations where results actually matter, such as farming, manufacturing, and the military. Sure, it's wrong to take someone's hard-earned money and give it to someone else as a matter of principle, but it's also wrong because it doesn't *work*.

You give free money to hobos, and you end up with drunk and stoned hobos. And ruined shoes.

Conservatives do not believe that people are inevitably good. We are not cynical, but we aren't fuzzy-minded Pollyannas either. A liberal will tell you that a criminal is not really a criminal because he had a tough upbringing and America is racist and there's no economic opportunity. A conservative will look at the same perp and see a car thief who belongs in jail. And, incidentally, the crook better not try to jack the conservative's Ford Explorer because the patriot has a 12-gauge solution to that problem.

It doesn't take a guy with a doctorate in political philosophy who wrote a dissertation on Edmund Burke to see what conservatism means. That's the thing about real conservatism: it's not *hard*. There's no real mystery to it. Sure, the intellectuals can analyze and hold forth on its subtleties, but at the end of the day, conservativism is based on natural law and life experience, while leftism is based on self-serving wishful thinking justified by the tenets of an ever morphing and invented morality. That's why five years ago, someone who insisted that a man could get pregnant was a nut. Today, someone insisting a man cannot get pregnant is Ted Bundy.

The establishment conservatives lost touch with the lived experience of millions of Americans, and as a result, they lost touch with the base. Conservatism has to be based on a common sense understanding of the real world accessible to everyone. You don't need a conservative clerisy to explain common sense; it's right there, based in the real world. In the real world, if you fail to do the things you need to do to raise a crop, no crop grows. If you are a soldier and you aren't better trained and armed than your enemy, you die. And if you fail to build a building right, no one buys it.

Donald Trump was a real estate developer. He built and sold buildings. If the building was not perfect on the walk-through, then it didn't get sold, meaning Trump didn't get the money he needed to keep paying his lenders their vig. Failure had consequences.

That's not true in Washington, where failure often gets rewarded. You can fake it as a conservative scribbler, living a sheltered life in academia or some think tank. If you write something that's just mediocre, it will be forgotten. You'll still get your paycheck, and you'll publish something else next week.

Anyone who's been in business knows that the real world doesn't work that way. Business is binary: you succeed or you fail based on measurable criteria. And failure will make it difficult to provide for your family or keep a roof over your head. The real world is Yoda 101: "Try not. Do... or do not. There is no try."

Liberals shrug if their latest policy doesn't work because working or not working is not the point. The feels are the point. But results are the point in conservatism, and Trump was the first guy in a long time to get that.

Conservatism must be more than abstract policies passed around among D.C. insiders. It must be more than arcane wonk-speak compiled in Heritage Foundation white papers, as useful as they are, and set forth in the moist pages of the sunken *Weekly Standard*, as useless as it was. Conservatism must be relevant, accessible, and appealing to the people whose problems it claims to solve. An ideology no one will vote for is dead, and a party with a dead ideology will soon be dead too. Trump made conservatism relevant again by talking about the issues people cared about, and he brought accountability back by holding the feet of Washington failures to the fire.

If you don't think the conservative establishment was built on failure and empty ideology, then just take illegal immigration as an example. Illegal immigration should not be a tough issue for conservatives. There's the national sovereignty angle, always a conservative favorite. There's the law and order component—after all, illegal aliens are aliens who are here illegally. And then there's the cultural disruption angle. You can't pour a couple dozen million foreigners into a culture and not have an impact, especially when you have not bothered to ask the people being impacted if doing so is okay with them. Yet the establishment managed to tie itself in knots figuring out ways to sweep it under the rug. In fact, it didn't just try to sweep it under the rug, it wanted to actively promote it!

"Well, you see the market says yada yada yada."

Sure, the market's great. Everyone loves the market. But everyone also loves to have a say in who comes into our country. The definition of conservatism can't be "Milton Friedman would approve." That's just not going to cut it.

And yet, the D.C. conservative mandarins said Trump wasn't conservative despite the fact that he was the only one calling to end illegal immigration. They botched a sure thing, and it did not help that much of the conservative donor class had a vested interest in an open border, and everyone noticed that the donees seemed to bend over backwards for their donors' positions until their noodle spines snapped. Trump called them out for it, and they responded by questioning his conservative bona fides. At least they managed to keep a straight face.

In the end, conservatism shares a lot with what the elites lump under "populism." At its best, conservatism is concerned with the wisdom of regular people and focuses on their concerns rather than the concerns selected by their elite betters. That's what conservatives have always called for, and what our most conservative presidents all did.

Trump is able to explain his agenda to a truck driver or an ironmonger because he knows actual truck drivers and ironmongers and their problems. They are the kind of folks Trump came up around on work sites and at building projects. Truck drivers and ironmongers see the problems with unfettered trade and illegal immigration. They live those problems every day. It's not hard to understand. But instead of sticking with commonsense solutions to commonsense problems, the conservative establishment offered convoluted, hard to understand explanations that were really meant to convince the base that their problems didn't exist, or that what they thought were problems are actually unalloyed goods.

Oh, and then they called the base "racist" and insisted that it shut its collective mouth.

One of the least attractive qualities of the conservative establishment, especially those members fired by the conservative base and replaced with Donald Trump, is the tendency of these grifters to fall back on the leftist slanders about racism and other bigotry to explain their own summary termination as conservative leaders.

Donald Trump's conservatism brought back to the fore concepts like patriotism, the primacy of American workers, and the understanding that people are not perfectible. Walk into a bar somewhere between the coasts, strike up a conversation with a local, and that's usually the gist of what they'll say. That's conservatism, pure and simple, and Trump channeled it all the way to the White House.

The conflict with China? What was the coherent conservative case for rubber-stamping trade deals that let China treat the U.S.A. like a Bill Clinton intern? If American conservatism wants to get anything done, or at least anything that's going to get support beyond the narrow band of conservative Poindexters, it has to take America's side. But some donors liked China on top in their dealings with America, and the donees deployed a lot of shaky arguments designed to explain how America was not being ravished, and even if it were being ravished it should just lie back and enjoy it.

The wars? What could be less conservative than marching off to the benighted corners of the Third World and trying to convince the locals to send their entire way of life in a brand-new direction? Regular conservatives, many of whom had the dubious pleasure of spending a tour or two in the sketchy precincts of our globe, immediately understood that nation-building was not going to work unless the nations in question wanted to be rebuilt in our image. Germany and Japan were rebuilt according to American ideals, but that was after we leveled them. We started from scratch. But not so in, say, Iraq. We were not going to level it. In fact, we were going to put in rules of engagement that limited our ability to level anything and put our troops at risk in order to try to make the Iraqis into something the Iraqis did not want to be: us.

Again, Trump mortified the conservative establishment by wondering what the hell our smart set was thinking. How did they think that they could solve Iraq's problems when they couldn't even begin to address our problems at home? And how that was conservative in any sense was never explained.

So, when the liars say that Trump and his supporters are not conservative, they reveal that they misunderstood conservativism all along. Conservatism is not a bunch of donor-approved policy prescriptions bundled together by D.C. swells. It is the natural instinct of normal Americans to approach issues with common sense and a cognizance of the flawed nature of humanity.

Regular Americans don't want to make people better, not here at home and not overseas. They want a stable society, with law and order, that allows them and their fellow citizens to support themselves. They want a government that puts their interests first, not those of foreigners and not those of the ruling caste. Politics is not something they use to fill their empty souls, like the godless left. It's a tool, and a regrettable one, to protect their rights and keep things running smoothly so they can get on with their lives.

In Donald Trump they found a politician who would do those things without hesitation or apology. And if those things are not "conservatism," then it's conservatism that's wrong, not the people.

CHAPTER 11

Trump Hates the Free Press...
and So Do You
Media-Hating Beasts!

No tyrant has done a worse job ruthlessly suppressing the free press than Donald Trump. For all the alleged oppression Trump inflicts upon the brave scribblers of our glorious media, he has thoroughly failed to silence its deafening chorus of hate, abuse, and lies. Journalists don't stand quivering in fear that the midnight knock on the door will be a squad of the president's secret police coming to drag him away to some gulag in—*horrors!*—Wyoming.

When Trump designated the mainstream media "the enemy of the people," he gloriously dropkicked the hornet's nest. Those pretentious bastards and presumptuous hacks had pretended to be disinterested, honest brokers while putting their thumbs, their butts, and the rest of their useless carcasses on the scale to help their liberal allies. They cloaked their naked partisanship in sanctimonious babble for too long, as if they weren't just another band of Official Truth bullshitters.

The hell with them.

A free media is crucial to a free republic, but who thinks our current media is "free"? There's no government control, that's true, but is it "free," in the sense that the mainstream media can publish whatever is in the public interest without favor or restraint? Yeah, sure, okay.

There are clear limits on what the "free press" can publish, but Donald Trump doesn't define those boundaries: powerful liberal elites do.

Just look at Harvey Weinstein. He was a big liberal donor and a friend to the folks who run our giant media conglomerates. His reign of pudgy, sweaty terror was no secret. Our moral mentors in Hollywood joked about what they all knew was going on for years before the dam broke. And our "free" press knew all about it.

NBC News, that crown jewel of the establishment media, refused to let Ronan Farrow's report see the light of day. Instead, they drove a stake through the heart of the story. Was it unimportant? Was it not in the public interest? It sure attracted a lot of public interest once Farrow got around NBC's defensive line and scored his touchdown.

How about Jeffrey Epstein, who totally did not kill himself even if he did? ABC News kept his story in the bag when their reporters had Bill Clinton nailed. They spiked the story to protect Bill and Hillary, the darlings of the establishment press. We only know about the scandal because an alternative media outlet, the hated Project Veritas, leaked a video clip of anchor Amy Robach spilling the beans on how they had the dirt on the bigwigs involved in the pedophile parade—including Mr. Hillary—and how the network killed it. So much for respected journalists.

But in the media's arrogance, journalists think information that hurts liberals shouldn't be released to the public. In their minds, they need to play gatekeeper and decide which terrible truths stay within the palace walls. After all, only the wise members of our elite can judge whether revealing the obscene moral bankruptcy of their clique is in the public interest.

The Great Whistleblower Mystery of 2019 demonstrated how far the media is willing to go to skew narratives and control the flow of information. As the media told it, the story starred a courageous truth-teller who stood up to President Trump's terrible misdeeds and abuse of power. But when questions emerged surrounding the whistleblower's personal connection to 2020 Democrat candidates, the talking heads decided to stonewall attempts to learn more about the whistleblower. When push came to shove, providing cover for the Democrats was more important than investigatory journalism. The powers that be placed a moratorium on publishing the whistleblower's name, despite the fact that everyone in Washington knew it, and the Democrats played along. All the while, they continued to insist they are the guardians of democracy while lambasting Trump's "assault on our institutions." Moon Unit Zappa summed it up best: "Gag me with a spoon."

According to the press, disclosing suspected whistleblower Eric Ciaramella's name to the public would put him in grave danger. They all knew his name. But you? You didn't get that privilege because you cannot be trusted with prized information. You are not special. They are.

The same journalists who refused to publish the whistleblower's name routinely wet themselves with delight at the thought of revealing confidential information leaked by Deep State bureaucrats. Those same journalists jumped at the chance to plaster the face of a Covington teen on every headline, prime time show, and front page across the country for holding his ground against the fake Indian elder and faker-still Vietnam War hero who beat his ridiculous drum in the kid's mug. Demonizing a teenager in a MAGA hat is fair game; investigating a Deep State liberal trying to take down the president of the United States is not.

And definitely pay no attention to the disastrously flawed Bat Biter Flu models behind the curtain.

Trump is right: the media is the enemy of the people.

They showed their true colors in their coverage of the Russiagate hoax. Instead of reporting facts, so-called journalists released anonymously sourced BOMBSHELL! reports week after week promising that "the walls are closing in" on President Trump. After forty-five years of Watergate fantasies, they thought that they were on their way to claiming another scalp at 1600 Pennsylvania Avenue, despite the fact that most of their stories crumbled within forty-eight hours. When the story began to fall apart, the press followed the same script for over two years: first they qualified their allegations, then they quietly issued a minimal correction, and then they restarted the process with the next BOMBSHELL! revelation.

They never issued an apology or took time to reflect on their reckless behavior. Instead, they doubled down on the boldfaced lie that "journalists don't take sides!"

That's bogus. The newsrooms, packed with half-wit grads boasting degrees in Advanced Wokeness and life experience consisting of, well, getting their degrees in Advanced Wokeness and nothing else, did away with the idea of objectivity a long time ago. Objectivity is an obstacle to advocating for their preferred policies, and they don't like obstacles. So, they jettisoned objectivity because being a raw partisan is a lot more fun.

But while they jettison objectivity, as they eagerly did daily for all to see during the Chinese coronavirus press conferences, they still demand the respect that a nonpartisan, objective observer would enjoy. They haven't realized that they lost their claim to respect the second they left their standards behind. You would treat a campaign spokesperson lecturing you on the airwaves with scorn and contempt; why shouldn't you treat today's journalists the same way? They want to have their cake and eat it too, before redistributing your cake to people whose political allegiance Democrat officials want to buy.

Our media demands respect that it hasn't earned, which is why it considers Trump's attacks criminal. Trump refuses to honor people who don't do anything. But as with so much of America's terrible, useless, and smug elite, posturing stands in for achievement. Today's journalists demand glory and honor just for holding their positions, not for practicing real journalism.

And Trump refuses to give it to them. Trump doesn't want to destroy the press; he wants to reform it. Plus, the media is perfectly capable of destroying itself. While newspapers across the country shut down their presses, alternative conservative outlets covering the stories our media overlords refuse to run are flourishing. They are eating into the mainstream media's profits, and the chances are that your current newspaper—if you even see it in that form anymore—is an anorexic wraith compared to ten years ago.

The unremitting, tiresome bias drove away the audience. CNN? The Hamster Channel gets more viewers, and the Hamster Channel does not even exist, though it should. Ever since CNN went all in on woke politics, its ratings have stayed at rock bottom of the cable news ratings, and if it weren't for the possibility of your being trapped at an airport, your chances of ever stumbling across its shrill propaganda would be vanishingly small.

Trump pushed back against the woke mainstream media, and he pushed back hard. Keep in mind his background: Trump has been dealing with the press for longer than a good number of the reporters out there have been alive. He knows their business better than they do. Heck, he probably knows how they think better than they do.

Donald Trump is better at using the press for his own ends than most people who work in the business. And not a little bit better—he's a master of the art form. He knows what story will run, can anticipate spin, and has the patience to counterpunch at just the right time to level his foe.

The media tries to stop him, but he's always one step ahead. Back in 2016, Trump's ability to game the press was a big reason why he ended up winning the White House. Blinded by their own biases, journalists initially thought that airing his raucous rallies would dampen Trump's popularity. They gave Trump all the coverage he wanted, in the hopes that Trump would talk himself into defeat. But that did not happen. People listening to Trump saw for themselves that though he was certainly unconventional, he was no dummy. He was funny and entertaining unlike the snooty establishment stiffs the media preferred. Moreover, he was talking about forbidden subjects and rejected political correctness. With Trump's larger than life personality, the combination was destined for ratings gold.

The moment the big networks figured out that more exposure to unadulterated Trump increased his popularity, they cut him out. Now, they blackball Trump and put his words through the spin cycle as soon as they come out of his mouth. Conservative outlets are the only outlets willing to give their audience unadulterated Trump. That's why they're doing so well.

Trump's not against the free press; he loves free press more than anyone. But acting as the public relations arm of the Democrat Party doesn't place you above criticism. In fact, the Fourth Estate's nakedly partisan machinations need to be corrected. That will only come after the strong and sustained criticism Trump taught conservatives is levied against journalists.

The media is the best punching bag in American politics. Everyone on the right sees the games they're playing and wants to bring the journalists to heel. Even Senator Martha McSally of Arizona got in on the action, bringing her dying Senate campaign back to life by calling some nattering CNN reporter a "liberal hack." Instead of hanging her head, McSally owned her outburst and rejuvenated what seemed like a death march to defeat.

Donald Trump showed establishment types that fighting the media is vital to the conservative movement's future. Remember George W. Bush? He bought into the media's mystique and treated it as an institution worthy of respect. They responded by barbecuing him for eight years straight. He should've known that the press needs to be confronted with a whip and a chair. Mitt Romney did the same thing, and he still does not get it. Even after the media clobbered him with secret recordings, gross insinuations, and petty scandals, that impotent sap still cannot get it inside his head that the media is just another partisan enemy that needs to be treated accordingly.

Treating the press accordingly is exactly what Trump and his supporters do. Their harsh and unrelenting criticism is the best thing that could happen to the allegedly free press. Maybe under intense criticism, they'll start acting in the public interest again instead of continuing to serve as bag boys for the Democrat party. But so far, the chances look slim, as the media has thoroughly rejected the opportunity to take a long look in the mirror and do a deep personal inventory of its failings. Accordingly, the floggings will continue.

When your job is to serve the citizenry and half of America hates you, you can respond in one of two ways: you can realize that you're doing something wrong or you can decide that half of America's opinion doesn't matter. Guess which path our media chose.

One of the consequences is people cheering when Trump calls them "The Enemy of the People."

It's not about destroying the "free" press. It's about treating the "free" press as it really is instead of as it pretends to be.

Trump has fought unfair coverage far more than his predecessors, cutting off access to press briefings and exiling particularly obnoxious reporters from the White House. He's shown the media that two can play their game, at least until Hawaiian judges discover a constitutional right for journalists to act like jackasses and order them readmitted.

We should applaud Trump's efforts, not criticize them. He simply refused to play along with the fantasy that active partisan players are disinterested custodians of the public welfare. If they aren't reporting the truth back to their audience, should they receive privileges? He treats him like the hacks they are.

It's refreshing and honest. If journalists want to be activists, they don't deserve the special privileges we afford them. And they're not fooling anyone. People see what is happening. They listen. They know that the press is overwhelmingly liberal, and polls from newsrooms indicate that Republican journalists are essentially unicorns. Nobody would care if the reporters tried to be objective, but they don't. And, at least among themselves, they agree that they must be political players rather that neutral arbiters.

In an August 8, 2016, *New York Times* piece titled "Trump Is Testing the Norms of Objectivity in Journalism," one Jim Rutenberg bemoaned the nightmare Trump has inflicted upon the paladins of the press:

If you're a working journalist and you believe that Donald J. Trump is a demagogue playing to the nation's worst racist and nationalistic tendencies, that he cozies up to anti-American dictators and that he would be dangerous with control of the United States nuclear codes, how the heck are you supposed to cover him?

Because if you believe all of those things, you have to throw out the textbook American journalism has been using for the better part of the past half-century, if not longer, and approach it in a way you've never approached anything in your career. If you view a Trump presidency as something that's potentially dangerous, then your reporting is going to reflect that. You would move closer than you've ever been to being oppositional. That's uncomfortable and uncharted territory for every mainstream, nonopinion journalist I've ever known, and by normal standards, untenable.

But the question that everyone is grappling with is: Do normal standards apply? And if they don't, what should take their place?

Notice a problem with this, besides the author's manifest bias? Start with the title: "Trump is Testing…," Trump. This is all Trump's doing. *He's* forcing us in the media to abandon our objectivity by being so, so…Trumpy!

TRUMP MADE US DO IT!

But if the problem is that the media is presented with a politician it really, really dislikes, then doesn't that make the whole pose of objectivity a sham from the beginning? After all, objectivity and neutrality don't really matter when the subject falls within the scope of what is acceptable to the media. Objectivity only matters when the media is challenged by someone that its members really, really don't like.

That's what happened with Donald Trump. The media decided that objectivity was fine when there was no risk that someone outside what they deemed the mainstream would come to power, but once that became a possibility, the risks of objectivity were too great because those stupid readers of theirs might, without guidance, come to the wrong decision.

It's the model of the media as shaper of opinion. Hard pass.

As the rest of Rutenberg's article demonstrates, there is a lot more about Trump that he disapproves of. A lot more. And a fair reading of the column is that he is ultimately cool with ditching objectivity. Now, he and others do not say that. Instead, they try to abandon the responsibility to keep their own views out of their reporting while still keeping the moral high ground. Explaining why strict objectivity is inapplicable, he cloaks his support for agenda-based reporting in this verbal goo:

> This, however, is what being taken seriously looks like. As Ms. Ryan put it to me, Mr. Trump's candidacy is "extraordinary and precedent-shattering" and "to pretend otherwise is to be disingenuous with readers."
>
> It would also be an abdication of political journalism's most solemn duty: to ferret out what the candidates will be like in the most powerful office in the world.
>
> It may not always seem fair to Mr. Trump or his supporters. But journalism shouldn't measure itself against any one campaign's definition of fairness. It is journalism's job to be true to the readers and viewers, and true to the facts, in a way that will stand up to history's judgment. To do anything less would be untenable.

Yeah, true to the facts. Sure. And guess who decides what is true, and therefore what is a relevant fact? Hint: It's not you. If it were you, the media would not have been demanding that no media outlet run the president's pandemic press conferences live. When he speaks directly to the people, it's hard to decide what parts of his speech you get to hear. But they try spinning him anyway—remember how he actually totally really told everyone to drink Lysol?

A free press is crucial to our democracy because people must be informed in order to rule themselves. They must be able to make informed decisions at the ballot box based on deliberation with their friends, family, and fellow citizens. Citizens have to look at facts and determine what those facts mean. The press's job, at least on the news pages, is to provide the facts that allow the citizen to conduct analysis for his or herself. That is not to say that the newspaper cannot provide arguments about what the facts show, but that debate is properly conducted in the opinion pages. There, columnists take the facts and, like lawyers at a closing argument, advocate for their interpretation of the facts.

So, when opinion and argument migrate out of the opinions section and onto the front page, and people are no longer making decisions informed by facts but, rather, by the approved arguments offered by the elite media, what do we have?

Well, not the kind of "free press" that is crucial to our democracy. After all, we already have partisans, candidates, and apparatchiks making arguments. Why do we need to add a redundant layer of horse hockey to the big steaming pile of it that we already face?

American democracy needs journalists who provide pure, unadulterated facts to the citizens to help them make informed decisions. More argument, more advocacy, and more elite opinion provides nothing citizens don't have in spades. When the press joins in the mud wrestling, it becomes just another hack. Actually, it's even worse, because while shills admit their partisanship, the press pretends to act from unbiased neutrality and the public interest.

They join the mud wrestling, but they pretend they're still the referee.

Trump does not hate the free press, nor do his supporters. Nor is he or they a threat to it. After all, by abandoning neutrality and embracing partisanship in favor of the liberal elite, the mainstream media has made itself worthless.

CHAPTER 12

Trump Is a Tool of the Rich...
and You Suckers Fell for It!

You are too dumb to know that you are taking home less money under Donald Trump than under Barack Obama. You are also too dumb to realize that Donald Trump is sitting in the Oval Office right now, Gucci loafers parked up on the HMS Resolute desk, lighting Cohibas with $100 bills, and laughing at you poor saps. He may, or may not, be wearing a golden monocle encrusted with diamonds.

Those of us who support the president ought to encourage the lie that Donald Trump is a tool of the rich waging war upon everyone but his billionaire buddies. While leftists think you are too stupid to realize that you are being suckered, truth is, they are too out of touch to see the prosperity Trump provided ordinary Americans, at least until the pandemic stuck. Still, anyone pushing the tired cliché used against every Republican since Honest Abe just looks like a fool.

The liars want to believe it; they want and need it to be true. But it's not, and everyone can see it with their own eyes.

Trump is a businessman, not some hack who spent his whole life drawing a paycheck from Uncle Sam. He understands what business needs. He also understands that the business world is the source of jobs, at least jobs that matter, unlike most civilian government jobs. So, he came into office, cut regulations and red tape, slashed taxes, and let the business community know that it has a friend in Washington instead of an enemy demanding tribute.

The economy exploded, just like when Ronald Reagan did much the same thing forty years ago. The Democrats may scream about "trickle-down economics," but the pre-COVID economic gains weren't trickling under President Trump—they're pouring down. And those same policies will supercharge the post-pandemic recovery.

We have been reliably informed by liberal "experts" that the tax cuts were a giant giveaway to Trump's wealthy pals at the expense of regular folks. According to our betters, the tax cuts were a moral monstrosity, even though they have demonstrably spurred the economy and created millions of jobs. Plus, the liars conveniently forget to mention that Trump has far fewer wealthy pals than the average Democrat zillionaire. Why would he want to give money to a group of people who hate his guts?

So how did the tax cut affect regular folks? Well, it…cut their taxes. Every working-class taxpayer got a tax cut. How big is really a matter of perspective. Nancy Pelosi, a multimillionaire who owns a winery, scoffed at the fact that some taxpayers would save a few hundred bucks. Nothing demonstrates the common touch like someone whose hobby is owning a vineyard waving off the value of a few hundred extra bucks to a working family.

Moreover, many working class folks learn their trade and then start to work for themselves. The tax reform law made some changes that gave small companies and sole proprietorships an opportunity to get on an even footing with the corporations against which they compete. Small companies tend to pass through taxes to their owners. The taxes are calculated off the owner's income, using individual rates. Individual tax rates are higher than corporate tax rates, so big corporations in any given industry paid a lower effective tax rate than smaller companies working in that same industry. This is a huge deal to the small contractors, truckers, and others who had been overlooked and overtaxed for too long.

Corporate tax rates went down too, meaning businesses could give bonuses and raises (which many did), expand (we saw the unemployment rate drop), and repatriate cash they had held overseas to avoid the formerly high tax rates (billions and billions have returned). Sounds like a pretty good deal.

As it so happens, the losers of the changes to the tax code are the same people who want you to believe you got screwed. Thanks to a provision eliminating the State and Local Tax Deduction (SALT), wealthy people in big blue states like California and New York can no longer make the rest of America subsidize their expensive government programs. The same demographic that never tires of howling about people paying their fair share was horrified to find that they themselves would finally be asked to pay their fair share. Oh well.

President Trump's economic reforms haven't been a cash grab by the wealthy; they've helped ordinary Americans most. Everyone knows it, including the people the Democrats desperately need to keep disaffected. Minorities, who have been a reliable Democrat voting block for decades, are better off under President Trump than any President in recent memory. That's bad news for a party which survives on its ability to keep minorities toeing the party line.

Sometimes the black vote for the Democrat in presidential elections exceeds 90 percent. The Hispanic vote—a silly concept, because voters of Latin heritage are not interchangeable, as the Democrats imagine—also trends toward the Democrats. And the old GOP was baffled about how to break this headlock.

For years, Republicans talked about "outreach" and "going into the communities" in order to entice minority voters out of their long-standing habits. It was a bit condescending, as if these voters were going to be talked into voting Republican if the GOP sent a minority party representative to mime the same old Republican talking points. But reaching out was not a crazy notion. Breaking the stranglehold on minority voters would doom the Democrat Party. As the party is currently configured—we'll discuss the abandonment of the predominantly white working class in a moment—any failure to achieve stratospheric numbers with minorities means the Donkey Party never wins a national election again.

The problem was that the old school Republicans offered minorities the same bland feel-good talk about "empowerment" and "entrepreneurship" that it gave to upper–middle class voters. That strategy went nowhere because minority voters often face different challenges than existing Republican constituencies. Unemployment, for example, was epidemic, and the old solutions were not working. Minority voters were hungry for jobs, and the Democrat policies they had long supported were not providing them. But the GOP brains trust never thought about what minority voters actually wanted, they just tried to offer them the same ineffective programs Democrats had put on the table.

Then Donald Trump came along, and despite being falsely and mercilessly tarred as a racist bigot who was practically Robert Byrd reincarnated, he offered action on jobs. He offered concrete solutions instead of big talk.

By the end of 2019, the minority unemployment rate was at its lowest in fifty years. That is tangible and more than just talk. It means real people getting real opportunities to take real jobs. And the news that, for the first time in decades, the real wages of non-supervisory workers were going up was the cherry on top. More people were working for more money.

Action, not words.

If Donald Trump was waging war on the working class, he lost gloriously.

Who was the working class's advocate in the decades before Donald Trump anyway? There wasn't one, at least not among the political establishment. Reagan famously won over the "Reagan Democrats," the culturally conservative, economically moderate blue-collar workers. The Democrats had already started leaving them behind in favor of the white collar professional and management class back then, as well as the liberal billionaires who ran out of material goods to buy and decided that it might be fun to buy the culture.

So, who spoke for the guy who drove a truck or raised corn or built television sets after Reagan left office? George H. W. Bush? The closest he ever came to a working man is when he passed a gardener on his walk into the country club and mumbled an awkward "Hello."

How about his son? His Texas twang notwithstanding, Bush 43's policies were aimed straight at advancing the globalist consensus that looked down on working Americans. His administration thought that the jobs working class Americans did were second-tier occupations that would soon die out. Dubya was all about "free trade," which was hardly free trade at all. "Free trade" meant American corporations got to send well-paying American jobs overseas, give them to foreign, near–slave labor, and then import the products back home to sell at Walmart. That guy who built television sets? He doesn't do that anymore—nobody builds television sets in America anymore. And while the globalists told us he would learn to code, he probably took a much crappier job and cursed the bigwigs in both parties, neither of whom cared about him or his struggles.

Once upon a time the Democrats claimed to care, but that was before the party got woke. After that, the Democrats stopped even pretending. The white working class was deemed surplus to the requirements of the new liberal coalition of white collar, credentialed, and cosmopolitan professionals, government union drones, and minorities. The credentialed class was moving left on social issues. If you want proof, just compare that quaint formulation by Bill Clinton about abortion being "safe, legal, and rare" to today's "Shout your abortion!" Working-class voters remained culturally conservative, and their stubborn insistence on clinging to their God, flag, and scary bang sticks made them an awkward fit in a Democrat Party that was against all those things.

Bill Clinton talked a good game for the working class, but he knew where his globalist bread was buttered, and it was not in Michigan. During the Bush years, the liberal intelligentsia argued that the party could finally free itself of these sweaty Neanderthals in the hinterlands. Hillary Clinton's campaign never even tried to reach out to the group that had been the Democrats' mainstay for decades after FDR. The Smartest Woman in the World™ famously did not bother to campaign in Wisconsin, following the advice of her geniuses in Brooklyn who thought those backwater rubes didn't matter.

Who is mattering now, you snobs?

Without an advocate in Washington, the American working class went into visible decline. The mortality rate rose, and suicide and opiates filled the void that came with being left behind and forgotten. Meanwhile, academia helped make a bachelor's degree in Anti-Colonialist Marketing necessary for the new jobs, not because it guaranteed competence (often it was the opposite) but because a diploma was a secret handshake that showed you were part of the clique. Outside the flush blue cities and suburbs, towns died, and main streets became ghostly stretches of empty storefronts.

But the fat, dumb, and greedy elites never noticed the crisis, regardless of whether they were Democrat or Republican. This was happening out in the wilds of flyover country, and fly over it the elites did. The Democrats were busy catering to their new faculty lounge dwellers and big city swells, while the GOP was still focused on budget cuts, tax cuts, and foreign wars that the sons and daughters of the forgotten Americans enlisted to fight.

Any astute GOP politician could have run on solving the problems facing middle America. But instead of addressing the working class's issues, GOP candidates listened to the conservative think tanks funded by oligarch donors. Republicans tried to compete for the same white-collar suburban types the Dems had taken from them with stale neo-Jack Kemp cant about "empowerment" and "entrepreneurship." Many Republicans were already gainfully employed or owned their own businesses. So while preaching to the choir got a receptive audience, it ignored the rest of the congregation whose jobs rolled off to Oaxaca and whose kids died of oxycontin overdoses, if not from roadside bombs outside of Ramadi.

Donald Trump was the only GOP candidate in 2016 who recognized the plight of the American working class and made their cause his own. And since he was the only one talking to these citizens, they listened to him.

MAGA—"Make America Great Again"—seemed like a hack cliché to the new class managers, lawyers, and consultants who had made a killing over the last couple decades. But to the forgotten Americans it was a chance to return to the prosperity and respect that working people had once enjoyed in their homeland. To them, America's greatness was inextricably linked to the status of regular Americans, not just the wealthy and connected.

Unlike generic Washington politicians, Trump respected working people. You could see it at his rallies. He spoke to them directly in a way they appreciated. He was honest, funny, direct, and sometimes righteously outraged. For the first time in decades, someone in power treated them like something other than buffoons, hicks, and canoe-tour ambushing, backwoods inbreds. And they returned his respect with their fervent support.

Most New York billionaires are more comfortable with other big city tycoons, but Donald Trump is a unique case. Trump was at the height of high society, but not because of his temperament or adherence to its norms. He was a brash, vulgar Queens real estate developer whose tastes were more in line with the ironmongers and teamsters he interacted with than those of the rarified, snooty elite who ruled polite society.

Trump did not win access to the crème de la crème of the culture because he was witty or charming (though his ability to charm is woefully underestimated by those whose blind hatred keeps them from accurately assessing their opponent). He was invited into high society because he had so damn much money and celebrity, and he was not afraid to use either one. He bought his way in with cash and fame and was tolerated, though never loved.

Trump's lifestyle resonates with the working class because it is so over the top. He lives on his own terms, not according to the genteel codes of the upper crust. Working stiffs dream of living like Donald Trump when they have a mountain of cash and a TV show, tagging

Playboy models included. That's why Trump never gave off the impression that he thought he was better in some cosmic sense than regular folks just because he had more money than they did. Regular folks don't see Trump's lack of modesty as hostile because he doesn't come across as condescending (as Hillary Clinton, for example, does). His wealth doesn't generate resentment. He is funny, tough, and living the dream.

That's why working people love him while other billionaires hate him. Trump's living on his own terms—"A Big Mac? Oh, well, I never!"—is a rejection of their clique's norms. Trump refuses to play the big money guy game. He refuses to conform to the rules of the Davos set, he refuses to offer his obeisance by uttering all the right liberal platitudes, and he refuses to sit silently when under attack. He broke their rules, and they hate him for it. They finally found someone they couldn't buy, and it gnaws at them to this day.

The coastal elites pretend that the weather is going to kill us all in a dozen years unless ordinary people give up their money and freedom. Their lies are a dagger aimed directly at the heart of America's working class, and Trump's refusal to play along was one of his greatest acts of service to families across America.

Joe Biden, in a burst of rare coherence, let the cat out of the bag on the campaign trail. During a debate, moderator Tim Alberta asked Biden whether he would "be willing to sacrifice some…growth, even knowing potentially that it could displace thousands, maybe hundreds of thousands of blue-collar workers in the interest of transitioning to that greener economy?" Biden responded with a resounding yes.

Blue collar Joe Biden would give up millions of working-class jobs to quell his liberal handlers' apocalyptic nightmares. And what would Joe Biden have those out-of-work men and women do? Learn to code, of course. He said so himself at a later campaign event, telling the crowd that "anybody who can throw coal into a furnace can learn how to program for God's sake."

The pandemic lockdown gave us all a taste of the nightmare that those oil and gas workers would experience if Biden got his way.

Democrats dream of impoverishing millions of Americans to pacify the angry weather goddess and please her Swedish teen high priestess. Think of the devastation and heartbreak that Biden and his cohort would eagerly inflict on working people for the sake of a hoax. And once they left working Americans jobless and without future prospects, they'd try to turn them into Brooklyn hipsters or simply abandon them to poverty and opioids.

Trump, meanwhile, has made energy cheaper for American workers and business. Liberating the oil and gas industry from burdensome regulations that limit technological innovations, like fracking, has given birth to an American energy renaissance. Trump has not only freed America from reliance on foreign fossil fuels, he's given millions and millions of families the chance for honest, good-paying jobs. It's a win-win-win-win.

The Democrats would crush the dream of energy independence and crush those working people. It's just a bunch of dirty knuckle-draggers out there in those weird states in the middle of the country. The current crop of Democrat voters never met the people who work on oil rigs. They've never even driven through coal country. They sure as hell don't think about what's in their interest. If those workers are ruined, well, that's a small price to pay for the weather cultists to feel good about themselves.

Trump is not having that. What he is having is the backs of his supporters.

And his supporters know it. They understand that their interests have been shunted aside by a Democrat Party that looks at them like the embarrassing uncle, probably played by Randy Quaid, who is sure to ruin a family gathering by saying something outrageous. The old Republican Party felt the same way and tried to keep the forgotten men and women out of view. Only Trump paid attention to them, and only Trump promised to defend their interests.

Trump's decision to champion the working class set off the biggest transformation of our political landscape in decades. Trump is remaking the GOP as the party of the working class, taking what used to be the Democrat's base out from under their feet. He didn't just champion the working class in terms of its generally conservative social views; he made their economic concerns the center of his domestic policy. He changed the game, creating economic opportunities and working-class jobs by slashing regulations and ignoring cries for a climate jihad that would ruin the middle half of the country. Now, finally, the economy is working for everyone. And that infuriates the liars who still claim that somehow Trump is the enemy of the working man.

CHAPTER 13

Trump Is a Climate Denier...
and You SUV-Driving, Cheeseburger-Gobbling Climate Criminals Are Too!

No list of lies about Donald Trump would be complete without the fashionable fib that the president is a "climate denier." In fact, no one can point to a single instance in which Donald Trump, or anyone else, has denied that there is a climate.

That, of course, is obtuseness in the service of battling the obtuse. But then again, this is the Age of Obtuseness, so when in Obtuse, do as the Obtusens do.

Everyone knows that when the liars use the term "climate denier," they don't mean it literally. No one denies that a climate exists. But the awkward construction isn't a mistake; it's meant to evoke Holocaust denial. When some fringe weirdo mouths off about how the Nazis were misunderstood and that the Final Solution was a giant fraud disseminated by Big Zionism, the term "denier" has a clear meaning: it means that the person spouting off his delusional fantasies is a loathsome mollusk.

When the liars call people "climate deniers," they hope that a bit of the contempt we all have for Holocaust deniers rubs onto people who refuse to accept that the weather will kill us all within a decade. They want to heap moral opprobrium on us because we refuse to embrace all those Marxist fantasies that can't win at the ballot box in normal times.

It's a scummy little rhetorical play by scummy little people. They often pair it with the epithet "science denier," as if Trump and those who support him hate science. Since they don't know any religious people, they think that anyone with a believing bone in their body wants to retreat into some sort of Luddite utopia where everyone wears black, never has sex, and only talks about Jesus.

It's so tiresome and pretentious.

Climate change is the fetish of bored Westerners and canny Third World rulers who see a chance to cash in on the bruised consciences of cosmopolitan elites. It's always dressed in flexible and inexact language, which is appropriate for a set of claims that are themselves inexact and flexible.

That's on purpose.

The meaning of "climate change" is intentionally elusive. You see, climate change doesn't imply a central claim that can be affirmed or denied. Does it mean that global temperatures will increase? Or does it that we'll enter a new ice age? Will the world turn into a giant desert, or will New York City be underwater in ten years unless we accept the left's government takeover?

When Trump supporters speak of climate change as a "hoax," we don't doubt that the climate changes. Of course the climate changes—that is why the premise underlying the climate change panic-mongering is so obviously a fraud. The Earth's temperature cycles through hotter and colder periods. The fact that many of you are not reading this book under a mile of solid ice proves it. The idea that "climate change" is bad assumes that there is a temperature that is a perfect temperature that it's man's job to preserve. Watch the fun begin when you ask one of the weather cultists what that temperature is. Exactly what climate should the Earth have? What's the right temperature, since getting hotter is bad?

You are not going to get an answer, because no perfect climate exists. The Earth isn't your living room, where you set the thermostat to seventy-two degrees and all your problems melt away. If they were serious, they would recognize that man has always adapted to a changing climate.

But you cannot expect the people crying wolf about climate change to be serious. They don't want to be taken seriously on the merits of their claim; they want to seriously scare you into accepting their ridiculous policy prescriptions.

The Gordian knot of lies about "climate change" and "science" serves the same purpose as the other lies we've covered. The liars want to bend you to their will. Here, they want you to accept a smorgasbord of nonsense that you would never accept in normal times. So they tell you that these are not normal times, they are desperate times—and desperate times demand desperate measures. If we don't *right now no time to think how dare you pause to think things through* comply with every pinko nostrum and mandate that couldn't otherwise be aired outside a faculty lounge without the audience breaking into hysterics, we're all going to die.

In fact, we are already supposed to be dead, frozen solid like Han Solo due to the ice age that all the best people confidently informed us was sure to descend upon us before the seventies were out. You may have missed the ice age that all the genius scientists assured us was on the way, since it never happened.

But forget all the past's failed predictions (and don't be a spoilsport by pointing out that we recently crashed our booming economy because of scientific models that were totally wrong). This time, the predicted disasters are totally a sure thing. Sure, the ice age never arrived, nor did any of the other environmental Armageddons the liberals threatened us with when we did not do exactly what they demanded. If you grew up in the seventies, you remember them. There was the population explosion that never detonated. The world was supposed to be overrun with babies, causing starvation and poverty and a litany of other bad things to overwhelm us. Instead, food production and wealth has increased, those babies got fed, and as their parents got richer, there were fewer of them.

Today, the population is still on an upward trajectory in some Third World countries, but in the developed world, the birthrate has dropped below replacement level. Places like Italy and Spain, formerly fecund Catholic countries, have largely given up on having babies. Within a few decades, Japan is going to be all old people and sex robots. At this rate, all their boy bands will be made up of dudes in their fifties singing about arthritis and prostate issues. Those screaming that the population explosion would destroy us all were not merely wrong. They were absolutely, totally 180 degrees wrong.

But then again, that's hardly a surprise to thinking adults. The doom hustlers are always wrong.

The ozone hole has not killed us. Acid rain has not killed us. The Alar apple apocalypse that Meryl Streep prognosticated never came to pass. So when, in the late eighties, they started pushing the idea that we were all going to fry unless we immediately went fully Marxist, ordinary folks were unconvinced.

But the elites jumped aboard the global warming bandwagon. It was not until years later that "global warming" would be replaced with the more rhetorically flexible "climate change." The problem with global warming was that it contained a concrete prediction. If it didn't start warming, people would notice. Every time some global warming conclave was convened in a roiling blizzard, people laughed. We were assured that scientists were tracking the relentless upward trajectory on our thermometers, but it did not seem to be getting any hotter. In fact, we were setting new record cold temperatures—because every year, some places set new records for cold—and that was just not helpful to the narrative.

Hence, "climate change."

The term "climate change" was far superior to "global warming" because it's much more pliable. If climate change is bad, then *any* change in the climate is bad, and labeling the problem "climate change" ensured that no matter what happened, the proponents would be proven right. When global warming was falsified, the liars replaced it with an unfalsifiable theory. A surprise early or late snowfall would doom the global warming narrative. But when it comes to climate change, it serves as perfect evidence! Sunny or rainy, cold or hot, weather proves climate change. How convenient.

But despite this clever rhetorical maneuver, not all of the liars played by the new rules. Some of them forgot that they were supposed to remain as vague as possible and decided to set deadlines. By 2000, there will be no more snowfall. By 2004, all the polar bears will be cinders. By 2009, Boston will be underwater. If we don't act by 2016, we're all doomed.

DOOMED!

After a while, even the most devoted acolyte of a cult gets a bit tired of getting all ginned up for the arrival of the Four Horseman just to end up twiddling their thumbs.

Alexandria Ocasio-Cortez made this classic mistake when babbling about her Green New Deal in 2019. She put another time limit on civilization, giving us 10–12 years before we are all toast. Except this time, people knew they couldn't take her seriously. Some even ironically started countdown clocks. After being told for decades that destruction was lurking down the road, people got hip to the fact that these predictions were never true. The terrifying warning of a horrible fate became yet another punch line.

AOC's Green New Deal wasn't just a disaster because of its ludicrous fearmongering. She also made the mistake of proposing "solutions" to the crisis. The "solutions" were always the point of the whole climate change hoax. The fright wig fantasies about flooding and heat waves and mass extinction were just the boogeymen designed to get people to agree to stuff they would never, ever accept unless they were staring down the barrel of an apocalyptic .44 magnum. Enacting those solutions quickly, when there's no time to debate or read the fine print, is convenient to our elite, since normal people hate the ideas and know they will inevitably pay for them.

The proposed solutions to the climate crisis read like a Christmas list for radical leftists. Look at what AOC wanted to do. She wanted to ban airplane travel (at least for you), and cows (no beef, at least for you), and eliminate the entire fossil fuel industry (no jobs for you). Oh, she denied it all. Apparently reading her plan and reporting what it said was hopelessly passé and bourgeois. But sometimes they just can't keep themselves from saying what they actually mean.

Greta Thunberg, the creepy Swedish teen icon of the climate deranged, put it this way:

> Schoolchildren, young people, and adults all over the world will stand together, demanding that our leaders take action—not because we want them to, but because the science demands it.
>
> That action must be powerful and wide-ranging. After all, the climate crisis is not just about the environment. It is a crisis of human rights, of justice, and of political will. Colonial, racist, and patriarchal systems of oppression have created and fueled it. We need to dismantle them all. Our political leaders can no longer shirk their responsibilities.

Did you get that? It's not about the degrees; it's about the dismantling. Welcome to social justice science, where leftists can control the weather through their very wokeness.

And Pinko Pippi was serious about enforcing her brand of neo-Marxist ideology. She was deadly serious, threatening to "make sure we put world leaders against the wall" if they don't play ball. Her handlers later had her walk back this inadvertent confession by saying she really wasn't talking about shooting her political opponents, but when it comes to communists talking about gunning down their opposition, well, let's just say they have not earned the benefit of the doubt.

Those not clued into their game may stop and wonder at the fact that everything "science" demands is something the left has wanted for decades. Apparently, science states that redistributing, regulating, and reorganizing our entire economy into a socialist non-workers' paradise will make the Earth colder.

They're waging war on average Americans in the name of their elite daydreams. One of Donald Trump's greatest achievements was the deregulation of the American energy industry that has allowed America, for the first time since the forties, to become not merely energy independent but a net exporter of petroleum. Millions of Americans have found good, high-paying jobs to support their families, while making our country stronger by weaning us from our reliance on cheesy foreigners squatting on oil lakes.

And because of the weather forecasted for a century from now, we need to give that all up? Joe Biden must have taken a big hit from his no-good son's crack pipe before he spoke up during the December 19, 2019, debate and made it clear that he would sacrifice hundreds of thousands of American families on Gaia's altar. Just think about that—this guy, "Middle Class Joe," would toss "hundreds of thousands of blue-collar workers" out of jobs because of the climate change hoax. And people wonder why the Green New Deal got a reception comparable to the feminist *Ghostbusters* reboot.

This is all in the name of transitioning to the new "green economy," which means pouring money into the pet projects of Democrat donors. Some of us like our cars and do not want to throw them away for expensive, useless electric shitboxes because a bunch of toffs in Santa Monica and Brooklyn say so. Out in the Real America, people need big butch cars to perform their jobs, to move their families, and to do, well, whatever the hell they want to do. City dwelling swells don't get a veto over my transportation decision.

With green regulations, the left gets to wield their significant cultural power over regular Americans. When these local loonies ban plastic bags or make you use a straw that disintegrates in your Pepsi, they know full well that they aren't saving the planet. (From a purely Darwinian perspective, a turtle stupid enough to impale its nostrils with a straw probably should be dragged out of the gene pool.) They do it because it is fun. It's fun to put people to petty and not-so-petty inconveniences, especially when those people are, in your view, benighted slobs in need of correction.

A dime for a bag at Trader Joe's is nothing to the people pushing this kind of smug virtue-signaling garbage. But a dime means something to other people, and that knowledge makes their jerk power plays that much sweeter to the weather bullies.

The climate change hoax offers a way to expiate other sins as well. There was a giant uproar about how Trump, putting into effect the will of the people who elected him, pulled America out of the Paris Climate Accords. The Paris Accords were amazing because they really did nothing to rein in China or India, who are actually the biggest "carbon criminals" out there. They were about clicking the fetters on America's wrists, though we were about the only folks making progress on carbon reduction.

But in addition to demanding ritual economic suicide, the elites demanded money transfers. See, by their reasoning, the West needs to pay climate reparations to a variety of Third World countries for our crime of being a modern society. And when the dictators of those seedy hellholes figured out that stupid, Western, elitist guilt meant checks, they got woke on climate quick. Apparently giving your money to foreigners will get the climate back to its optimal temperature, whatever that is.

Of course, as Greta sternly insisted, this all goes hand in hand with dismantling the patriarchy and overthrowing the tyranny of biology. How dare you not comply! How dare you!

Remember, it's *science*. And you are a notorious science-hater.

Now, our common frustration with the lies told about Donald Trump and his supporters is that the liars only assume what they claim to prove and then slander anyone who points out their shoddy logic. That's in full effect with this fib because, as we have seen, the climate change hoax is itself a rejection of science. Instead of science, the liars advance a predetermined outcome that justifies their political preferences. Those preferences have a tenuous relation to the weather at best—but saying that means you hate science.

Oh, how we hate science!

Where is the science in climate change anyway? Sure, we are duly informed that 97 percent of scientists agree with something about climate change, but we're never told what that something is. Are 97 percent of scientists down with reducing the Earth's average temperature by crushing the patriarchy? That seems unlikely. "97 percent of scientists!" is always followed by the command that we accept any left-wing dream that has the label "Climate Change Remedy" stuck to it.

Let's look at that 97 percent figure we hear all the time. What does it mean? That's unclear. According to the poll the liars cite, 97 percent of scientists think the climate is changing and that humans play a role in that change. But 97 percent of scientists only agree on the most vague and general characterization of that change. Sure, most scientists agree that the climate has changed in the past thousand years. But that doesn't mean they believe the polar ice caps are going to melt in the next decade or that we'll all be ice sculptures next week.

And of course humans have an effect. A butterfly flapping its wings has an effect. Remember that trippy sci-fi story where a guy goes back in time, gets chased by a dinosaur, steps on a bug and comes back to the present and everything is different? No? Okay, remember the *Simpsons* "Treehouse of Horror" episode where Homer did that?

Everything has an effect, but not all effects are created equal. The question is whether mankind's use of carbon fuel has a significant effect, and there is no "97 percent consensus" surrounding that. Instead, the 97 percent figure gets morphed into some sort of white-jacket, peer-reviewed stamp of approval pressed on everything anyone claims about climate change, especially when accompanied by a Marxist wish list of remedies. Those remedies are really what the climate change hoax is all about, and it's rhetorically useful to clothe the proposals in scientific garb instead of presenting them as political choices. If it's science, well, you can't argue. But we do argue, despite their name calling, because we recognize that political questions must be solved politically. The strategy of defining these policy choices as "scientific" questions is just a way to take those decisions out of your hands. After all, you can't be trusted to make these calls. We need experts, science experts! And if we have already vetted those science guys to make sure they conform to our opinions, well, the fix is in. So, shut up and obey.

Nah. We refuse to submit to this clever, but not that clever, hustle.

That's why we elected Donald Trump. He has the unique ability not to care what the smart set folks think, in large part because he has dealt with them and knows that they aren't all that smart. But they are smart enough to try to manipulate us by claiming that *we* aren't smart. That's where the "You deny science!" nonsense comes from. Why, there's a scientific consensus, you uneducated dolt! If they can define opposition to their position as opposition to science, then people who oppose them must oppose science, and we all know that people who oppose science are dumb.

This weaselly ploy works on those more interested in maintaining their class credentials than on thinking for themselves and doing the right thing. It's a lot easier to nod along to the nonsense masquerading as science than to buck the current and point out the unclothed Emperor's genitals.

Reality is reality, and Trump supporters generally live in the real world, not ideological constructions. If you are a farmer, you live science every day. An engineer? Science. But if you are a blue/pink-haired barista with a dual major in Contemporary Bolivian Rap and Anti-Colonialist Comic Book Studies, then maybe science is not your thing. Maybe your thing is actually just genuflecting to odd Scandinavian teens who dispense climate diktats to waiting suckers across the Northern hemisphere. The liars love science when it is useful, but they think "science" is a set of predetermined leftist policy positions instead of a process of measuring and analyzing data to prove or disprove theories about how the universe works. They don't understand that a "scientific consensus" must ultimately be verified by real life experience. Or maybe it's that they don't care.

They pose and posture and swoon over mundane, clichéd tweets from Neil deGrasse Tyson, but they don't love science. They don't even know science. They don't want to. Here's an experiment: the next time some hipster doofus accuses you of denying science, ask him how many genders there are. But be prepared, because he may scream, shout, and try to get you cancelled. He, she, or xi will probably call you "racist."

CHAPTER 14

Trump Obstructed Justice...
and You Lawless Co-Conspirators Don't Care

"Donald Trump obstructed justice" is an article of faith among leftists and cackling Never Trumpers, and they hold you accountable because they think you law-hating monsters who support him simply do not care. The first part is false; the second part is true.

While you may think obstructing a corrupt investigation is perfectly fine, that's not actually legal. Obstructing an investigation is not legally defensible on the grounds that the subject under investigation is a farce that makes a mockery of everything America stands for. That's why the liars turned to obstruction of justice when their sham collusion investigations crumbled. While the underlying probe came back with nothing, they hoped they'd caught Trump in a process crime at some stage of the ordeal.

It may be hard to believe, but for the left, legal proceedings, like war, are politics by other means.

The "obstruction" allegations against Trump are political allegations. But as political allegations, they need to convince voters that they are serious or worthy of their consideration. They must at least *appear* to have some basis in reality. The problem for those pushing the charges, though, is that the allegations can't even meet that low threshold. In fact, millions of Americans think that what the left calls "obstruction" is a perfectly legitimate and reasonable response to an investigation that was so damaging to the country. As with most Democrat hoaxes, the nation ultimately foots the bill for their delusions.

Let's review what occurred. A bunch of bureaucrats who hoped to get their gal into the White House decided to use their positions in the FBI, CIA, and elsewhere in conjunction with an eager media to stack the deck against Donald Trump.

First, they had to make Hillary's massive violation of the most basic laws governing the use of classified material disappear. If she were anyone else, Hillary's conduct would have sent her up the river. Fortunately for her, professional courtesy led James Comey literally to invent a new test for the application of unequivocal federal laws. When the results came in—shocker!—she was good to go. Comey said in his televised press conference that no reasonable prosecutor would ever bring charges against Hillary, right before he performed a giant stage wink on national TV.

All right, that last part did not happen, but there's no way he believed any of the nonsense he spewed in service of the woman he expected and hoped to be his next boss.

Ironically, Comey's performance did not ingratiate him with the liberals. In late September 2016, when noted high school–girl connoisseur and husband of Hillary's closest gal pal Anthony Weiner finally had his computer searched by the FBI, the feds stumbled on a bunch of improper emails. Comey told Congress that the FBI had reopened the investigation he had prematurely closed and quickly concluded the whitewash required to pronounce Hillary clean again. Even though Comey's antics were clearly designed to boost Hillary, liberals still inevitably blamed him for her eventual defeat.

Everyone hated Comey back then. Contempt for that looming doofus was the only thing most Americans agreed upon for a fleeting moment. Then the soft coup plotters hatched their plan to trash Trump, and the liberals canonized Comey as the patron saint of the #Resistance as well as of lame tweeters.

The conspirators had been sowing the seeds to take down Trump long before he was elected president. Through leaks, public statements, and investigative jiujitsu, rogue intelligence agents and Deep State bureaucrats had been connecting Trump to Russia for months. (It's always Russia, isn't it?) The plan was *perfect*. They could pretend they were protecting American security from evil foreigners who had... done what exactly? Gotten a hold of the incriminating materials that Comey said were good to go?

It was never quite clear how Russia was "hacking our election." "Hacking" certainly sounds nefarious—it's all high-techy and scary. But when you ask what exactly The Bear did, you rarely get anything concrete. Instead, the liars call you a "pawn of Putin" for your trouble, because apparently it helps Putin to ask what apocalyptic danger he poses. In other words, seeking specificity is now treason.

The FBI's initial suggestion was that the Trump campaign hacked the Democratic National Committee's servers in conjunction with the Russians, the Knights Templar, and the Saucer People. When the Russians stole communications showing that the DNC was a festering cesspit of evil, the Trump campaign collaborated with them to make sure the emails were released to the public.

But alleging that Russia had hacked the DNC was always meant to cover up the obvious and flagrant corruption the leaked emails revealed. It was like a teenager who shrieks "I can't believe you went in my room and invaded my privacy, Mom!" when confronted with a little plastic baggie of Kush.

The allegations didn't stop there. In fact, it was just the beginning of the deluge of accusations intelligence officials leaked to the press. The Trump campaign may have helped the Russians hack the server Hillary kept in her basement. Or maybe the Russians hacked the server independently, but were waiting for Trump to give them the signal before releasing the emails to WikiLeaks. Or something. Oh, and the Russians were behind a bunch of Macedonian nerds who bought a few thousand dollars of Facebook ads that said mean things about Hillary.

Whatever.

The pro-Hillary FBI bigwigs thought they had hit the jackpot when some shady Brit offered them a dossier full of stuff they wanted to hear, including great stuff about Trump hiring hookers to pee on him. The fact that the dossier was paid for by the Clinton campaign didn't seem relevant to them, because darn it, sometimes a story is too good to check. And golden shower trollops are far too good to check—or to fully inform the Foreign Intelligence Surveillance Court about.

We now know that the FBI bullshitted its way into spying on the Trump campaign. We also know that there were countless leaks about the terrible collusion between the Trump organization and the dirty nasty Russians. As it turns out, all those leaks were baloney stories by Deep State bureaucrats intended to sully Trump's name. They wanted to boost Hillary by making it seem like Trump was also a target of investigation, and they justified their investigation by leaking stories to the press that they knew were false.

Trump won anyway, despite the best efforts of these incredibly inept coup plotters. Luckily our best and brightest are just as lousy at framing people as they are at doing their actual jobs. Comey only lasted a few months under Trump, but that didn't stop him from working double time to move against the sitting president. He was still trying to set Trump up even after the president unceremoniously fired his ass.

Comey, that moral paragon, shamelessly manipulated the news cycle and pressured Congress into appointing a Special Counsel to investigate Trump. He illegally leaked documents, editorialized his #Resistance conspiracy theories, and gave misleading testimony to raise suspicion around President Trump. His shady efforts culminated in the appointment of his friend, the somnolent Robert Mueller, as Special Counsel. Mueller ceded authority to the Democrat operatives on his team—that is, his entire team—and took a nap for nearly two years. He woke up to find that his team's report grudgingly conceded that there was zero evidence of the collusion that formed the basis of their whole sordid scheme.

But obstruction? Hey, maybe that was a thing! Maybe Trump obstructed the investigation into what never happened by…what?

Firing Comey? As we already mentioned, everyone hated Comey. Hillary would have canned him on day one. She may yet arrange for him to be found lying stiff in some park with six self-inflicted gunshot wounds. Democrats on the Hill were calling for Comey's head whenever he testified to Congress. Plus, Trump was the president of the United States. You know, the FBI director's boss. Trump had the authority to fire Comey for whatever reason he wanted, even if he just thought that Comey sucked.

But that doesn't take the Trump Exception™ into account. You see, there's an unspoken rule that makes any exercise of the powers invested in the presidency by Trump a national scandal and a sign of an imminent fascist take over. Thanks to the Trump Exception, the president obstructed justice by doing exactly what the Constitution allows him to do.

In fact, he obstructed justice even more flagrantly by denying his guilt. The narrative found that Trump was a Russian asset, so proclaiming his innocence had to be an attempt to corrupt the otherwise independent justice system. Acting like the innocent man that Mueller's cast of angry Democrats later found him to be was an impeachable offense. What an interesting obstruction charge.

The report the Mueller posse released left the decision on "obstruction" to William Barr, who had replaced the AWOL Jeff Sessions as attorney general. Barr had previously written a memo that detailed how the theory of obstruction the Mueller team used was nonsense—before he was attorney general and before the Mueller team had made their interpretation of the obstruction of justice statute known to the public. When that memo leaked, the media lambasted Barr as a paranoid old man. There was no way the Mueller team was making that ridiculous an argument, they said.

But when the report came out and the legal theory Barr had skewered formed the cornerstone of the Mueller team's case, the same people who had roasted Barr went suspiciously silent. Instead, the media and the

Democrats, to the extent the Venn diagram of the two don't make a single circle, both decided that the unprecedented obstruction interpretation was not only sound, but that Barr's decision to not press charges was evidence of the most obstructiony obstruction ever. What a joke!

But the elites weren't done making a laughingstock of themselves. Instead of just letting the obstruction case hang, Congressional Democrats dragged Mueller in to testify. The long-awaited day had come—it was Muellertime at long last! Here comes the truth, Bad Orange Man! Mueller will have the evidence! Mueller will avenge! Mueller will make it all better!

Mueller looked more like an aging beagle who had broken into its master's Ambien stash than a #Resistance hero. Mr. Impeccable Integrity fumbled and stumbled through his testimony, presenting himself like the old establishment hack he is. It was clear he was not the engineer on the investigation train. He wasn't even the conductor. They just put him to bed in the caboose and woke him up once they pulled into the station.

Mueller managed to get out that Trump had not been "exonerated," a line that the mainstream media and Democrat leadership had clearly cued up for him. In that respect, Trump was like every other suspect investigated by American law enforcement. Prosecutors don't "exonerate"; they either get enough goods to file charges or they don't. So, the liars doubled down on their deceptive narrative-building by asserting that there must be a ton of evidence of wrongdoing even though Mueller could not find any.

And then Mueller staggered off stage and the Ukraine "scandal" broke. What impeccable and fortuitous timing! The saga made one thing clear: the Democrats have a deep bench of partisan bureaucrats willing to take on the president of the United States. When one fails, another immediately steps up to the plate. So as soon as Robert Mueller broke millions of Democrat hearts, the establishment activated their sleeper agents on the National Security Council, in the State Department, and in the intelligence community and told them to get the next plot rolling.

Apparently it's illegal and morally reprehensible to ask a foreign government racked with corruption why the former veep's son was scoring over fifty grand per month in their country. Hunter Biden is no boy scout. His track record includes strip club sex toy antics, misplaced crack pipes, paternity suits, and being kicked out of the Navy for dope, and this achiever was scoring fifty grand-plus a month from a Ukrainian oligarch. According to the Democrats, calling for an investigation into *that* guy's shady business dealings is adequate grounds for impeachment and removal from office.

The liars want you to believe that Donald Trump is the ultimate scofflaw, flaunting the processes of justice for his own advantage. Trump isn't just skirting the law; he's undermining the very idea of law by refusing to submit to the forces of truth and rightness and goodness.

Pass the barf bag.

In all the lies we've covered about the president and you, we keep coming back to one central theme: projection. All the lies point out conduct the liars themselves routinely participate in. Part of this is just good old-fashioned distraction. If we are talking about how Trump perverted the course of justice, then we are not talking about the Democrats' manifest criminal behavior. That's a pretty standard ploy for the kind of petty authoritarians who make up our establishment. But there is a more troubling possibility: maybe they don't think they've done anything wrong. All's fair in love and war and in trying to lynch The Donald.

Oh, is there ever some projection going on.

If you want to see real obstruction of justice, just look at how members of the ruling caste respond to an investigation.

Hillary got a free pass on crimes that would have Cool Hand Luked anyone else. So did the former intelligence chiefs now leading the #Resistance on cable news, who manufactured predicates for an investigation to spy on and defame a presidential campaign. Officials at the highest levels of the Department of Justice set up a Special Counsel team rigged with staff who hated their target's guts. Nothing about these miserable shenanigans bears any resemblance to "justice," and yet the liars want you to think Trump is undermining the rule of law by calling out their transparent machinations.

The people responsible for our security knew exactly what they were doing. They circulated and perpetuated the lies from the get-go. They all knew this Russia collusion thing was garbage. Just look at the texts of guys like FBI bigwig Peter Strzok, who texted his mistress and fellow FBI agent Lisa Page: "I want[s] to believe…that there's no way [Trump] gets elected—but I'm afraid we can't take that risk. It's like an insurance policy in the unlikely event you die before you're 40." Why would one need an "insurance policy" if Trump was actually taking dictation from the Kremlin? An insurance policy is something that comes into effect only upon the culmination of some misfortune. One would think the applicable misfortune would be the revelation that Putin is pulling his puppet strings, but in fact the misfortune appears to be that the American people decided to elect Donald Trump president. What, would they have just shrugged and ignored Trump's alleged sedition if Hillary had won? This text only makes sense if it was referring to framing the president.

There was plenty of *ex post facto* explaining of this text by Strzok and his gal pal Lisa Page. (How the hell do people with security clearances not get fired for committing adultery *within their damn agency*?) They testified that the text message was just a hodgepodge of words that may as well have been compiled at random. You are crazy for assuming their manifest and obvious meaning. Your eyes are lying to you.

The Strzok-Page correspondence showed the world one thing: senior members of the Intelligence Community thought that it was their responsibility to prevent Donald Trump from taking office. The fact that he was duly elected by the American people didn't matter. In their minds, that responsibility included framing President Trump for an unprecedented act of treason.

The whole sordid affair made it clear that there are two systems of justice in our country. One is for us normal Americans, where a complex web of laws, rules, and regulations assures that the powers that be can strike down anyone who gets uppity. The other is for the elite, which explains away all wrongdoing as par for the course. Ordinary American citizens live in a world ruled by the infamous quote of Soviet secret police chief Lavrentiy Beria: "Show me the man and I'll show you the crime." The elites, meanwhile, get to make the rules and enforce them, and they never rule against their own.

Hillary Clinton's casual disregard of basic laws that get other people felony convictions is just one example. Look at the Internal Revenue Service scandal under Barack Obama. The IRS targeted conservative organizations for special harassment, and neither the media nor Democrat politicians cared. In fact, they *supported* the IRS's actions, carrying its water and protecting the wrongdoers. Unfortunately, these cases are the rule, not the exception. Selective enforcement is part and parcel of the bureaucracy's standard operating procedure. When someone comes along threatening to hold them accountable, they'll bury him.

They did it to a sitting President of the United States, a guy over 60 million Americans voted for, and if you don't think they can do it to you too, talk to Mike Flynn.

It is not an accident. It is policy. At least under a Republican administration, some of the worst of the abuses can be contained. There is some potential, however vanishingly small, for accountability. But under a Democrat administration?

Think of that.

This oppression would be policy.

Trump has stripped the masks from his enemies. Watching their wrongdoing come out into the open has been one of the most beautiful parts of Trump's presidency (next to the waterfall of liberal tears, of course). Despite the fact that Hunter "Snort" Biden was peddling influence around the world throughout the Obama years, the elite still has the audacity to claim that the Obama administration was "scandal free." But to the elite, Hunter's corruption is politics as usual. They're all on the same take, sitting on the corporate boards of companies they're supposed to regulate.

Hunter's case is so blatant and manifest that it serves as a litmus test. If you can look at Biden II's antics and not concede that his in-your-face graft is appalling, then you'll never censure your political allies. And if you would tolerate corruption among your own, you would not hesitate to make it up about your opponents. We've already seen that happen.

A long march of garbage humans like John Brennan and other Intelligence Agency mandarins have ambled over to Capitol Hill, lied through their weasel teeth under oath, and walked off scot-free. Meanwhile, harmless eccentrics like Roger Stone get dragged out of their homes by FBI SWAT teams for exaggerating their own importance to the media. And then they get judges who ask, "So what?" and jurors who tweet about how much they hate the president. Is that justice?

If anyone is obstructing justice, it's not Donald Trump or his supporters; it is the political and media elite that shamelessly manipulate the system to protect their own power. They leverage the full weight of the government against their enemies and never pay the price for their own wrongdoing. Then they have the audacity to say that anyone who defends himself against their baseless accusations is undermining the rule of law.

They tried to frame the president of the United States. They almost pulled it off. What could they do to you? What will they do to you if they ever take unrestrained power again?

If what they're doing is "justice," then thank the Lord that Donald Trump is there to obstruct it.

CHAPTER 15

Trump Is a Pawn of the NRA...
and So Are You Gun Nuts!

Most Trump supporters wish this lie were true. If Donald Trump were a puppet of the National Rifle Association, then we might get some of the gun reforms America really needs. Instead, we're stuck with fascist gun laws that trample our Second Amendment rights. A puppet of the NRA would make sure concealed carry reciprocity was passed through Congress. He might even mandate that every healthy, law-abiding American citizen have a real assault rifle in their home in order to defend themselves, their families, their communities, and their Constitution.

Just the thought of getting our Switzerland on is enough to cause uncontrollable tingling. Hey, don't we always hear about how we have much to learn from our European friends? The Swiss have assault rifles in their houses—why don't we? Why do xenophobic liberals hate the Swiss so much?

The liars don't focus on the positive legislative agenda of America's foremost civil rights organization. They don't even recognize that gun advocates have a vision for America's future. Instead, they focus on the NRA's steadfast defense of our Second Amendment rights.

Defending rights troubles them because they think that our rights are purely optional privileges to be granted or revoked at the whim of government flunkies. The NRA is an obstacle to unlimited power by the left. So while they may not be able to fight the NRA with guns, the liars can target them with round after round of slander.

Ordinary Americans know that keeping our guns is key to keeping our liberty. Our refusal to lie down like a bunch of serfs and accept disarmament galls them to no end. Our weapons give us the dignity of citizens and provide a hot lead backstop against the Venezuela-style tyranny our elite dreams of imposing. They know how important our weapons are to resisting their project, which is why they'll say anything to turn the pack of AR15-wielding attack dogs into a passive flock of neutered sheep.

They accuse you of murdering innocent people and take special delight in claiming that you are responsible for the killing of children. They blame you for the world's problems while calling you a terrorist with the blood of children on your hands. Go to hell, gunfascists.

Blaming gun owners for the murder of children is a brazen and irresponsible attack on American patriots. Armed citizens make up the backbone of our country. Instead of recognizing our free choice to own guns, the left prefers to disseminate a literal blood libel that refusing to knuckle under their fascist erasure of our rights has made us responsible for children getting shot. If you were to make the case that our political discourse is leading us down a dark path, then this would make a good place to start.

Every time some freak decides to take out his personal failures on innocent bystanders, liberals blame Trump, the Republican party, and the millions of Americans who support those organizations. It's as if the president is standing on some street corner passing out rifles to every loser, malcontent, and weirdo who wanders by. It's a lie, and they know it's a lie, and they don't care. They want Trump out, the NRA crushed, and you submissive.

"Let the Kids Die, the NRA Says—and Here's Money," reads the headline of a February 23, 2018, Courthouse News Service article by one Robert Kahn. "Near as I can figure it, the NRA's response to the latest mass murder in a public school is this: Screw those kids. Let 'em die. Don't kiss your children goodnight; kiss them good-bye. Here's some more money for Congress and the President of the United States: Now kiss our ass."

If you dare to defend your natural right to protect your life and liberty, expect a downpour of abuse from our liberal elite. They'll call you all sorts of craven names and accuse you of unbelievable crimes. It's always the same. If you aren't willing to disarm yourself and place your life and liberty in the hands of our ruling caste, you've gone full Moloch. And you should never go full Moloch, except when it's fetuses that are inconvenient. Then Moloch away and shout your Moloching in the streets.

Now, Trump is not a stereotypical gun guy. He's a city guy and the image of him tramping through the wilderness with a deer rifle is pretty far-fetched. (His sons, though, are both avid hunters.) It's a bit surprising that a guy without the personal experience of collecting and using guns understands how vital bearing arms is to our citizenry. He knows that guns are the only thing able to deter both crime and tyranny. That's why he has been immune to the liars' skeevy campaign to shame him into submission.

Trump refuses to take moral lessons from the people who lecture us about evil guns. Most GOP marshmallows (read: Mitt Romney) would fold to the gunfascists in a heartbeat. Trump is immune to their moral blackmail and doesn't fall for the theatrics that accompany their push to erase our rights. It's not that he's full of hate or lacks compassion; he simply refuses to be manipulated by liars trying to game him for their own ends.

And you feel the same way. You understand that the gun issue is a foundational debate in American politics, a question whose resolution will determine what kind of country the United States of America is. Are we a nation of citizens who reserve to ourselves the ultimate power to reject and remove a government that has strayed from our consent? Are we a nation of citizens where criminals fear *us*, and not vice versa? Or are we a nation of craven serfs stupid enough to think that our government will rule us for our benefit and with our consent for the rest of time? Are we a nation of servile inhabitants who cower at the thought of taking our safety into our own hands?

Just like every other policy our elites want to enact, this proscription increases their power and takes away yours. What a coincidence!

Trump understands gun politics despite the fact that he is not a gun aficionado himself. He knows that the gun question is existential, and that once the establishment disarms the populace, the American experiment is over. Instead of a nation of self-sufficient citizens, people would be at the mercy of the one group left with guns: the ruling class who control the military. And what kind of idiot would want to be at the mercy of America's inept, self-serving, quasi-fascist, twenty-first century ruling class?

The liberals also think of the gun debate as an existential struggle. Guns are the big score. They know that taking the guns away will break the will and the strength of the American people once and for all. Doing that is necessary for them to actualize the leftist dystopian America of their dreams. And they have to do it soon, before Trump can ensure the Supreme Court has a majority of justices who defend gun rights without worrying about what *Washington Post* editorials say about them. Count on John Roberts to resist the country club clique at your peril.

So, we get the lies.

Most of the lies we have reviewed leverage social and cultural power to delegitimize Trump's administration and his supporters. By shaming you through defamation, the establishment wants to intimidate you into silently acquiescing to their demands. Maybe if you get called "racist" enough, you'll stop sticking up for your own interests.

But this lie, this grotesque blood libel that says standing up for your rights means butchering babies, targets weak-willed and foolish people who never understood why we have guns because they never understood what it means to have a personal, individual role in defending society.

Many of these vulnerable suckers are well-off, affluent, coddled, and protected, and it has never occurred to them that the stability and freedom they inherited did not just spontaneously generate. It was established by men with guns, and it was defended by men with guns.

But the kind of people whom Mike Bloomberg and the rest of the gunfascists make overtures to don't think about that. They are soft, sentimental, and stupid. Gosh, if we just beat all our swords into plowshares, everything would be peachy. That is, of course, until somebody shows up with an unbeaten sword. Then you're pretty much screwed.

And you, the uppity American who insists on his rights, are the villain. You, the guy who works and supports his family. The guy who did a tour in Afghanistan. The guy who votes and answers his jury summons. The guy who knows that if he is packing when something bad goes down, maybe he'll miss the bad guy, but the bad guy will pump bullets into him rather than some kid who is running away and that's better than nothing.

You are not the bad guy. To say you are is a lie. You are a law-abiding citizen who stands to protect his family, his community, and his country. You deserve the respect of your fellow Americans, not their ire. And you support Trump because he gives you the credit you deserve.

Name the NRA member who ever went on a mass killing spree. Just one will do. The NRA member, not the radical jihadi, who shot up a San Bernardino Christmas party. Not the radical jihadi who shot up a gay nightclub. Not the Obama supporter who shot a reporter and cameraman on-air. Not the teen who shot up the Florida school after the FBI got a bunch of warnings about him. Not the trans teens who shot up the Colorado school.

It's hard to think of one, right? That's because there are none. If any mass shooters were NRA members, you would hear about it so much that you'd never forget it. The liars try hard to find people they can use to make you look crazy. They thought they had it with that creep in New Zealand, except his idiotic manifesto trashed Trump. They were gleeful at the Texas border killer until that guy's similar eco-fascist screed was published. The nearly simultaneous Dayton shooter was a straight-up leftist. Once it comes out that any given shooter is not a dyed-in-the-wool Trump supporter, he is no longer useful to the liars, so his story fades away.

But while no NRA members have orchestrated mass shootings, several NRA members have capped some mass murdering degenerate before he could get his murderous rampage off the ground. That's what NRA members are for.

It's disgusting to tie the evil monsters who murder the defenseless to the law-abiding patriots who are members of the NRA. Mass shooters are evil, deranged nihilists who want to wreak as much havoc as they can before they end their pathetic lives. Comparing the one to the other is a disgrace, and yet the elites beam with self-righteous pride whenever they do.

If they're willing to demonize you and suppress your right to bear arms, what would they be willing to do if you didn't have guns? After all, the people seeking to steal your rights are not deterred from their quest to disenfranchise tens of millions of Americans by simple honesty and decency. If they were, they wouldn't baselessly defame you. Their own behavior proves that if shit hits the fan, we better be packing something a bit more decisive than words.

The gunfascists have no interest in stopping gun violence. They just want to use instances of gun violence to defame their fellow Americans. The policies they propose would do nothing to prevent the particular incidents that they use to whip their base up into a frenzy. Nearly every single time there's a shooting, the perp is some felon, nut, or minor whom existing laws bar from owning or possessing a firearm. Or the shooting takes place in a "gun free zone," which shows the real value of banning guns.

But hey, a law that keeps you and your family from defending your lives and freedom, yeah, that would have deterred him.

"Gosh, I'm a felon who isn't supposed to have a gun, and I'm going into this place where guns are illegal, and I'll be committing murder, but I really don't want to push it by breaking this other law."

The liars don't care whether the law prevents violence. That's beside the point. Their goal is to disarm and humble you, their cultural enemy. If they take your guns, they take your self-respect, and if they do that, they can take everything else you care about.

No one has ever disarmed people for their own safety. The liars are no different. They would rather you die than successfully defend yourself. While they may not put it that way, it's the logical conclusion you can draw from their actions. If they succeed in taking away your guns, law-abiding citizens will die. Do you think criminals will turn in their guns when liberals make possessing firearms illegal? They don't follow the law—that's why they're criminals.

Take the White Settlement, Texas, shooting as an example. A criminal who was legally prohibited from owning a gun walks into a church with a shotgun—a kind of gun they do not demand be banned (yet), and which was even recommended by senile Joe Biden as a home defense weapon— and without warning, he brandishes the weapon and kills two parishioners. Before the shooter was able to claim any more victims, an armed parishioner put a .357 slug in his noggin at fifty feet while a half-dozen other parishioners produced their pieces. That's how it should be: American citizens standing up to defend themselves and their loved ones.

The gunfascists hate those stories. They were horrified that an American citizen dared to defend himself. They howled about how guns should not be allowed in churches, as if the man about to commit cold-blooded murder stopped and thought, "Gee, I guess I can go inside with my gun. Phew, didn't want to break the law."

They would rather leave you disarmed and defenseless, which really means that they would rather see you suffer the foreseeable consequences of being disarmed and defenseless than be able to protect yourself.

That's sick.

And evil.

But is there any clearer sign that their priorities do not include keeping you safe?

If you really want to see what a fraud the fake concern over gun crime is, look at the streets of Chicago. It's no coincidence that dozens of shootings go down every day in the Democrat city with the tightest gun laws imaginable. But those gun crimes are not important to liberals. If they were, they'd either insist on arming the law-abiding populace or sending the National Guard to restore law and order.

Chicago proves that liberals only want to take the guns out of your hands, not the hands of criminals. The numbers prove that same fact. The *Washington Times* reported on July 23, 2014, under the Obama Administration, that gun crime prosecutions dropped substantially: "The 2013 totals represent a 42 percent decline from the record number of 8,752 prosecutions of ATF cases brought by the Justice Department in 2004 under Mr. Bush, according to the data." But Barack Obama was so very, very concerned about gun crimes, we were duly informed. Heck, he was so concerned about them that he even told his Justice Department to send a bunch of guns to Mexico as part of the Fast and Furious operation.

But Barack Obama wasn't worried about the guns criminals possessed illegally. He wanted to take away the guns you rightfully own. There were fewer prosecutions because Barack Obama wanted to put fewer inner-city criminals in jail. The Obama Justice Department was swept up in the "mass incarceration" rage, which demands that we set criminals free or not jail them at all. Enforcing the law is racist, according to our betters in California, New York, and other places dumb enough to elect leftist governors and prosecutors.

The thugs aren't dangerous, they're just misunderstood. The real danger is the law-abiding, largely middle- and working-class people who legally own firearms. Those people think owning a weapon is a key part of what it means to be an American citizen—what backwater hicks! Those people are the real threat.

Of course, they define the "threat" not as some rampaging punk— those rarely get into the kind of neighborhoods that Mike Bloomberg, Shannon Watts, and the rest of the delegates to the Gunfascist Reichstag live in. No, the definition of a threat is *you*, the Trump voter, the citizen who dares to demand to retain his or her power to control his own destiny not only with a ballot but, if it comes to it, with a bullet.

The lies accusing decent American citizens of causing the acts of vicious criminals because we won't disarm at the behest of people who despise us is tiresome, but fortunately the lies are not working. Donald Trump has resisted all efforts to convert him into some sort of gun-banning freak. He has declined to make a .30-06 political error that would make George H. W. Bush's "Read my lips—no new taxes" betrayal look like a .22.

But he's been under pressure. The other side has its scheme locked and loaded. He just refuses to buckle.

A horrible event that has nothing to do with Trump, you, or the NRA happens and the Democrats blame him and try to get him to fold on demands that never have anything to do with the crime that just occurred. Their ghoulish delight is obvious despite their fake outrage—they see each crisis as an opportunity and gleefully wade into the blood to try to leverage the carnage to steal our rights. The president, understanding that human beings experiencing the shock of a horrible tragedy are vulnerable to emotional appeals, makes noises as if he is listening to the liars and taking their nonsense seriously. He knows he is speaking to all Americans, not just those who care about the Second Amendment, and he wisely gets ahead of his opposition.

And then the media eagerly writes up reports from its impeccable sources in the administration that Trump is about to stab the NRA—by which the media means Trump's constituents—in the back by accepting some new useless law. And then he doesn't.

The media soon moves on to some new story about something that will totally do Trump in, and the gunfascists are left with nothing but the hope for new murders that they can exploit.

Trump understands he'll get tossed out of office, and then it'll be open season on him and his family by his liberal enemies. It's literally a political life or death question for him. And the NRA understands that

Trump is the only game in town. A lot of soft Republicans would be only too happy to sell out the base by sucking up to the establishment with some law banning scary-looking firearms.

But just because the lies have not succeeded so far does not mean that we will not hear the lie again and again. Watch for it the next time that someone who has nothing to do with Trump, the NRA, or you, commits a crime and the liars blame you. They'll tell you that blood is on your hands. If it were so, the one finger salute you shoot back would be red.

CHAPTER 16

Trump Is a Bully...
and You Are Part of His Gang of Thugs!

Is Donald Trump a bully? The liars say that he is a vicious thug abusing innocent folks for his cruel jollies, taking their figurative lunch money, giving them wedgies, and stuffing them in their lockers. Oh, and you're a big mean bully too because you support him.

That's the claim, all right. Yet, if it were true—and the evidence shows that it's not, but let's get hypothetical for a moment—so what? Maybe we need a bully right now.

After years and years of watching leading conservatives politely gentleman themselves into utter submission, maybe normal Americans need a bully. Sort of like that old movie *My Bodyguard* where the little kid hires big old Adam Baldwin (a spectacular real-life conservative, by the way) to protect him from the punks who were pushing him around. Sometimes you have to fight fire with a flamethrower. The guy we elected in 2016 is that flamethrower.

Still, if we are to indulge in the ancient and obsolete bourgeois premise that words have objective meaning, then we need to acknowledge that Donald Trump is not a "bully." He's undeniably rough and tough, and he's certainly not afraid to throw a rhetorical haymaker, but he does not go out of the way to hassle people to puff up his own ego.

Trump is a counterpuncher, a guy utterly incapable of walking off an insult, who is at his best when taking hammer and tongs to someone who started trouble with him. He doesn't take grief on the chin, which drives the liberal elites up a wall. For decades, they took full advantage of guys who had their faces buried inside the covers of the non-existent *Marquess of Queensberry Rules of Politico-Cultural Combat* while the other side pummeled them into a pulp. Trump ticks the establishment off by not assuming the role of punching bag for every lib, pinko, internet scribbler, semi-literate actress, and social justice warrior who wants to take a swing.

Words do mean something, and the word "bully" has a specific definition. A bully enjoys tormenting people for the sheer joy of exercising brutal power over the weak. That does not fit Trump or the normal Americans who support him. There's no evidence that Trump gets pleasure out of using his social media sledgehammer on someone who did not lob an insult at him first. There's no evidence that he revels in beating down people who did not wrong him. The phrase "don't want none, don't start none" was invented to describe guys like Trump. And in a lot of ways, the phrase describes the American character writ large.

The elites often portray Americans as bullies both domestically and abroad. According to their court philosophers, Americans take cruel pleasure in being mean to nice people—you know, illegal aliens, welfare cheats, criminals, and other key Democrat constituencies. We enforce our borders because we delight in tormenting desperate people, not because we're a sovereign nation with a duty to protect our territory. We demand people support themselves because we enjoy seeing our own country's Oliver Twists walk away dejected with empty bowls, not because we want middle class Americans to be able to survive without the crippling demands of supporting an underclass. We lock up criminals because we think sending people to jail is fun, not because we want to keep Americans safe and deter people from a life of crime. And we do all this because we are nourished by evil.

No, it does not make a lot of sense. When you consider the facts, Americans are exceptionally good people, not evil. Americans' per capita charity giving dwarfs the rest of the world's. If you have ever served overseas, you know that the Ugly American stereotype is just a hack cliché. But, in keeping with the basic principle that Trump and his supporters are everything wrong in the world, we get the bully lie.

Maybe they hope that by characterizing perfectly normal reactions to politico-cultural stimuli as "bullying," they can get us not to react to their provocations—or better yet, to react with ashamed, abject acquiescence.

As conservative comic Evan Sayet keenly observed, two words sum up Donald Trump's great appeal, and they just so happen to be title of his viral July 13, 2017, Townhall.com article: "He Fights."

Trump fights, and his opponents hate that. The same counterpuncher's instincts that make him such a deadly opponent in a media dust-up immunize him from the effects of the "bully" label. He doesn't care if they call him a "bully" because he doesn't care what they think. He instinctively recognizes it's all bad faith baloney anyway.

Of course, if Trump were a bully instead of someone who is just gloriously indifferent to the accusations of his enemies, then he still would not care about being called a "bully." But a lot of other conservatives *do* care about being called names, which is a problem. And it's a much bigger problem than people think.

The idea of being a gentleman, of not stooping to the level of one's enemies, of maintaining civility even in the face of abuse, has some residual appeal today. The siren song of civility is powerful, harkening back to a more genteel time. Many Americans yearn to return to a time when ideas were debated, the issues addressed, and herds of snowy-white unicorns romped on the Washington mall.

I hate to break it to you, but it's not happening.

It didn't even happen back in the days when we think it happened. Let's look back to the time when the gracious Ronald Reagan was supposedly battling it out with Tip O'Neil by day and sharing a nip of whiskey with him in the evening. O'Neil and the Democrats hated Reagan. They called him an idiot, a cowboy, a Nazi, and a racist, and if we now forget their vitriol today it's only thanks to time. Plus, there was no social media back then to sear it into our consciousness.

Reagan was the master of the gentle jibe, the "there you go again" that would turn his opponent into a huffing, puffing punchline. But that was a conscious tactic, and the good-humored, good-natured Gipper act was astonishingly effective. That was not necessarily the real Reagan. In private, the man was tough as nails, as his ruthless and systematic destruction of the USSR unequivocally demonstrated. Reagan was a determined fighter for what he believed in at home too. The only difference was that at home, he killed his enemies with kindness.

The problem is that the ranks of the Republican establishment are filled with guys who don't fight with kindness or with anything else.

Look at George H. W. Bush. Boy, he was genteel. He was the pride of the prep school set, the perfect gentleman. And he got rolled time and time again.

Bush Senior was physically brave and certainly knew how to fight in war. The guy was a Navy pilot in the Pacific for crying out loud. And he was not a sissy when it came to our engagements overseas. After all, he sent your author and a half million other soldiers to the Middle East to wipe out the Iraqi military. But when it came to domestic political battles, 41 didn't have a drop of fight in him. Crossing over the Beltway into the D.C. fishbowl can turn otherwise butch players into gelatinous cubes of weak-sauce goo.

Bush 41 got bullied into his most famous fumble, the one that brought him from wild popularity (his approval rating was nearly 90 percent during the Gulf War) to a drubbing by some priapic ex-governor from Arkansas. Bush was never a true fan of Ronald Reagan's conservatism, and he never really understood all the ideology stuff. The Gipper picked Bush as his veep because he needed to nail down the moderate wing of the GOP. In the end, Bush's party was quickly becoming unfamiliar to him with its fixation on conservative principles rather than the gooey go-along to get-along politics Bush was used to.

So, when Bush said, "Read my lips, no new taxes," it did not come from the preppie's gut. It came from expedience. The people whose votes he needed wanted to know that he shared their principles. He thought he could give them some of their crazy conservative talk, and they would nod and elect him. And they did.

But apparently, he did not think the electorate would remember his promises after Election Day. Maybe he thought that voters mistook his promises for empty words, just like he did. It was certainly not a promise that he would defy the establishment bullies to make good on.

The establishment put incredible pressure on Bush to raise taxes. After all, the Reagan "supply side" tax cuts still baffled much of the Republican establishment. Bush himself had labeled it "voodoo economics" before he joined Team Ronnie. Plus, cutting taxes was outright anathema to the Democrats. So the political opposition, the soft Republicans, and the media banded together to push Bush into raising taxes. They bullied him into doing it, or rather, he allowed himself to be bullied into doing it. And then Bill Clinton and the Democrats absolutely pummeled him for it in the 1992 campaign.

Eight years later, his son came along. Where daddy had promoted a "kinder, gentler nation"—a sop to the bullies on the left who were ganging up on him—W decided to trot out some abomination called "compassionate conservatism." Real conservatives were appalled that their leader felt the need to apologize for their views. ("Hey, our new conservatism is okay because it's *compassionate*, unlike the kind our voters believe in!") The liberals saw it for weakness, and they let Bush have it.

After the post-9/11 rally around the flag interregnum came to a close, George W. Bush endured stomach-turning abuse. Even conservatives who were disappointed by the Bush presidency found the constant flow of attacks against the president of the United States was unprecedented.

There were assassination porn and Hollywood movies about Bush's perfidy, while Democrats abused him daily on the floor of the Congress. There were endless talking heads calling him a "war criminal" and so forth, while others called him "Chimpy McHitlerburton." He's a monkey! He's a puppet of Halliburton! He's Hitler!

He said nothing.

He did nothing.

He just took it.

He was very concerned about the dignity of the office, you see. But real conservatives found that what may have started out as dignity ended up as weakness. Real conservatives hit back for Bush. We fought against the endless smears and made the case for his leadership that he refused to make for himself. As he let himself be dragged through the mud without resistance, we tried to intervene. But you can't defend a guy who won't defend himself.

Maybe he didn't see that by refusing to defend himself, he tacitly refused to defend his supporters. Letting insults slide didn't uphold the dignity of the Oval Office; it tarnished the dignity of Republicans across the country.

The head of the party always stands in for all of us. When he lets himself get trashed, he lets the people who stand beside him get trashed. That's no way to stand up for your own, and it's no way to conduct politics.

Morale matters. It matters in war, and it matters in politics too, not merely because, as Clausewitz pointed out, war is an analogue for politics. Morale requires leadership, steadiness, and a command presence. It also requires victories. Not always, not every time, but you gotta put some points on the board or people are going to wonder just why the hell they are following you.

Where were W's points on the board? Medicare Part B? No Child Left Behind? Iraq? If you can't make any policy progress, you can at least smack around the people tormenting you. But Bush 43 didn't even give his people that.

He sat there and was bullied and bullied and bullied and never smacked the bullies in the face. And after a while, his followers were demoralized. Bullying only works if you let yourself be bullied.

And as if things couldn't get any worse, the establishment decided to follow up W's weak performance by giving Republicans John McCain. McCain was another guy who combined great personal bravery in the face of foreign enemies with just as great a capacity to submit to the establishment. For a so-called "maverick," his maverickry always mirrored exactly what the Democrats wanted. They played him perfectly, and even got him to close down his presidential campaign because the economy was imploding.

Not all political bullying is calling your opponents names: sometimes, it's the threat of withholding establishment approval. McCain, the guy whose heroism and perseverance in Vietnam made him seem immune from pressure, could be bullied in a snap by invoking "honor" and stock phrases like "that's not who we are." With that kind of pressure, the elites could get McCain to do whatever they wanted. That's why his last significant political act was breaking his promise to his constituents to repeal Obamacare: he wanted the approval of the establishment, who eventually returned the favor by giving him an endless funeral not long after.

Actual voters never seem to carry as much influence with these soft conservatives as the mean girls of Beltway High School. At the end of the day, those softies care more about what their swamp buddies think of them than the people they're supposed to represent. They can be bullied, manipulated, and worked by the elite, and that's why the elite keeps holding them up as "principled" conservatives.

Trump can't be bullied, and that won him the election in 2016. The entire elite tried its hand at defaming our president, but he shut their lies down and put them in their place. Rosie O'Donnell, that smarmy Tinseltown nag, stepped into the ring. Trump laid her out. McCain tried to play the war hero card, and Trump cut to the heart of it with his "'I like people who weren't captured" retort. The establishment lost its mind, but the people didn't. They saw McCain's rhetorical jab and didn't care that Trump deflected it.

Megyn Kelly wrecked her career when she tried to take on Trump. After she took shots at him on the debate stage, he fired back and was condemned by all the right-thinking people. Meanwhile, real Americans shrugged, voted Trump in, and tuned Kelly out.

Trump refuses to recognize the unwritten rules that the elites only enforce against Republicans. Name an instance when the establishment spasmed in outrage over something uttered about Trump or his family. The left trots out a Gold Star family to trash him and Trump is supposed to stand silent with his head bowed, cowed and shamed. That's not happening.

Some seventeen-year old Swedish weather cultist who is being used as a ventriloquist dummy by leftist activists spouts off, and Trump fails to respect the new rule that she is off limits. He gently mocks her neurotic outrage, and the establishment gasps in horror. He doesn't care, and neither do his supporters. In fact, we like the fact that he punches back against those willing to defame us.

According to the usual script where the elites get Republicans to squish with lies and defamations, Trump was supposed to fold like a house of cards when some unstable liberal claimed that Brett Kavanaugh had assaulted her more than a third of a century ago. Trump shrugged, bucked the establishment pressure, and *voila*—Justice I Like Beer is on the Supreme Court.

Trump refuses to be bullied by slanders or by appeals to amorphous "principles" that always require what leftists want. If you want to talk smack about Trump or his supporters, you better prepare for the smack that will fly back. And if you can't handle it, you won't be able to declare yourself out-of-bounds—you had the chance to do that before you said anything.

The left does not just bully presidents: they bully all their political enemies, no matter how big or small. Everyone from "Cocaine Mitch" McConnell, who cannot be pushed around either, to the average Joe in a MAGA hat is fair game. When Trump fights back, he gives all his allies more room to breathe. His supporters adore it because someone is finally standing up to the real bullies. After all, his supporters are the targets. What's a more powerful power move than co-opting an epithet against you for your fundraising? Ask Supreme Court Justice Merrick Garland or Nancy Pelosi if the Murder Turtle can be intimidated.

Since Trump is immune to pressure, the left has changed their tactics. Now, in addition to launching volley after volley of defamation against the president, leftists attack Trump supporters directly. They try to intimidate supporters by confronting them on the streets or in restaurants, by stealing their MAGA hats, by punching them, by canceling them on social media, and by trying to get them fired from their jobs. Maxine Waters explained the game to whomever was bored enough to listen:

> Let's make sure we show up wherever we have to show up. And if you see anybody from that cabinet in a restaurant, in a department store, at a gasoline station, you get out and you create a crowd. And you push back on them. And you tell them they're not welcome anymore, anywhere. We've got to get the children connected to their parents.

Gee, that seems a lot like bullying. And you know what else sounds like bullying? Suing nuns to force them to fund birth control. Or sending gay activists to harass wedding photographers and cake bakers. Or passing laws designed to infringe upon the rights of citizens to keep and bear arms, while threatening to turn the National Guard on them if they don't comply. Or maintaining a social media gestapo designed to ruin the lives of anyone who refuses to toe the liberal line.

There is a bullying problem in America's culture and politics today, that's for certain. But the problem is not Donald Trump. He is the solution, someone immune to the power of the establishment bullies. He will take the fight right back to them. He's fearless, and that is why they hate him so deeply.

The liars want to stop Donald Trump from normalizing resistance to their punk pressure tactics. By calling him a bully, and you a bully for supporting him, they hope to get ordinary Americans to submit to their agenda. But Donald Trump is not a bully, and neither are you. And after years of humiliating submission by erstwhile Republican leaders who melted under the glare of our finger-wagging socio-political elites, would it be so wrong for regular Americans to shrug and think, "Better a bully than a beta?"

CHAPTER 17

Trump Loves Dictators...
and You Do Too!

The lie that Donald Trump is some sort of buddy to the world's dictators—*shouldn't Vlad be jealous that other strongmen are hitting on his bae?*—is a lie that our ridiculous foreign policy establishment would be ashamed of it had the moral capacity to recognize just how incredibly shameful it is. Maybe I'm a bit biased, having led young Americans to war, but I'm sensitive about our troops' getting killed, and I deeply appreciate leaders who prevent that from happening.

President Trump has tried the radical idea of communicating diplomatically with world leaders who want to kill us. Instead of sticking to the foreign relations playbook that has failed American citizens for decades, Trump has expressed a willingness to try new ways to secure agreements with foreign nations in our mutual interest. That's driven our foreign policy elite nuts, especially after the president's approach started to deliver results.

We've already dispelled the lies surrounding the Trump–Russia conspiracy theories, so maybe we should begin with the second autocrat Trump expressed a willingness to negotiate with: Kim Jong Un (who may very well have checked out of this mortal coil by the time you read this).

When Donald Trump took office, the situation on the Korean Peninsula was dire. After years of Washington failures, Kim Jong Un had developed and improved his nuclear arsenal and was threatening the United States and South Korea on an almost daily basis. If things got messy in Korea, we would have been in major trouble, propelled into another war on the other side of the globe that could drag on for decades.

Donald Trump talked tough to Kim Jong Un, and the establishment freaked out. Then, when Trump's hard-line rhetoric paid off, forcing Kim Jong to reconsider his course, the establishment began calling Trump a friend to tyrants.

Luckily, President Trump doesn't pay much heed to their lies, because the political establishment is certainly willing to sacrifice American lives in the name of their Trump Derangement Syndrome. Don't you think those smug elitists who purport to oversee our nation's diplomacy should be a little more circumspect when trashing the guy whose hands-on interaction with the loathsome Kim Jong Un has not only kept Kim Jong from popping off more ballistic missiles, but has also deterred the puny butcher from starting a war that would paint the Korean peninsula red with the blood of millions, including tens of thousands of American soldiers and airmen?

A lot of people talk about this being a short war. Don't bet on it, unless your gut tells you the people who told you the wars in Iraq, Syria, and Libya would be quick are due to finally be right about something.

They aren't. And if we were to steamroll the Norks quickly, we win the much-coveted prize of bringing North Korea into the twenty-first century.

Now tell me that we shouldn't be on our knees thanking Donald Trump for making nice with that tubby sociopath.

Trump's overtures to Kim Jong Un helped correct one of the major blunders the best and the brightest continue to make. If you thought the wars in Iraq and Afghanistan were bad, just look at the Korean War. Despite nearly seventy years having come and gone, the First Korean War has still yet to end, in large part because our establishment's diplomatic geniuses failed to take any meaningful action since the war devolved into a stalemate across the Thirty-eighth Parallel in 1953.

Instead of remaining content with maintaining the *status quo*, Trump set his targets higher. Thanks to his unique diplomatic style, Trump might actually end the war on the Korean Peninsula. A peace treaty may soon be on the table. Unlike the Republican chicken hawks and the Democrat kumbaya NGO experts who staffed previous administrations, Trump knows how to deal with tough guys, a skill honed by decades of dealing with other tough guys in the high-stakes international real estate and media arenas.

The liars know what they are doing when they push false narratives on the American people. They know that they make arguments based on false premises. But they push them anyway. In this case, the premise is that Donald Trump admires Kim, and Turkey's Erdogan, and China's Xi, and all the rest. The liars pretend that being pleasant, even flattering these dictators, in order to secure a deal that would help the American people exposes Donald Trump's secret desire to be a dictator. Give me a break.

The truth is, they're terrified that Donald Trump's success will expose their decades of failure. Remember, these liars have repeatedly made a hash of our relations with these dictators. The suave, urbane pros who know how to deal with foreigners have routinely failed to accomplish anything even remotely resembling a victory in their entire lifetimes. Unlike the dregs who check the ballot for Trump, they are the educated, witty, charming members of our glorious foreign policy elite. If Trump and his supporters solve problems that they couldn't crack, then they'll start looking real bad.

That, at its core, is the big difference between this lie and the others. When they call him a "racist" or a "homophobe" or "a bad Christian," the liars want to humiliate Trump supporters into submission. This lie, meanwhile, isn't about you. It's about them.

Trump has done what these pompous dweebs have only dreamt of, and they've gotten jealous. While Trump made progress, they continually made fools of themselves. In one term as president, Donald Trump has achieved more on the Korean peninsula than every president combined since Ike drove those commie bastards back across the Thirty-eighth Parallel.

It gnaws at them. It eats at them. They got degrees in international relations at Georgetown. They worked in the foreign service. They were distinguished fellows at the Institute of Appeasement and Mediocrity think tank. And everything they touched turned to Iraq.

Then Trump came along, this vulgar, uneducated brute, and did more with a couple tweets to promote America's interests in the western Pacific than a thousand Foggy Bottom Yalies previously thought possible. For all their credentials and all their delusions of competency, he showed them as the inept gaggle of pompous buffoons that they are.

How does Trump do it? Flattery mixed with toughness. His flattery is often ridiculous, to our ears at least, but to the ears of the thugs across the table it sounds like a sweet symphony. In June 2019, he said about China's leader, "And I like President Xi a lot. I consider him a friend, and—but I like him a lot. I've gotten to know him very well. He's a strong gentleman, right? Anybody that—he's a strong guy, tough guy."

Just a few days earlier, Trump made similar remarks about Turkish President Recep Tayyip Erdogan: "It's my honor to be with a friend of mine, somebody I've become very close to, in many respects, and he's doing a very good job."

And in April 2017, Trump commented about Philippines President Rodrigo Duterte and his innovative solution to the addiction crisis there, which is essentially shooting dealers, "I just wanted to congratulate you because I am hearing of the unbelievable job on the drug problem."

Trump's dramatic overtures are effective, and that's why he keeps coming back to them. Does anyone think that Trump means these comments wholeheartedly? No, but that doesn't stop the liars.

According to these savvy experts who claim to have mastered diplomatic communications, our discussions with our opponents must always reflect our true feelings and intentions. Moreover, where those true feelings are negative, we must speak those feels loudly and proudly because, as no one has ever seriously contended in the entire history of mankind until Trump came into office, diplomacy is the art of pissing off foreigners.

As it turns out, the liars' beef with Trump is that he is too diplomatic, which proves that he doesn't know what he is doing. But other times he is too tough, because he is Trump, and everything Trump does is wrong even if he is doing precisely the opposite of what the liars contend Trump was doing wrong thirty seconds ago.

Trump's negotiations with Chairman Xi of Red China make a great case in point. Thanks to the folly of the experts now making a living out of criticizing Trump, this administration has had to repair the disastrous relationship with the ChiComs that locked America into a permanent disadvantage. Trump is constantly extolling Xi's leadership and wisdom before "reluctantly" imposing a tariff on the Chinese. After showing the Chinese that we're willing to deal out some economic pain for once, it's back to the table and *voila!* A new trade agreement where America stops getting grifted like the guy who bought the Brooklyn Bridge.

These trained and Harvard-approved negotiators imagine that they are the experts at negotiating, but the preppies who helped wrangle the last Danish Bernstein Grubé cheese protocol have got nothing on the guy who bargained his way into building a tower on New York's Fifth Avenue. And dealing with guys who shoot people they don't like is a bit different than sitting across the table from some dudes from Copenhagen.

Let's face it: these bad guys are tough and serious in a way that the pampered prisses who used to conduct American foreign policy just cannot comprehend. Their big worry is that someone will report them to the State Department Undersecretary of Diversity and Complaining. Kim Jong Un, meanwhile, had to smoke his half-bro in a Malaysian airport to make sure said sibling doesn't come home, launch a coup, and feed the Dear Leader feet-first into a wood chipper.

You need a guy like Trump to handle these thugs. And Trump does not get rolled. How many "Peace in our time!" moments have we had where our super-competent experts have come home certain and smug about our last deal and a few months later the bad guys are building a new bomb, or doubling their carbon dioxide emissions, or just plain laughing at those American saps they just skinned?

Trump is not interested in the big moment where the agreement is made, and that's another difference between him and the experts. The agreement is the goal for our professional diplomatic corps, the follow-through not so much. But Trump won't make a bad deal just to get a deal. He's picky about deals as only someone for whom deals are—forgive me—an art can be. He canned and replaced NAFTA because it stank. He trashed our deals with China and the EU because they stank. He trashed the Paris Climate Hoax Agreement and the Iranian Money Pallet Deal.

When Trump did that, the diplomats wet themselves, America's enemies took notice, and the American people loved it. And now he's negotiating new deals that will discredit those small-souled whiners for a generation.

Perhaps it is small and petty to point out that the critics of the president seem to have their own fondness for foreign tough guys. For instance, the media and not a few Democrats, like the obnoxious Bernie Sanders, fawned over Fidel Castro and his allegedly wonderful free health care and literacy programs. Of course, none ever actually went to Cuba to see a doctor or publish a book. Hugo Chavez got a lot of love from the smart set too, with Hollywood's finest heading down there to visit the socialist paradise; unlike the locals, none of them had to raid the zoos for food.

But it's more than just a quasi-erotic fascination with swarthy, sexy Marxist *caudillos* from the South. If you hate America, you'll always find some of America's elite who will love you. The Obama administration absolutely adored the Muslim Brotherhood-approved Mohamed Morsi right up until current Egyptian President Abdel Fattah el-Sisi deposed that anti-American creep in 2013. Now that Egypt is an ally again, Trump is awful for saying nice stuff about that vital country's leader: "We agree on so many things. I just want to let everybody know in case there was any doubt that we are very much behind President el-Sisi. He's done a fantastic job in a very difficult situation."

Of course, the lie that the dictators and Trump are sitting in a tree, K-I-S-S-I-N-G, is also a lie about you. They say you don't care if Trump cavorts with these criminals. At best you're morally blind, at worst you yearn for a strongman to rule over you. That especially goes for those of you who went overseas to fight for freedom. You vets are the worst.

Of course, maybe instead of channeling the wisdom of the Einsteins who flew a billion bucks to the mullahs in Tehran, you prefer the insights of the warrior-statesman Winston Churchill. Churchill was a guy who knew war up close and bloody, and his oft misquoted observation still resonates in its actual form: "Meeting jaw to jaw is better than war." The kind of Americans whose kids end up wearing combat boots in the mud, not Che t-shirts at college anti-patriarchy rallies, are perfectly willing to have Trump sweet talk the scumbags if that keeps their kid from getting an AK-74 round through his forehead.

And despite Trump's alleged fondness for international bad boys, he does not appear to be taking any hints from them. Journalists, as well as people who work at CNN and MSNBC, continue to report unrestrained by Trump's secret police, who are so secret that no one has ever seen them. Perhaps Trump looks at these other leaders and sighs, daydreaming about what it would like to be able to crush all opposition and rule by decree, but he has yet to succumb to the temptation to give it a try.

Instead, he deals with these dictators the same way he dealt with powerful bullies and creeps back when he was doing deals in the no-quarter world of business. Sometimes he butters them up, sometimes he beats them down, but he plays for keeps, and he gets what he wants from them.

Maybe instead of trashing the president, the amateurs masquerading as pros ought to study a true master of getting what he wants from an opponent. But they won't. They can't. They can't because to learn from Trump is to admit that there is something that they could learn from Trump, which itself is a concession that maybe our best and brightest aren't either of those things.

Well, that won't do. No, conceding that won't do at all. So they lie, because without any significant foreign policy achievements on their collective resume in the two decades preceding Donald Trump's taking office, all they have to assuage the agonizing sting of their failure are the lies they tell themselves.

CHAPTER 18

Trump Betrayed Our Allies...
and So Did You!

As I write this chapter, a dress blue uniform with a rack of ribbons pinned to it hangs just ten feet away. One of those medals is a NATO service medal from my years in units integrated into the NATO command structure. Other medals and ribbons represent service overseas with other American allies like Saudi Arabia, Kuwait, Kosovo, Germany, Japan, and Ukraine.

I'm not the only one who wears service awards from nations around the world. Millions of Americans have similar decorations in their closets. And for those of us who support President Trump, it's annoying to hear people who should know better spread the disgraceful lie that Donald Trump hates our allies, and that we do too.

Trump supporters do not hate our allies. Millions of us have risked our lives alongside allied soldiers to defend our mutual interests. We just want some of our allies to stop playing us for suckers.

The establishment, though, is not only content to let the United States of America be exploited, they think accepting the former status quo is a moral imperative.

Here's the thing: for all the lies about Donald Trump's wrecking our relationships with our allies aside, he is the best thing to happen to the NATO alliance since Ronald Reagan unceremoniously tossed the Soviet Union onto the ash heap of history.

When the United States was first founded as an independent nation, America really did not have allies in the modern sense. No less an authority than George Washington warned us against "entangling alliances," telling Americans that "it is our true policy to steer clear of permanent alliances with any portion of the foreign world" in his final public address.

When the cherry tree-chopping big daddy of America talks through those wooden teeth, you should listen. And he was unequivocal: don't get wrapped up in the antics of those weaselly foreigners. If you must, then do the bare minimum alliance-wise for as little time as possible. Don't get bogged down in their euro-messes.

Sure, we let the French help us out in the Revolution, but that didn't sign us to a mutual defense pact with the French for the rest of time. The frogs had their own beef with the limeys, and helping us redden English redcoats served France's own interests. Once that period of mutual benefit passed, the alliance ended. We Americans kept doing our own thing, and the French returned to doing what the French do, like gobbling camembert and appreciating Jerry Lewis unironically.

That didn't mean we became sworn enemies of the French. Friendly relations short of a formal alliance led us to buy much of our country's midsection from them. It just meant that we were on our own, playing by our own rules, like the nineteenth century's edgy loner with a bad attitude. We consolidated our power even as we wrested the continent from Elizabeth Warren's great-great-grandparents.

Being the globe's bad boy was cool. It left us free to do as we pleased. But like most bad boy phases, ours could not last very long, especially as America blossomed into a massive maritime trading power. The world was out there, and we were going to have to interact with it. Between 1800 and 1916, we invaded Mexico half-heartedly a couple times and full-heartedly once, resulting in the distinctly mixed blessing of the state of California. We grabbed Cuba and Puerto Rico and gave Cuba back (except for Guantanamo—take that you commie bastards). We took the Philippines from Spain. We forced Japan to open its doors to our traders and got a taste for multinational coordination when we helped the European armies settle the Boxers' hash in China at the turn of the twentieth century.

And then Woodrow Wilson with his unerring knack for terrible decisions allowed America to be sucked into World War I. Suddenly we were entangled in Europe's quarrels via the barbed wire strung across the Western Front. The injection of American forces into the exhausted allies turned the tide of that meat grinder masquerading as a war, and soon President Wilson found himself leading a debutante great power that loomed over the bled-out nations of the Old World. He went full internationalist because he was so much wiser than that knucklehead Washington (or so he thought), and ended up pushing for us to join the League of Nations. America was not ready to abandon its traditional reticence regarding alliances, and the Senate refused to acquiesce to Wilson's demands.

And then, a couple decades later, the Japanese attacked Pearl Harbor, and any chance of an isolationist America sank with the USS *Arizona*. By the end of the war, the Allies had created the United Nations, which was the League of Nations 2.0, and this time the Yankees were all in. The UN eventually founded its headquarters in New York City, where obnoxious foreign bureaucrats with diplomatic immunity would come to demonstrate why George Washington was absolutely right to counsel against entangling alliances.

World War II ended with America alone among the main combatants, exponentially more powerful than before we got roped into the conflict. The Soviet Union also emerged from the war as a major power, but at the cost of tens of millions of dead and the utter pulverization of its western territories. The stage was set for the conflict that would dominate the remainder of the century, as the Soviets fought to export communism around the world.

The communist threat truly changed America's behavior on the international stage. Though the Soviets initially stayed in the Eastern European countries they had recaptured on the road to Berlin, it wasn't long before communism started to expand beyond neighboring Soviet satellite states with communist governments. The reds wanted to swing the unoccupied western electorates to the hammer and sickle by hook or by crook and began plotting regime change in Western Europe.

The looming Bolshevik menace meant that America could not go home again back over the Atlantic, as it did after World War I, and leave the smoking ruin that was Western Europe to be gobbled up by Uncle Joe Stalin. We had to stay and give the fledgling democracies a fighting chance to be free, independent, and hopefully not anti-American—for our sake as well as theirs.

The fight against communism called for the creation of a complex web of alliances and treaties across the Western world. First, there was the Marshall Plan, in which America spent a towering pile of cash rebuilding a ruined continent in order to lift Europe out of poverty and keep them from going red. It worked. And soon after that came the North Atlantic Treaty Organization, a military alliance designed to stave off the USSR's military might. Built on a foundation of American money, arms, and troops, NATO fulfilled its apocryphal purpose of keeping the Americans in, the Russians out, and the Germans down.

As we created a system to fight the reds in Europe, we began to spend blood and treasure fighting them in East Asia. The Korean War, which has still not officially ended, was the first engagement, and our plans would come to include the Vietnam War, which everyone apparently forgot about when we went into Afghanistan. And, as time went on, there was the Middle East. Our friendship with Israel grew to include a friendship—well, some kind of -ship—with Saudi Arabia, Iran (that ended poorly), and many others.

Somewhere along the way, the foreigners figured something out: America was still learning the ropes of being a great power. The older nations had centuries, in some cases millennia, of experience dealing with other nations. America did not. The great powers of old were cold and cynical. America was, well, American.

In a century, America went from being a suspicious outsider to the world's soft touch.

Wilson, among his myriad faults, promulgated the naïve view of international relations that caused America a century of problems until Donald Trump tossed out his model. Wilson was an innocent. He believed that relations between nations could be based on lofty principles instead of raw power. His followers made the same mistake, and even America's foreign policy realists often displayed that they lack the cynicism necessary for a successful dive into the pool of foreign relations.

In the 1940s, America needed to foot the bill for NATO. After all, Germany was flattened, Britain was still rationing food for years after Hitler offed himself, and the French were, well, the French. In the 1950s and 1960s, things were still getting cleaned up over there, but conditions were getting better. Germany was starting to rebound, putting out millions of Volkswagen Beetles. The British were invading our airwaves with their mopped-top musicians. The French by then had pulled out of NATO's integrated command structure, though everyone knew that if the Soviets got hinky they would have no choice but to fight alongside the allies to prevent *Vichy 2: Sacre Bleu, Here We Go Again.*

America paid up while also taking on the burden of building a space program and a nuclear deterrent. (The Brits and frogs had a few hot rocks themselves, but they were marginal in the great scheme of things.) While the other NATO countries may not have invested as much cash as we did, they were certainly contributing bodies. Most of them still had conscription, and Tommy, Pierre, and Fritz were all stationed in Germany with guns prepared to fight back the Russian hordes, should they come, right along with GI Joe.

The 1970s and the 1980s came and went, and lo and behold the communist Soviet Union crumbled like the Potemkin economy it was. NATO worked. Its mere existence helped take down Lenin's Abomination without firing a shot.

But after it had achieved its purpose so admirably, what was its use? With the Soviets gone, NATO no longer had a clear function. In the 1990s, Russia was too busy drinking itself to death to invade anyone except its weaker former countrymen. Yet anyone who understands bureaucracies realizes that none of them ever announce, "Finished!" and close up shop. As Reagan once quipped, "a government bureau is the nearest thing to eternal life we'll ever see on this earth."

After the fall of the Berlin wall, our allies noticed that America's checks kept coming. Its men were still stationed in their countries, tasked with protecting the Europeans from invasion. Now, the number of American soldiers stationed in Germany certainly went down after the Soviet Union's close (in the late 1980s there were half a million soldiers and dependents and entire American communities across the Federal Republic of Germany), but American troops still made up a big chunk of the NATO fighting force.

The Europeans saw American soldiers sticking around and decided they didn't need their militaries anymore. One by one, the Europeans ended conscription. When they looked at America for our reaction, we handed them a check. Then they started cutting force structure. They looked at America. Here's a check! So they cut more. And more. And more.

Many considered the arrangement a win-win. The Europeans let America pick up the tab for its defense while they pushed more money into the soul-killing welfare states that were destroying their societies, and the American foreign policy establishment got to feel important by playing empire.

By the 2010s, the vast German tank army of the Cold War years had shrunk to a fraction of its former size. German helicopters and fighters were grounded for lack of parts, and its troops were more focused on social engineering than on killing invaders. Most NATO countries let their militaries rot, happy to ride on the back of American waste, while they turned their gaze towards the leftist policies NATO was supposed to fight against.

"Security? Oh, Uncle Sucker from across the ocean will see to that. Let's invite in a million refugees with the money we should be spending protecting our own country."

Americans noticed. Millions had served overseas and saw that NATO forces consisted of Americans, some Brits, and not many others. Americans serving in Germany or with our allies in Afghanistan got to see the state of NATO for themselves. American soldiers in Afghanistan often fought alongside NATO allies who were ill-equipped or straddled with rules of engagement that kept them out of the fight. Now this was not true of all our allies—many served with courage and honor even if their chains of command did not support them literally or figuratively. But firsthand experience taught many Americans that our allies were simply not carrying their weight.

Which is, again, just fine with our foreign policy establishment. In their eyes, we should put our blood and treasure on the line for Europe while they sit back and enjoy the show. Letting the rubes from flyover country carry the rucks of our allies lets our diplomatic mandarins avoid uncomfortable confrontations at cafes and parties. We couldn't have that, could we?

American voters look at this and balk, but they're too stupid to know that all this is actually good for them. Washington bureaucrats don't want these policies for their own gain. How dare voters, with their short-sighted balking!

Donald Trump likewise balks, and as a former New York real estate developer, he balks hard.

Trump came into office flying the "America First" banner. That outraged our mandarin rulers. For decades, the establishment had put the needs of other countries ahead of the needs of Americans. They never articulated a reason why ordinary Americans should underwrite their globalist policies. And while there were some pretty good reasons for America to shoulder the heaviest load seventy years ago, now it's not so clear.

But, like all establishments, our current establishment is conservative in the sense that it wishes to conserve the status quo. The establishment has no interest in upsetting the pre-Trump arrangement where America's interests are often of secondary importance to our own policy makers. But the American people wanted to scrap that arrangement, hence the appeal of "America First."

One amusing aspect of this upsetting of the apple cart was the freak-out over the term "America First." The establishment tried to link it to the pre-World War II isolationists, some of whom were Nazi sympathizers in the interwar years. But that didn't matter because Trump obviously didn't use it to connect with Nazis; he used "America First" because it expressed a solution to our disastrous foreign policy. And as it turns out, "America First" sounds pretty good to normal people. After all, should some other country be first? Which one? Burkina Faso? Liechtenstein?

The establishment had no real answer to that question. You see, the foreign policy elites in many ways feel more attuned to their eurotrash friends across the pond freeriding on the lives and livelihoods of American workers. Members of the foreign policy elite had spent so long soaking in the waters of the bipartisan establishment foreign policy consensus that they never felt compelled to defend that consensus. Accordingly, when Trump came along and asked a really good question—"Why again are we paying to defend a bunch of rich countries after the Soviet Union disappeared over a generation ago?"—the establishment was unable to provide a coherent, effective argument.

So instead of argument, they turned to lies.

"Trump hates our allies! He's destroying NATO! He's betraying our friends!"

Others started asking tough questions. Tucker Carlson asked a really good question when Montenegro was being considered for entry into NATO. To paraphrase, Carlson wondered, "Why is America promising to go to war to protect Montenegro? Why is Montenegro worth American lives?"

Again, there were howls but no substantive answers, despite the fact that it was a pointed and worthwhile question. And there are possible answers. But the foreign establishment, flabby and intellectually bankrupt from three generations of unchallenged assumptions and premises, could not come up with one. Instead, it presented more fussy outrage over someone's daring to ask the question.

Trump reconsidered existing relationships with nations outside of Europe that were more than capable of paying their own fare. He demanded that South Korea, an industrial powerhouse, start picking up its own tab, and the same with Saudi Arabia. The bizarre part about all this is that, until Trump, no one seemed to even ask them to pay for their own defense spending. Some allies offered token payments in exchange for massive defense spending, but no one pushed a harder bargain. It was easier to just pass the bill to the American people and enjoy Davos free from awkward confrontations.

The elites even started perverting the term "ally." In Syria, Turkey's dictator announced he was going into Northern Syria to set up a security zone to prevent attacks by Kurdish communist terrorists. Trump, not particularly interested in getting in the middle of that conflict, ordered the American forces inside the area out. The establishment melted down. Why, we were betraying our allies the Kurds!

As we've already mentioned, our only allies in this mess, the only combatants with whom America has a formal treaty ratified by our representatives in the Senate, are the Turks, allies via the NATO treaty. Suddenly, NATO became much, much less important to the establishment, so much so that some thought we should risk war with a NATO ally to defend a bunch of Kurdish communists.

We had no formal alliance with "the Kurds." Even an informal alliance with "the Kurds" would be very difficult because calling them one people assumes a homogeneity that does not exist. As it turns out, the Kurds are hardly a unified ethnic group. There are Iraqi Kurds, Syrian Kurds, Turkish Kurds, and a bunch of other Kurdish factions. Very few think of themselves as a unified people, and they fight among themselves as often as they fight other ethnic groups. Plus, does anyone think that an agreement to enforce the northern Syrian border against a NATO ally would ever get the stamp of approval from our senators?

But since *Trump* decided to leave the Middle East to solve its own problems, it must have been bad. Naturally, all the howls of betrayal and warnings of impending genocide were forgotten when the apocalypse never happened. The Turks and the Kurds skirmished for a bit then worked out their differences, as peoples have done in that region of the world for eons.

Trump's real crime was accurately assessing that America had no interest, at least none worth fighting and dying over, in refereeing a border dispute halfway across the globe, especially when the same people calling for Syrian engagement routinely tell us that defending our own border with Mexico is a crime against humanity. And while our betters fumed, most Americans were quite pleased that their sons and daughters were not involved in another Middle Eastern dustup.

Trump's shocking and overdue assertion of American rights and interests also applied to trade. Trump challenged the idea that in 2019 we needed to have the same economic relations with Red China the emerging superpower as we did with Red China the backward strategic counterweight to the Soviet Union. He tussled with the EU over trade as well and forced Mexico and Canada to renegotiate NAFTA. And Trump, noting how the world's biggest climate criminals, China and India, skated while America was going to be sent to figurative solitary confinement via the Paris Accords, pulled out of them.

We have been told that all this shows that Trump and his supporters hate our allies. That's a boldfaced lie. It's not hatred to demand the respect you deserve. It's not hatred to demand that allies do their part and that they take the lead in their own defense where they can. It's not hatred to insist on equal terms in trade. And it's better for the allies in the long run. Their freeloading is unsustainable, and better Trump offer them a chance to do the right thing than a disgusted America tell them to kiss its red, white, and blue ass somewhere down the road.

The elites spread this lie because their position is indefensible. Why should America do the heavy lifting in war and peace while our allies laugh at how Uncle Sam has allowed himself to be played for decades? "America First" is so appealing because it perfectly encapsulates exactly how the United States should proceed in its international relations. We should be guided by what's best for our people, not someone else's. Trump believes that. You believe that. Only our alleged betters do not. And because they can't make a compelling argument that we should continue subsidizing our friends, all they can do is lie.

CHAPTER 19

Trump Is Tearing America Apart...
and You Are Complicit!

Remember the wonderful days before Donald Trump came along and tore America apart? There was lots of hugging, laughter, and singing of "Kumbaya." Our politicians reveled in our differences, and our cultural institutions celebrated the unique contributions of all Americans, hip urban smart setters and churchgoing flyover folk alike. Barack Obama enlisted diverse elements of our society in a consensus campaign to fundamentally change America, which was weird because America was already a wonderful lovefest. And Democrats were eager to take the hands of their Republican leader friends, like Mitt Romney, and stride together toward a brighter tomorrow in an atmosphere of mutual respect and fellowship.

Not a thing.

That's not even close to how it was, except perhaps in the mind of the GOP soft boys who spent decades in denial about the deepening schism in our politics and society. They did not want it to be true, so they willfully ignored the indisputable evidence that our culture was coming apart. The country club gang wouldn't recognize that they were in a fistfight until their mouths were bereft of teeth. At that point, they would typically issue a heartfelt apology for allowing their faces to get in the way of their liberal abusers' fists.

Donald Trump was a product of the divisions in America, not the cause. And you, the normal citizens, did not tear your country asunder by supporting him. You were given two options: Donald Trump or the people who never hesitate to express their contempt for you. One promised to make you rich and respected, the other intended to disenfranchise you and dispossess you of the fruits of your labor. You chose wisely.

Trump was a human stop sign in the war on regular folks. He brought the endless onslaught to a halt. But the liars say that by standing up for your interests, by refusing to sheepishly acquiesce to the elites' aspirations, you are somehow disrupting the flow of progress. Your selfish refusal to bear the blame for every problem facing America is itself the problem.

That is, if you buy the lie.

You are not shredding the fabric of American society, nor is your avatar Donald Trump. That accusation is utter nonsense. To prove it, let's examine the premise that began this chapter.

According to the elite, there was a wonderful consensus about where we were going as a nation and how we would get there. Now ask yourself, do you remember that time? When, precisely, was this moment when America was reveling in its glorious unity? And if that were so, why did that Bad Orange Man appear and shatter it into a zillion pieces?

I'll wait. Think about it.

Nothing, huh?

Still coming up blank?

Of course you are, because the idea is ridiculous. That time never existed. There was no golden age of socio-political cohesion, at least not in recent memory. Back in the fifties, maybe, and early sixties, America had a moment of exceptional cohesion. There was a consensus on the big issues, even if that consensus would soon break down. Everyone agreed on the basics, regardless of what party they supported. Republicans were the party of the educated and the big and small business people. Democrats were the party of the working man and a few eggheads in the faculty lounges. But Democrats were also segregationists, and they operated the machinery of Jim Crow, while a significant number of minorities would reliably vote for the Party of Lincoln. Today, the Republicans are the party of small business and the working class, while Democrats have a lock on the credentialed class—these people used to be called "educated" before one could get a sheepskin for majoring in Marxist Mime—as well as minorities. Today, there's a big sign on the front door of the Democrat Party reading "No admittance to anyone who sweats when he works."

But in the fifties, everyone agreed on the basics. Religion in general was favored, and most people were religious and actively attended services. Family was considered a good thing, as were patriotism and self-sufficiency. Also, everyone knew which bathroom to use.

These are all generalizations of course. When you talk about whole nations, you naturally talk in generalities. You could find beatniks in Greenwich Village who shacked up because marriage was a drag, daddy-o, as well as rustic baby mamas out in the country who didn't show up to their Sunday church services. Not everyone went to church, and not everyone was a patriot. But, when you talk about whole nations, you have to speak in generalities.

Despite the fact that the overwhelming majority of folks shared a general moral orientation, adherence to those morals was not perfect. There was plenty of hypocrisy, but as a French aristocrat once wrote, hypocrisy is the homage vice pays to virtue. No adulterer would pretend to be a devoted spouse if he or she were not ashamed of committing adultery. The fact that a lot of people don't practice what they preach doesn't make their preaching wrong. That was certainly true of Americans in the fifties, who had their fair share of secret vices. But they agreed those vices were wrong, and they were generally ashamed of them.

American culture agreed on what constituted right and wrong sixty years ago. Today, we don't even agree on whether right and wrong exist.

The late sixties, the time people typically have in mind when they talk about "the sixties," is when the first real fissures in the post-war cultural and political consensus developed. Two events shook the established consensus to its foundations: the civil rights movement and the Vietnam War. The shameful official treatment of black Americans by Democrats ate away at faith in the goodness of American life. Moral people saw the horrific treatment of blacks and began to wonder if the principles of American life could be justified. Vietnam, meanwhile, channeled the increasingly prominent Frankfurt school's theories into the natural cowardice of far too many young people. You could be an edgy rebel by not taking the risks that those crew-cut squares did—a win-win. You were a hero, or at least you got to score with hippie chicks, by not being brave, while the brave came home to long-haired slobs who spit on them when they disembarked from the plane.

As soon as the draft died out, so did all the Vietnam protests. The protesters were more motivated by fear than a sense of injustice. After the draft, millions of Southeast Asians also died at the hands of communists, but whatever. It was all groovy.

The Sexual Revolution furthered the breakdown of the consensus, with people pledging their lives, fortunes, and sacred libidos to undoing the button-down repression of prior decades. This struggle achieved broken families, massive unwed motherhood, and the fetish for abortion. A whole socio-political constituency was born, dedicated to excusing, if not outright promoting, the attending social pathologies.

And again, it was the best kind of edgy, one where the more *avant-garde* you were, the more action you got. You really have to hand it to the left—it's astonishing how they always manage to turn doing things that are fun and/or self-serving into selfless heroics.

The fracturing of the cultural consensus coincided with massive political shifts. At the beginning of the decade, John F. Kennedy was only a few degrees different from his foe Richard Nixon. JFK was arguably more of a hawk than the Republican and one of his premier accomplishments was an economy-spurring tax cut. From our perspective sixty years later, there was little real difference between the two, or as little difference as there could be between a guy who sweat through a debate and a guy who nailed Marilyn Monroe.

But when JFK was assassinated by a scuzzy little Marxist creep (almost certainly without the aid of Ted Cruz's dad), Democrats and Republicans went their separate ways. Lyndon Johnson was significantly more liberal than JFK, and his Great Society vision redefined the role of government in American life. The program wasn't popular, and combined with the increasing discontent over Vietnam, LBJ decided not to run again in 1968.

Richard Nixon got elected by promising to end the war and to clamp down on the hippies. He took an active political stand in the ongoing culture war, which was spilling over into everyday life. Things were falling apart: there was a series of assassination, mass riots, and general chaos across the country. America was looking for a strong hand to right the ship, and Nixon promised to bring back order.

The division was happening.

In 1972, the left took over the Democrat Party over and sealed the former consensus's fate. They nominated George McGovern for president, a hardcore lefty who promised to wage the culture war and advance leftist policies. Nixon crushed him, but by then he was the object of active political hatred by the elite. He was not just an opponent; he was an enemy. The hip comics roasted him. The cool crowd showered him with contempt. Pauline Kael, the New York film critic, famously (and maybe apocryphally) wondered how Nixon got elected when no one she knew voted for him. Of course, outside New York City, pretty much everyone voted for Nixon. The election was one of the biggest landslides in American history. The urban swells were pulling away from the rest of America.

Watergate was a cute little scandal where Richard Nixon allegedly leveraged the power of the federal government to spy on a political opponent. You see, once upon a time, an administration's spying on a political rival was considered a bad thing. This may be lost on people today, in a time when our patriotic intelligence community "protects" Americans by spying on the elite's enemies. But in the dark times of the 1970s, it was considered a grave offence for which a president could be impeached and tossed out of office. Now, the only thing that can get you impeached is investigating a corrupt former vice-president and his crack-huffing progeny.

They drove Nixon out of office and turned their hate onto the affable Jerry Ford. Nixon had gotten America out of LBJ's Vietnam mess. With us gone, the communists were—and this may shock you—shitting all over the Paris Peace Treaty they had signed and invading our allies in South Vietnam. The Democrats, dominated by a new generation of leftists, had control of Congress, and when Ford moved to do what we had promised to do and support Saigon in the wake of red treachery, they stopped him. South Vietnam fell, and the American left smiled. This would have been incomprehensible a generation before, illustrating just how deep the rift in the Great American Socio-Politico Consensus had become.

The 1976 election of Jimmy Carter was an attempt to return to normalcy. Though it was doomed to fail, voting in a Democrat Georgia peanut farmer who taught Sunday school was the last real gasp of the prior consensus. Actually, it was more of a death rattle. Jimmy Carter may have been an Annapolis grad who served on nuclear subs, but he governed like McGovern with exponentially more sanctimony. Under Carter's watch, the Soviets took ground all over the world. America's military accelerated its post-'Nam decline, and the punk-ass mullahs in Iran (who that insufferable twit felt morally obligated to allow to take over from our loyal ally the Shah) grabbed a bunch of American hostages and paraded them around on camera.

In other words, he was exactly the kind of sap you would expect from the modern Democrat Party.

Then came the Reagan Revolution. Contrary to the popular portrayal by superficial people, Ronald Reagan did not want to return America to the fifties. He understood the socio-political consensus of the fifties and did not seek to reimpose it. Remember, Reagan was with Barry Goldwater in 1964, famously speaking at the GOP convention to support the controversial Republican nominee. Goldwater was no fan of the status quo. Reagan was conservative of course, but he didn't just want to preserve the institutions as they existed. He was, rather, a radical who sought major changes to America's sociopolitical arrangements.

Reagan came to heighten the contradictions of the current regime, not to unify. (But in 1984 he would unify the entire Electoral College with the exception of Minnesota and those government flunkies in the District of Columbia.) The first item on Reagan's agenda was returning to a sound foreign policy. In the fifties, American foreign policy revolved around containing the Soviet Union. That paradigm broke down in the seventies, when Carter let the Bolsheviks run rampant and unopposed around the globe, even allowing the Russkies to invade Afghanistan.

Reagan had no interest in containment, he wanted rollback. He fired the first shot at the motley Caribbean Marxists and their Cuban puppet-masters on Grenada in October 1983. Then he set his sights on Moscow. Reagan's strategy to take down Moscow was nothing short of brilliant. With a military in disarray following years of budget cuts, Reagan saw an opportunity to apply massive pressure to the Soviet system. Reagan was not going to use the American military to beat the heirs of Lenin into a pulp; he was going to use the *rebuilding* of the American military to do it. By his calculus, the Soviets could not keep up with the United States when it put its mind and money to spending big on boosting our military forces. And it worked. When the reds tried to keep up with our growing armaments, they sent their entire economy haywire.

All this time, the Democrats were falling for KGB sucker ploys like the "nuclear freeze." Yes, this was before the Russians suddenly became bad in the mid-2010s when bad Russians became useful Russians. The smart set failed to see the strategic genius in Reagan's plan because they were too busy gulping down Soviet propaganda.

On the domestic front, Reagan was less of a cultural warrior than he is remembered as. While he took a stand against abortion but did not really do much about it. (He welcomed evangelical Christians into the Republican fold. Do not forget that Jimmy Carter was an evangelical, and until Reagan reached out, their vote was not tied to the Republican party.) But he's remembered as a fire breathing culture warrior because the flak he got from the cultural elites made their disdain for Nixon seem gentle by comparison. The nicer folks called him a "cowboy," which his supporters took as a compliment, but others called him "Hitler," stupid, and a warmonger. (*Der Fuhrer* is a common refrain from the left when it comes to Republican presidents.) Of course, he was such a stupid warmonger that he crushed the only other superpower without firing a shot, but whatever.

Despite the fact that Reagan's successor, George H. W. Bush, was a genteel moderate who had no intention of waging a culture war, the left treated him as a monster and vilified him shamelessly. Remember *Doonesbury*? Some of us do, vaguely, and Bush-bashing was an obsession in popular culture. Most actual conservatives would have been delighted if some of the grief heaped upon the preppy president for being a rightwing nut had a kernel of truth to it. The divide was such that simply not being part of the vanguard of the flower generation was enough to get you hated. You didn't even have to be a radical like Reagan.

Interestingly, the guy who beat Poppy succeeded as president when he crossed over the divide and took conservative positions. This was part of his famed triangulation strategy, aided by Dick Morris who, unlike Bill Clinton's harpy of a wife, knew and understood regular people. Clinton embraced welfare reform and championed the fight against crime, which was out of control in the early nineties. Clinton's law and order positions were a break from the traditional liberal view that criminals are oppressed victims of the system. By breaking from leftist orthodoxy, Clinton was able to bridge the divide, and he achieved great success. He even managed to skate on his Oval Office orifice antics. Ironically enough, Bill was always the quintessential sixties product.

When Bush 43 took the Oval Office, it was open season for hunting conservatives again, with barely a decent pause after 9/11. It's difficult to explain the full scope of the hatred Bush drew. It was constant, unrestrained, and almost unbelievable. Social media would not really take off until he left office, and the tornado of hate that would have barreled towards Bush from Twitter would be unimaginable if we had not already seen what Donald Trump deals with on a daily basis. In any case, W did not fight back, in part because of an obsolete vision of decorum, as we discussed above. Fighting the culture war required admitting there were cultural battle lines, and he did not want to do that. Instead, he preferred to dwell in his shrinking bubble of rectitude while the actions of the left wrecked the lives of his erstwhile supporters.

Barack Obama was sold as a great unifier. He spoke about unity and one American people and all that nice, goo goo stuff. But when he got into office, he promised fundamental change to our country, and told Republicans to go pound sand.

Obama was all about the identity politics that had sprouted up over the years. Rather than bringing Americans together, he wanted to jam his vision of America down the unwilling throats of his opponents. He had no respect for them either. They were stupid, bigoted, and lived out in the boonies. In 2008, at a fundraiser in (of course) San Francisco, he told his supporters: "They get bitter, they cling to guns or religion or antipathy to people who aren't like them or anti-immigrant sentiment or anti-trade sentiment as a way to explain their frustrations."

Nothing says "Let's come together" better than calling the people who don't support you stupid bigots. That's a war cry, not a rally cry.

At the same time, his opponent John McCain seemed utterly oblivious to what everyone else was seeing. The culture war was the only war McCain didn't want to fight. He felt it unseemly, and he really did not care about cultural issues. But the great divisions in the American sociopolitical milieu were real and devastating. Families were falling apart, jobs were shipping out to the Far East and Mexico, religion was under attack, and there was the realization among Americans who had (as Bill Clinton brilliantly put it) "Worked hard and played by the rules," that they were no longer being served by those in power. The Wall Street meltdown of 2008 reaffirmed that. The potentates of Big Finance who set fire to the whole shaky edifice were never charged with arson and, instead, presented the bill for the damage to the American people. Millions of Americans, meanwhile, lost everything they owned.

But McCain, whose contempt for the voters who (often reluctantly) supported him became manifest over his remaining years, did not give a damn. They begged for help with the border. He promised help and never delivered. They begged him to get rid of Obamacare. He promised help, and lied about that too, casting the vote that stopped its repeal in a fit of pique to tweak Donald Trump.

John McCain, in shafting the conservative voters who trusted him, was less a maverick than an archetype of the GOP establishment.

Oh, and Mitt Romney. "Romney" must mean "Gumby" in some language or another. This spineless carpetbagger, both geographically and ideologically, represented the opposite style of GOP failure. Where McCain refused to do what the voters wanted, Romney was as eager to please as a slobbering golden retriever puppy, albeit not one lashed to the roof of the family car.

When you truly believe in nothing, people notice. The guy who pioneered Massachusetts's Obamacare prequel was suddenly Obamacare's biggest foe. He was going to lock down that border, though nothing in his history showed that he cared about America's being overrun with uninvited foreigners any more than any other corporate-curious Republican. To finally win it in 2012, Mitt was going to be whatever the base wanted. Tell him a policy had tested well in focus groups and he was 100 percent in. Mitt was now "severely conservative," you know.

But he could not be the one thing that the base really wanted. He could never be a fighter.

The GOP gave the base a guy who would not fight back in George W. Bush, then a candidate who would fight, but only *against* the base in John McCain. Then the powers that be gave us this human sponge who couldn't even best Candy Crowley. The stage was set for Donald Trump.

Donald Trump understands that America is a divided country and behaves accordingly. A real estate developer deals with reality. A building is structurally sound, or it is not. It is ready for occupancy, or it is not. The buyer will pay the asking price, or he will not. The difference between Trump and his predecessors is that Trump feels no moral obligation to deny reality. Rather, like a paratrooper, he fights on the ground he was dropped on. This was a divided country when he got here. He simply accepts that, like Obama accepted it in practice (even if he sometimes made faux gestures toward consensus), and proceeds accordingly.

Likewise, Trump's supporters understand that the socio-political divisions define the cultural battlefield. Where the prior generation of GOP leaders covered their ears, squeezed their eyelids shut, shouted "La la la la la, I can't hear you," and tried to ignore the painful reality, Trump's base accepts it.

We have opponents in this struggle. That's how divisions work. And they want to win. They define "winning" as sending conservatives into permanent irrelevance. That means we don't just have to fight, we have to win, or else we'll be crushed.

The elite makes no bones about its goals. Its attacks on free speech, the free exercise of religion, on election security, and the right to keep and bear arms constitute existential threats to our ability to live as citizens rather than modern serfs. They want to relegate us to obscurity and despoil us of our heritage. If we don't stand up and fight, they'll have their way.

Trump did not create the divisions that beset us. The schism came along even before he started getting splashed across the front pages of the *New York Post*. But Trump also didn't pretend that the very real divisions in the American body politic don't exist. He recognized and accepted them, which took away the elite's advantage. That's why they got upset and blamed him for stoking animosity. It's a lot easier to beat your enemy when he won't even admit he's in a war. Trump knows he's in a fight, and acts like it. They will never forgive him for that.

CHAPTER 20

Trump Corrupts Christians...
and You Are All Bad Christians!

Donald Trump, so the slander goes, is an insidious poison who corrupts and destroys the souls of those benighted Christians who support him. He's not just evil; his evil is so all-encompassing and potent that supporting him makes you evil too. Especially when you refuse to vote for the party that thinks the Founders tucked the right to off your kid inside (or even outside) the womb into our Constitution via penumbras and emanations that only liberal judges can see.

For starters, you must understand that the left hates Christianity. Christianity is a threat to their leftist project. Religion is something the left cannot control, and, worse, it asserts the dominance of a higher authority than leftist dogma, which is itself heresy in their beady little leftist eyes. Christianity is a bulwark against tyranny—not the unread blog kind of *Bulwark*, but the kind of bulwark that conserves conservative things instead of grifting donors into subsidizing the unreadable rantings of Never Trump hacks.

This makes Christianity (and Orthodox Judaism) a target. But that's nothing new. Leftists have long seen religion as competition. In the Soviet Union, Cuba, and China, leftists tried to beat religion out of the people because they fear religion. They have good reason to look at religion and tremble. Just ask the Polish communists who were undone in no small part because of the Catholic Church's hold on the Polish people.

Religion isn't a threat to communists in Second World countries alone, it's a threat to liberals in the United States too. Religion is a competing power center to the liberal establishment; therefore, it must be undermined, and because Donald Trump has proven himself an indefatigable defender of religious people's rights, that connection must be broken. If they can break Trump's appeal to the religious right, they can break Trump. And if they break Trump, they can break the religious right once and for all.

It's not working, in large part because religious people are nowhere near as dumb as their cultural opponents think. Donald Trump is the best political gift to Christians and people of faith in decades. The lies to the contrary are expressly designed to shatter the defenses that the faithful have been holding against the secular left. If they can break the religious away from center right conservatism, the liberals will be much closer to their final victory. And their final victory means an America fundamentally transformed into something nightmarish. Think 1984, except with an obsessive focus on gender identity.

It's no secret that religion has become a key fault line in the schism between our two political parties. The Republicans are, without a doubt, increasingly finding religious citizens, including many Orthodox Jews, swelling its ranks. And the Democrat Party, with the notable exceptions of black churchgoers, is becoming more and more secular. This has been happening for decades, but the trend has only accelerated in the past decade. If you were to move to a town in Tennessee, in less than five minutes your new neighbors would ask you which of the town's dozen churches you would be joining. If you were to move to Santa Monica, the locals would ask you about your pronouns.

This fight has been brewing for some time. Back in 1980, the mainstream media obsessed over the "Moral Majority," Jerry Falwell's explicitly Christian group that scandalized the elite by injecting religion into

American political life. How dare these backwoods rubes (Christians who actually believe in Jesus baffle the New York/Washington axis of mediocrity to this day) flaunt Jesus for votes!

Religion has always played a big part in American politics. But in the years leading up to the Reagan Revolution, it was the liberals who won over small churches and America's Christians. The progressive era had a significant religious undercurrent. Traces of that older liberal type still shape the liberal self-consciousness, a sort of mainline church center-leftism that serenely imagines itself as a salvific force bringing redemption to the fallen. The conservatives, of course, are the fallen.

The folks we're talking about here are the marshmallow Christians whose churches avoid tough scripture, moral judgments, and whose pews are as empty as their declining parishioners' heads. They have long carried their social justice Christian heresy into politics, using gospel teachings to justify socialism. Unlike Falwell, they preferred social justice to social issues. With them, it's money and Marxism over morality. They were very concerned about economic redistribution and neutering America's ability to assert its interests internationally, but not too worried about stemming the moral rot that metastasized in the 1960s.

Now while these lily-white church ladies were condescending and tiresome, not all of their church activism was bad. The civil rights movement was a Christian movement. Dr. Martin Luther King was literally a reverend, and churches a century before had been the vanguard of the abolitionist movement. Later on, they helped organize and lead the fight to defeat the Democrats' Jim Crow regime in the South. This was an unalloyed good. What was an unalloyed bad, according to the left, was when churches started opposing things liberals support.

Abortion was the big flashpoint, though there were plenty of other signs of decay. Pornography and the decline of the family from divorce both contributed to the sense that society was falling apart. But abortion represented the worst of the sexual revolution combined with a grim contempt for human life. For years, the various states got their federalism on and addressed the question of pre-natal termination in different ways.

Some states had no truck with Molochism. Other states declared open season on fetuses.

The process was ugly and disorganized and exactly how daunting and divisive issues are supposed to be resolved within the American system. The abortion issue was getting worked out politically, via elections and legislation passed by those elected representatives. But the United States Supreme Court, in its finite wisdom, decided that these political machinations were unnecessary. It knew better and chose to cut to the chase, with the chase of course being the policy preference held by the liberal majority.

By a 7–2 vote, the Court ruled that everyone needed to shut up and do what the liberals wanted. This was the gist of *Roe v. Wade*. The Court decided that the Fourteenth Amendment contained an obvious and indisputable right to kill your baby, within specific time frames that were also somehow derived from the versatile Fourteenth Amendment.

Read the Fourteenth Amendment. See if you can locate the anti-fetus text purportedly lurking within. You might notice that something is missing. That would be the word "abortion," or any similar term. The word and the concept are simply not there. But SCOTUS found it there, or so the opinion said. But where? Sections 2 through 5 are directed at various post-Civil War issues. Perhaps there is something in Section 1?

Let's see. There's a sentence about "persons born or naturalized in the United States" being citizens. That's not it. There's one about "the privileges or immunities of citizens." That seems unlikely (and the Court, except for the great Clarence Thomas, has long studiously ignored the "privileges or immunities" clause). There's the Due Process clause that does not allow "any State [to] deprive any person of life, liberty" without "due process of law." No, nothing about abortion there. The same with "equal protection of the laws." You can see how people who suddenly found their right to have some input into the details of legalized kid-culling might have been a bit confused and put out when they were solemnly informed that this disenfranchisement was absolutely, totally right there inside the Fourteenth Amendment.

So how did the Court get around the problem of abortion's not actually being in the Constitution? Well, apparently it was there all along, you literal-minded saps. It was right there, lurking within the "penumbras" and "emanations" of the Constitution. The concepts of "penumbras" and "emanations" came from a prior case that the Roe Court relied heavily upon, *Griswold v. Connecticut* (1965). Griswold had to do with the right to buy birth control. The Court found a general right of privacy that would let you buy contraceptives. Then they extrapolated that out to letting you kill your baby, albeit within a rigid, trimester-based framework that likewise appears nowhere in the Fourteenth Amendment. Chalk that detailed schedule up to the "penumbras" and "emanations" too—boy, what can't those "penumbras" and "emanations" do?

Apparently, they can't allow a significant number of Americans a say in a divisive cultural argument. And that's the problem. Federalism presumes legal differences between states, based upon the differences between the states and the attitudes of the voters within them. Yet here, the Court—representing an elite consensus—simply snatched the argument away, declared it settled on the dodgiest of grounds, and thereby told traditional voters to go pound sand.

Except the voters did not pound sand. They chose instead to pound their political enemies by organizing. It seems unlikely that Ronald Reagan would have beaten Jimmy Carter, himself an avowed evangelical, without the Moral Majority and its sympathizers.

Interestingly, Ronald Reagan himself was Christian but hardly a stereotypical evangelical. He talked about God in general, even ecumenical, terms. There was neither fire nor brimstone. His generic Christianity was one of hope with little of the social issues fixation that the Republicans would be accused of for the next several decades.

But Reagan was also a sinner. Of course, all Christians believe they are sinners, though the left does not seem to understand that concept. The left seems to believe that Jesus is both a malicious avenger who consigns to Hell those who refuse to bow down to the aspiring theocrats between the coasts, and a neo-Marxist hippie demanding redistribution of the means of production and the beating of swords into plowshares.

Reagan was divorced. That was still a bit radical in 1980, not hugely, but enough to cause a stir. Nor was he a compulsive churchgoer. He believed in a generic, Midwestern kind of way, but he didn't make a big deal of it. Jimmy Carter, on the other hand, did. He taught Bible school and attended church every week, and he made sure everyone knew it. On the home front, he never divorced his wife, and his daughter, Amy, seemed normal. He publicly agonized over his own self-identified moral failings. In a mortifying 1976 *Playboy* interview, he admitted, "I've looked on a lot of women with lust. I've committed adultery in my heart many times."

It's interesting that Carter embodied the fundamentalist stereotype, while the fundamentalists largely voted for the guy with a second wife and a freakshow family. The reason was obvious: Jimmy Carter was not going to stand firm at the cultural Thermopylae and hold the line against the invasion of sixties immorality and petty anti-religious provocations. In the early sixties, Americans woke up one morning to find that the Supreme Court had discovered that the prayers they said in school as kids were verboten. Afterwards came an endless series—which continues to this day—of tiresome lawsuits about Bible quotes, nativity scenes, and the placing of "In God We Trust" on currency. The peanut farmer's party was not going to push back, and if Reagan was not going to turn the tide back to old school traditional values, at least he would not allow it to proceed apace.

Fast forward four decades to Donald Trump today.

There's no arguing that Trump is, to put it mildly, not exactly the stereotypical practicing Christian. His personal life is hardly textbook Baptist. He is on wife number three, and his tabloid lifestyle is about as alien to the evangelicals who support him as is humanly possible to conceive of. He likes the ladies, including at least one porn star and a Playboy Playmate. The *Access Hollywood* tape was the cherry on top of three decades of his breaking nearly every Christian rule (and a few vows) imaginable governing the relations between men and women.

But he was no hypocrite. Like Reagan, he offered no apologies for how he lived his life pre-White House. Church is not and still does not seem to play a huge part in his life. He doesn't relax by turning off Fox News, retiring the tweeting machine, and curling up with the Good Book for some in-depth study of Galatians.

But he makes a point to mention God and his providence without irony or a wink. It's impossible for mortals to know what is in anyone's heart, but it is entirely possible that Trump holds the same uncomplicated faith as millions of Americans. Sure, he is not exactly Bible-fluent. Famously, he referred to "Two Corinthians" instead of "Second Corinthians" during a January 2016 campaign stop at Jerry Falwell's Liberty University. His rivals for the nomination tried to make something of this, but the reason that it failed, and that Christians went with Trump and stick with him, was right there in that very same speech. Trump said, "We're going to protect Christianity. I can say that. I don't have to be politically correct."

Finally, an ally. Not a George W. Bush, whose principled paralysis led to eight years of unanswered assaults. Not a John McCain, who had no use for anyone who believed in anything but the glory of John McCain. And not Mitt Romney, himself the victim of shameful religious bigotry, but who could never quite bring himself to scandalize his social classmates by offering a full-throated defense of the right of every American to worship their God freely.

The calculus was simple. Better the sinner who has your back than the sinner who wants to plant a pickaxe in it.

Hillary Clinton made much more of her churchiness in 2016 than Trump. She wanted to appeal to the archetypal black churchwomen, the one part of the Democrat constellation of constituencies that still has not received formal notice that liberals aren't doing the religion thing anymore. She also wanted to draw off some Trump support among the religious with some fake "Hey, I'm one of you" pablum for the rubes.

The rubes, though, were wise to the scam.

The Pious Hillary act was a stretch from the outset. She had enabled her creeper husband's tawdry antics during the White House years, and her frankly bizarre marriage thereafter did not put her in a position to posture as the paragon-of-purity alternative to the guy whose sins had been splashed across the covers of America's papers for the previous third of a century. One way or another, the religious folks were getting damaged goods. The question was, which set of damaged goods would turn around and damage them less?

Here's the thing, and it's a hard and harsh thing, but a thing nonetheless. The liberal elite that owns and controls the Democrat Party despises believing Christians. It only puts up with black church-women—who were the primary reason the California anti-gay marriage referendum passed—because they show up to vote blue reliably every two years. But the rest of those knuckle-dragging Jesus freaks? The hell with them.

The mask really came off during the notorious "Democrats boo God" incident at the 2012 Democrat National Convention. There was plenty of unconvincing ex post facto explaining about how the Democrats really didn't boo God, but it did not undo the damage. These were the movers and shakers of America's party of the left, and those movers and shakers were in no mood to try to fake not having utter contempt for America's believers.

But that was only one incident of many. There were more court decisions, including the gay marriage decision in *Obergefell v. Hodges* in 2015. Once again, the political process was working out the issue when the Court stepped in and snatched it away. Some states were down with it, others not so much. People's minds were changing and evolving, but apparently not fast enough for the Supreme Court. By 5–4, the nation's highest court decided to take yet another divisive social issue out of the hands of the people and place it off limits to further debate on the basis of…well, nothing actually in the Constitution. As with abortion, there is no mention of gay marriage in the Fourteenth Amendment, and those who crafted the amendment would be a bit taken aback to find out that they had intended that dudes could get hitched when they drafted the text.

Once again excluded from decision-making about their own society by the robed druids' mysterious divinations of the meaning of the Constitution, the traditional religious contingent found itself under fire for not Obergefell-ing enough. The push for gay marriage was not merely to ensure that those two nice young confirmed bachelors living together in the cute cottage down the street could get married, as promised. It was to compel obedience to the full LGBTQetc agenda, or else.

Chick-fil-A, which would later disgrace itself with its shameful cowardice, became a rallying point for traditional Americans. It was not so much that Chick-fil-A hated anyone but that the purveyor of grossly overrated poultry sandwiches refused to knuckle under (for a time) to activist demands for obedience. Those demands became overwhelming, and combined with the power of the social media cancel culture, traditional Americans found themselves rapidly losing the space to think and live as they saw fit. It was not tolerance the activists sought but utter and complete submission.

You could see the change in regard to the Religious Freedom Restoration Act (RFRA), passed in 1992 at the behest of Chuck Schumer, of all people. Truth be told, the law was reasonable. At its core, it promised that the government will do everything it can to accommodate individuals' religious beliefs except where there's a compelling reason not to. And even then, when the feds absolutely must burden religious folk, they have to do it in the "least restrictive" way possible.

Seems about right in a pluralistic nation with a myriad of differing faiths. And, of course, now the Democrats have done a 180 and absolutely hate the idea of RFRA. What happened? Well, you darn Christians started using it.

See, the law was originally passed to help fringies and marginalized religious folks. It was a response to situations where one of Elizabeth Warren's distant cousins wanted to drop some peyote, or some dude in the penitentiary wanted to worship rocks and twigs. But liberal support for the law went out the window once regular Christians started pointing to it in order to avoid being complicit in feticide or to get out of some local requirement that they high-five gay couples.

Hey, wait a minute! The idea behind RFRA was to let strange cultists freak out the Christian squares, not to protect those very same squares from liberal social progress! The free exercise of religion is fine, until the wrong people start asserting their right to freely exercise it.

Remember how Barack Obama—whose churchgoing largely consisted of a few years of sitting in a Chicago church listening to a rabidly racist lunatic spew lefty hate—mourned the fact that so many Americans were bitterly clinging to their religion (and, not unrelatedly, their guns)? That sums up the most benevolent interpretation by our elite of our citizens' religious inclinations. At the other end of the spectrum, the elites consider religion downright evil.

So, it isn't surprising that the Obama administration was not interested in tolerating dissenting religious beliefs and demanded full and unreserved compliance with the agenda of the left. For years, these bigoted bureaucrats litigated and fought over attempts to force compliance, often in the most petty and malicious ways. They made a point of demanding that nuns provide birth control because Catholics are not down with birth control. It was a pure power move. What better way to assert your power than to force your opponents to bend to your will and repudiate their most sacred beliefs? After all, it's not like there are a lot of nuns out there getting preggers because their order's HMO refuses to spring for the Pill.

The faithful noticed the war on the religious by the cultural left, and they believed their lying eyes no matter how much the media tried to tell them they were hallucinating.

The left waged war against any institution that supported traditional values. As we mentioned above, they launched attacks on Chick-fil-A and lobbed bombs at Hobby Lobby. They repeatedly took peripheral wedding service providers to court for declining to participate in gay wedding ceremonies. Across the country, they tried to tear down memorial crosses, references to the Ten Commandments, and even the Pledge of Allegiance.

And don't forget popular culture. If Hollywood needs a villain, and there's no businessman or soldier available to trash, it goes with a kooky fundamentalist. Stephen King, when he's not howling like a nut on Twitter about Trump's perfidy, has made a career out of that hoary, hack cliché. To our cultural elite, half of America is just aching to impose theocratic government and the Christian equivalent of sharia law.

Or they ignore the religious and marginalize faith. Name some characters in modern, mainstream media, who go to church or the synagogue. Come on, just one. It's hard, isn't it? The left likes to talk about how the culture makes some groups "invisible." No one is more invisible in American pop culture than believers.

One exception is *The Simpsons*, but even that show has morphed. In the early, not awful seasons, Homer and the crew poked fun at religion, but the writing was not angry or bitter. It was somewhat sympathetic, and the comedy did not come from a place of contempt. But in later seasons, the religious references became downright hostile. The humor was no longer based upon the foibles associated with churchgoing; it was attacks on religion itself, the sort of atheist snark that millennials who can't tell Jesus from Santa Claus would dig.

Oh, and then there is the new atheism. Those militant God-deniers are worse than CrossFitters. They just can't shut up about it. If you venture onto social media and mention the Almighty, good luck. You will be swarmed with internet heathens instructing you in the essential meaninglessness of existence. And should you offer your prayers over some tragedy, you better seek some protection for yourself because that's chum in the water to the piranhas of godlessness.

It's all part of the cultural war. The enemy's objective is clear: We seek to destroy your attachment to your religion because that is one of the few remaining obstacles to our unchallenged political, social, and cultural control.

But, unlike their popular culture image, religious people are neither stupid nor blind. In 2016, they understood their situation. They understood that they had a choice. They could choose a flawed human being who would protect them, or a flawed human being who actively despised them and would unleash every weapon in her governmental and cultural arsenal to bend them to her will.

In retrospect, it seems like a pretty easy choice. You can pick the guy who will help you or the furious succubus who wants to destroy you. Gee, let me think that one over.

But what about the lie that observant Christians and Jews who have seen Trump bring America closer to Israel than any other president ever somehow pollute themselves by associating with the likes of the president?

Supporting President Trump isn't a question of preference for America's religious folk, it's a matter of survival. The anti-religious fervor of the left is a critical threat to the faithful. The left seeks to eliminate the competition faith poses to their monopoly on American beliefs. Faith is competition to the all-encompassing, all-consuming dogma of the left. The left doesn't just want to marginalize religious voters, they want to destroy their ability to seek refuge in their collective strength and defend themselves from within the fortress of their faith.

That's the origin of the lies about Trump's corrupting the faithful and the faithful's being complicit in their own corruption.

Nothing in the Bible requires the faithful's submission to earthly tyranny. Jesus said to love one's enemies, but that doesn't mean you have to vote against the guy who will keep those enemies from pummeling you into submission. Somewhere along the line, someone decided to push the idea that Jesus preached the imperative of losing. American Christians largely reject that particular heresy.

There is nothing un-Christian about refusing to provide political support to someone whose platform is the total marginalization and neutralization of Christianity just because the white knight has some baggage. And that's especially true when the black knight has her own baggage.

Believers support the guy who interposes himself between the forces of malicious secularism and the faithful. The fact that his past is a bit checkered means neither that his supporters approve of it nor that his opponents represent something different. In fact, the cultural elite would be perfectly accepting of Trump's pre-presidential antics if he were useful to them. Remember Katie Hill? She popped up a few lies back. She was the congressweirdo who introduced the world, kicking and screaming, to the term "throuple." Her bizarre lifestyle included posting pics on websites that catered to the cuckold curious. When it all came to light, she pulled an Al Franken and quit Congress. Soon after, she reinvented herself as a media martyr, a terribly wronged victim of a patriarchy that couldn't handle her unique sexuality.

Katie Hill, A-okay. Donald Trump, bad. What's the difference, besides Trump's militant cisgender heterosexuality? Katie Hill is a Democrat.

People see hypocrisy. They see that the cultural elite doesn't really care a whit about Trump's bedpost notchery. After all, these were the same people who spent decades taking Harvey Weinstein's dough and partying with Jeffrey Epstein on Pedo Island. It's not exactly remarkable that Christians are unwilling to commit cultural suicide at the behest of an establishment that demonstrably rejects the very principles that it claims compels Christians to commit *hara-kiri*.

In other words, is anyone shocked that believers aren't going to abandon the one person who has shown an unwavering commitment to protecting them, just because folks who don't believe a bit of Christian dogma insist that Christian dogma mandates it?

Donald Trump has, without meaningful dispute, been the greatest ally of the faithful to occupy the White House in decades. Is he perfect? No. But then again, the imperfection of man is the whole point of Christianity. And Christians know it.

CHAPTER 21

Trump Is the New Normal...
We Hope

L ike all good lies, this final lie has a kernel of truth to it. Donald Trump fundamentally transformed American politics. The liars want you to believe that Trump has destroyed the constitutional order our Founding Fathers bequeathed to us. Patriots, meanwhile, hope that Trump destroys the sclerotic institutions that stand between us and a functioning republic.

After all, Trump could be an aberration, and everything could return to regularly scheduled programming. Check back in a decade to see if America has reverted to the nightmare that was "normal" under George W. Bush and Barack Obama.

For the elite, a return to "normal" means going back to politics as usual. The elite wants to return to the decline and fall of the United States, eagerly embraced by the liberal faction of the establishment, while soberly managed by establishment Republicans. Before Trump, decline was on the menu, regardless of whether the chef was a Democrat or Republican. We don't want to go back to normal; we want to strive for greatness. That's why patriots support Donald Trump and thank him for disrupting the Washington status quo.

Is Trump a uniquely damaging figure in American politics? Those of us who support Trump certainly hope so. We hope he damages the special interests, party bosses, and media elites who have run this country into the ground. So while the liars consider Trump's ability to do damage a very, very bad trait, we think it's very, very good. The establishment needed to be destroyed for the sake of our collective health. When the liars claim that Trump has caused untold damage by disrupting the status quo, that's not all bad.

Plus, if anyone has destroyed norms, it's been the rabid establishment, not President Trump. In their vendetta against Trump, the establishment has shattered more unwritten rules than we knew existed. And it did so with such ease that we should doubt the level of devotion to those jettisoned norms that existed in the first place.

For one, the left enlisted the federal bureaucracy in a shameful and brazen attempt to frame Trump and his inner circle as traitors. Say goodbye to the neutral corps of Washington bureaucrats and hello to the steadfast legions of #Resistance heroes. Conservatives have long known that bureaucrats act as an organ of the Democrat party, but the extent to which career officials were willing to go to take on Trump offered irrefutable proof of their party allegiance.

Dozens of supposedly disinterested public servants took leading roles in the left's push to remove Trump. Lo and behold, the apparatchiks that Republicans had long complained about were more interested in their own careers under Hillary Clinton or a future Democrat regime than in providing their expertise to this administration. When a Democrat regime looked less and less likely, those deep state functionaries conspired, leaked, and lied in pursuit of the president's scalp—even after Trump took up residence at 1600 Pennsylvania Avenue.

The bureaucracy's intransigence caused a potential constitutional crisis when the Democrats allied with the Deep Staters to impeach Trump. Against bipartisan opposition, House Democrats rammed through stunningly vague articles of impeachment after conducting a truncated impeachment proceeding that made a mockery of due process.

And all the while, the hacks of the mainstream media revealed their own partiality by covering for Democrats and constantly putting their hands on the scale.

Thanks to their destructive reaction to Trump, the whole country now sees that the left has no compunction about abusing the apparatus of the bureaucracy and Congress to achieve its political goals. Media bias used to be a complaint reserved for those of us who followed politics most closely. Now, everyone can see that the press has embraced naked partisanship. And the left seems totally cool with it. Trump just tore off the cover and revealed the Dorian Gray-like decay of the liberal establishment's supposed principles.

The conservative establishment was, of course, less successful in exploiting the Trump insurgency. In fact, the rise of Trump destroyed the Republican establishment. Trump reconfigured the right, bringing long ignored and excluded parts of the base to the fore. He invited people pushing for immigration enforcement and reform back into the fold. He courted those who wanted a trade policy that favors people who work with their hands over people who work with their Bloomberg terminals. He promised to end the forever wars, appealing to people disillusioned by mismanaged foreign entanglements. And unlike the professional culture warriors, Trump reached out to the millions of Americans sick of constant retreat in the face of the culture war *blitzkrieg*.

Conservative institutions that found themselves on the wrong side of the future lost influence or failed outright, like the *Weekly Standard*. Those institutional gatekeepers of the zombie establishment—with apologies to that glorified donor cruise brochure's competition—attempted to stand athwart history shouting, "Orange Man Bad!"

They sank. Ahoy, losers.

The Trump normal reversed the decline presided over by establishment elites. Under Trump, America is resurgent. The economy is booming, and millions of Americans are getting the opportunity to work well-paying jobs again. Federally tolerated (or even sponsored) social dislocation is no longer the law of the land, and the great American middle is being restored rather than replaced—the Chinese coronavirus tangent being a bump in the road that we hope will disappear in our collective rearview mirror soon. And finally, American foreign policy is no longer the laughingstock of the world. When we engage, we mean business, but we don't have time for endless suicide missions.

The Trump era is no time for conservative sissies. The center left has freed itself of any constraints and is willing to punch anyone on the right well below the belt. Trump was the crisis liberalism needed as an excuse to finally throw off the old rules and norms that circumscribed its actions. Liberals have taken the gloves off, and they're trying to knock out conservatives. Too bad Trump is Mike Tyson, and they are Woody Allen.

So when the liberal establishment complains that Trump is the new normal, they may take some joy in that. The left is united in the struggle against Trump. They are on war footing, and there is no reason to believe that they would ever demobilize voluntarily. That is, of course, barring a massive electoral repudiation that leads to a likely temporary rethinking of the Democrats' leftward swerve.

If the Trump normal is open warfare between the American left and the American right, then it follows that it will only remain the new normal so long as the right has a warrior chief to lead the fight. And that is not guaranteed. Many of those nominally on the right tend to go AWOL when duty calls. And some of those are potential contenders to succeed Donald Trump, who will someday leave the White House and relinquish his leadership of the movement he has led since he rode down that escalator in 2015.

Which brings to mind a fraught question: Is Donald Trump himself the movement or the face of something bigger?

Many wrongly identify Trump the man with the movement he represents. It's an understandable mistake because Donald Trump was the first in a long time to advocate what the movement demanded. Moreover, Trump is such a force of nature, such a huge and unique personality, such a master of the media and messaging, that it is easy to allow the sheer bigness of him overwhelm the message he voices.

But the seeds of the movement were there long before Trump showed up. Populist movements—the term "populist" is not entirely accurate, but it is not entirely inaccurate, and it is generally useful in this situation—have sprung up throughout American history, and the indications of popular discontent were there for all to see in the run up to 2016.

The Tea Party was the first clear sign that something was rotten in these United States. While the Tea Party emphasized different policies from Trump, they both constituted a revolt against an arrogant, corrupt, and utterly incompetent ruling caste. The Tea Party was a true grassroots movement, not some Soros-funded Astroturf fraud. Its decentralized organization was its strength. Individuals with minimal help and little or no financial support spontaneously organized events using the skills they had learned in business, the military, and their communities.

But lack of leadership was also the Tea Party's Achilles' heel. The lack of leadership placed a ceiling on how high the Tea Party could rise. The merciless siege that the establishment laid on the Tea Party was enough to break the grassroots movement, which could never move from a series of protests to an organized attempt at institutional power.

In 2016, Trump was the only candidate who recognized the wide-open populist lane to the GOP nomination. As we all saw, he jumped into that lane and put the pedal to the metal. That's not to say he cynically scooped up the populist banner because he thought it was his best shot at power. Trump never ran for office as a typical Republican. Heck, he was a registered Democrat for much of his life. No, Trump didn't adapt his views to run for office; he ran on what he really thinks. His public statements from decades in the spotlight make that clear. Despite years of being on the record, he never varied significantly. You can track his views back decades and find that Trump was always firmly in the populist camp. Unlike most politicians, Trump believed what he was saying. People could see that and resonated with his message. Plus, politicians of conviction tend to draw ardent supporters.

Trump solved the problem that had stalled the Tea Party by giving the populist energy direction. Instead of a group of more or less talented amateurs, conservative populism was now in the hands of a media savvy, charismatic rebel who praised his supporters and utterly refused to give any quarter in the fight. Trump was a magnificent communicator, and he had a better understanding of the media than the corps of Ivy League liberals calling themselves "journalists." He skillfully exploited them for earned media—up to $5 billion worth, according to some analysts—and when they wised up and tried to starve him of attention, Trump figured out how to get around the gatekeepers, notably by using Twitter to connect directly with his supporters.

Trump didn't just know how to communicate; he knew *what* to communicate. Lacing policy proposals with humor and memorable slams on his punch-drunk foes, Trump understood what the people that establishment politicians had long left for dead wanted to hear. He talked to them about what they wanted to talk about, not what their betters had decreed they should hear. He validated their clinging to their guns and religion and honored their patriotism. You never got the feeling he was standing up for the National Anthem ironically.

Plus, he fought back and always gave back harder than he got. It's easy to underestimate the importance of morale to the members of a movement, especially one with high stakes and low odds. Demoralized soldiers don't rush into the breach when their commander tells them to charge; they shoot their officers and surrender. Demoralized members of a political movement don't write checks, man phone banks, or come out in the cold to vote; they stay at home and watch their party fail from the couch.

Republicans needed a boost in morale after the Bushies' indifference, McCain's disdain, and the sickening weakness of Mitt Romney. Trump boosted the morale of a Republican base habituated to disappointment by the party leadership. The grassroots had seen enough and wanted a man who could get them fired up about politics again.

And Trump had a bunch of money.

But most of all, Trump was a winner. He radiated it. He had the cash, trappings, and boundless optimism of a serial winner. Plus, he never wavered, and he never stopped wading into the mosh pit to slam his foes.

Those early supporters got what they had hoped for in Trump. Trump won, improbably, perhaps inexplicably, but decisively. And the tears of his formerly smug foes, immortalized in YouTube videos of herds of weeping, brokenhearted "I'm with Her" losers, made the taste of victory so much sweeter.

It's fair to say that without a champion with Trump's unique skill set, the populist revolt would have been strangled in its crib. None of the other Republicans running in 2016 could have done it, and none even tried. They would have lost to Hillary, the progressive transformation would have accelerated, and the anger of the unheard populist movement would have been built up as the abuses piled on. With or without Trump, the populist explosion was on its way, though it's not clear what form it would have taken. One thing is for certain: that explosion would have been a lot messier than the election of Donald Trump.

But while Trump was a prerequisite for initial electoral success, it's not clear whether Trump is necessary for the populist movement to carry on. Can it continue without him? Doubtless, while the liars want to pretend that Trump has dispensed with "normality" forever—thereby justifying their permanent abandonment of the norms and unwritten rules of normal times—they hope that the loss of Trump himself, in 2021 or (horrors!) 2025 leads to the movement's swan song, leaderless and rudderless.

It could happen. It absolutely could happen. But will it?

As of yet, no Republican has made an aggressive play for the Trump mantle. The potential GOP 2024 presidential candidates are all stepping gingerly around their rivals, biding their time without making any sudden movements. They are all smart operators—there is no total outsider like Donald Trump in the queue—and they all know that the Republican Party has embraced his populist vision.

But not all of them share it wholeheartedly. Many of Trump's would-be successors still want to revive the discredited establishment consensus. Remember, many "conservative" leaders are nearly as uncomfortable with Trumpism as the liberals are. Some on the right want to wait him out, and then get back to business as usual.

But that assumes the base is willing to be fooled again, and with the power of social media and alternative conservative outlets all watching the politicians for the slightest deviation from the new conservative wokeness, that seems unlikely. Jeb! Bush and his cohort are not going to waddle back onstage and take up failing where they left off.

The successor to Trump must be a worthy successor: not just a pale imitation, but someone with enough of the core attributes that made Trump successful. We need a leader who will keep the supporters Trump won in the fold and perhaps expand the movement.

Anyone who wants to walk in Trump's footsteps will have to match his policies. We can assume that any heir to the Trump mantle will take up the typical conservative positions. But there will be some dispute on issues where Trump deviates from past conservative orthodoxy. The foreign interventionism of the past will no longer pass muster. The "free traders" who refused to demand equality in our trade relationships with other countries (especially China) will get no traction. Immigration softies have no chance.

But having the right policies alone won't cut it. Any potential successor to President Trump needs to have some personality. Though it may come as a surprise, that's not a given. For a long time, stiffs and saps dawdled along unchallenged and sheltered toward the nomination. No more. The candidate has got to have the charisma to back up the policy vision we demand.

The winning candidate must be willing and able to reach out to the base. That means rallies, interviews with conservative radio, podcast, and television hosts, tweeting, and not catering to the liberal mainstream press. Traditional Republicans held a bizarre and undeserved reverence for legacy media outlets that led them to imagine they would be treated fairly and honorably. The 2024 Trumpist can have no such illusions.

And he or she must not only be a warrior, but a ruthless and joyful one. He or she must savor the adrenalin high of political combat while adhering to Conan's philosophy (via the great conservative screenwriter

John Milius) of what is best in life: "Crush your enemies, see them driven before you, and hear the lamentation of the women!"

Bush 43 didn't have any Conan in him. He had some Thurston Howell III. He thought it was unseemly and was hamstrung by a sense of political chivalry that belonged to a bygone era. Romney was just weak. He hit like a little girl who identified as a little girl.

Neither of those traits will do. The 2024 candidate must enjoy delivering a haymaker. He or she must delight in kicking in the liver the prone, quivering carcass of any opponent. After all, the other side feels that way. The enemy is serious, and in a serious fight you fight to win.

Trump did not make our politics into a brutal arena of ruthless combat, he just acknowledged the state of play, adapted to it, and emerged victorious. The 2024 winner will have to do the same in the face of unrelenting pressure from the entire media and D.C. establishment to be one of those good Republicans, like that nice, submissive Mitt Romney or that even nicer, dead John McCain. He or she will need an iron will in the service of not giving a damn about what the smart set thinks. A Republican can be beloved by the *Washington Post* or president of the United States, but never both at once.

So, who fits the bill? Who has the right stuff to grab the new GOP's baton and carry it forward? Half of Washington seems eager to take a shot. And Donald Trump has not picked a protégé—right now, he is not grooming anyone for the role.

It's wide open, so let's look at a few of the leading contenders.

There is Mike Pence, who would gently and kindly, after much reflection and prayer, disagree with the characterization of the field as "wide open." Pence has been a loyal vice president to a man who probably scares the hell out of him. That would normally put him ahead of the pack. But he's no Trump in any sense. He's not tough or funny. He would be inclined to reach across the aisle where Trump would happily throw something. Pence is nice, and that's bad because nice people tend to assume that other people are nice too, and that's a good way to end up wearing a vinyl body suit and living in a wooden crate in Chuck Schumer's Senate Majority Leader office closet. The base respects Pence and his loyal service, but he just does not have the covfefe that the base needs and wants in 2024. Too bad—he's a good guy who deserves our thanks.

"Little Marco" Rubio might try again. He'll fail. While he lived down his embarrassing performance in 2016—imagine his thinking he could go toe-to-toe with Donald Trump in a game of the Dozens!—he still can't seem to resist the opportunity to adopt some sanctimonious pose whenever someone shoves a microphone in his face. Once a Jebbite, always a Jebbite.

Rick Scott, Florida's other Senator, has potential. He likes to fight. He was soft on guns though, and the base won't forget it. He's not a stiff, and he's got a great life story. Best of all, he has money.

Ted Cruz is already angling for another run at the presidency. The man is a genius, but he's no Trump. While he is a reliable advocate on television and in committee and his Twitter game is top notch, he just does not get the pulse running for the base. Too bad. His politics are on-point, and there is zero chance Ted Cruz would ever go soft. He has probably lived down his inexplicable and grave error of not expressly endorsing Trump at the 2016 convention, but his razor-thin 2018 Senate win over the noted furry, Beto O'Rourke, was too close for comfort. If you can barely take Texas, forget the Midwest. Ted will probably run, but he's not going to win, regardless of how much we would like to see it happen.

Mike Pompeo, Trump's secretary of state, is another administration official who looks like he's preparing to succeed the boss. He's smart—number one in his class at West Point—and he's not weak. He managed to walk the tightrope between Trump's noninterventionist inclinations and the old school hawkishness of the GOP. But does he excite the base? Can he ladle out the red meat? Would he point out that Rosie O'Donnell is a hideous hag? He nicely slammed a scuzzy NPR reporter who broke her "off-the-record" promise to him. That's a good start.

Tom Cotton might fancy a run. He was an Army Ranger, which is good, but he looks like he's fourteen, which is bad. Cotton has the right positions, and he's never going to be tempted from the path by the prospect of a favorable write-up in the Sunday section. He gets huge props for being way ahead of the power-curve on the Chinese coronavirus. He is a sometimes-competent speaker but seems unable to adapt to a crowd. The idea of Tom Cotton getting a solid laugh from an outrageous observation is far-fetched to say the least. He is a Harvard guy and smart. But he may not be as smart as he thinks, as he has the reputation for not listening to other people who might be able to teach him something. Every Army officer needs a sergeant major who can shut the door and tell him he's stepping on his junk, and Cotton appears to lack one. If Cotton has a year, it's not 2024.

Nikki Haley is actively circling the idea, testing the waters with a book and television appearances, trying to decide if it's her year or whether she should wait for 2028. She wants it. She could get it. In fact, she is probably the best positioned to win the nomination in 2024—on paper.

She was the Governor of South Carolina and a damned good UN ambassador. In her latter role, she took no guff from corrupt bureaucrats or petty potentates. That's a big plus. She's apparently got no personal weirdness going on, and that's a big plus too. The media might think that the fact that she is a female of color is relevant, but that's only true to the extent that the base would delight in shoving in the left's scrunched, grimacing face the fact that the first female and first female of color elected president is Republican.

Side note—the first woman elected president will be a Republican.

Nikki Haley can speak clearly and coherently, but the content of her speeches should worry Republicans. Simply put, she is not conservative woke. She does not understand or accept that the left and right are in a death struggle and that opponents are not your pals. Sometimes this failure is manifest as hackneyed tweets about "unity" and aisle-reaching. Other times, she is totally tone deaf. For example, any Republican candidate should know that there is never, ever a good reason to stand there smiling in a photo with the venomous John Brennan.

But she did, and she was brutalized in the conservative media and on social media. Whether she learned the lesson—that this is a fight and you better be unequivocally on our side—remains to be seen. She certainly can fight, but will she? The base does not think so. They largely think of her as another globalist who might play woke for the election then start channeling the Bushes once she's done seducing the great unwashed.

The base needs to know that she will fight for their interests. Without the base, Nikki Haley is over before she starts. Time will tell whether she chooses wokeness or the same lame advice the same lame consultants have been dishing out for decades.

There is also a wild card, a very wild one. He is also a personal friend of the author, so you will need to judge for yourself whether this assessment is biased.

Having spent much of Trump's first term in Germany dealing the pain to our allies for their failure to pay their fair share to NATO, cavorting with the Iranian mullahs, and canoodling with Putin, Richard "Ric" Grenell is wildly popular with the base. When Trump tapped him as the acting director of National Intelligence in February 2020, the base was ecstatic, and the liberals were terrified, and for good reason. He proceeded to start rummaging through the Deep State's dusty files to uncover its staggering corruption.

He's Harvard-educated and as polished and charming as Trump is rough 'n' tumble. A familiar face to conservatives from his time as a Fox News contributor, he is conservative woke and delights in verbal combat. Moreover, he is as smooth as silk in front of a mic, funny, and cutting when appropriate. His Twitter game is mighty, but that's because he gets social media in a way consultant-driven pols can't. He has a compelling story as a cancer survivor, his pro-military stands have earned him a fanatical following among many vets, and he is an evangelical Christian. He is also a married gay man, which is the least interesting thing about him.

Another side note—the first openly gay man to be president will be a Republican.

Of all the major Republicans out there, Ric Grenell is perhaps the most superficially different from Trump, while being the most like him in the ways that count: the ability to communicate, understanding of the nature of the fight, and joy in engaging in political battle. If Grenell is not the GOP nominee for president in 2024, he will certainly be at the top of any short list for vice president.

The liars may not be lying this time. Perhaps Donald Trump is the new normal. Leaders like Ric Grenell and those in the populist Republican base will see to that. Plus, they like the new normal. Trump gave them the opportunity to drop all the pretenses they had to abide by for so long, to ditch the unwritten rules and norms that reined in their political id. And to meet the future, we need leaders who not only understand that, but relish the prospect of the fights ahead.

Epilogue

APRIL 2020

As this book's manuscript is being tuned up for publication, America finds itself in the middle of the Chinese coronavirus pandemic. And it should be no surprise that in response, our elites and their media stooges are falling all over themselves to trash Donald Trump with even more lies.

One of the lies stems from Trump's telling the indisputable truth—that the Chinese coronavirus came from China and probably arose either in some incompetently administered lab or in the infamous "wet markets" where the Chinese buy and sell weird animals to use as entrees for Far East foodies. Trump being Trump pointed this out and violated a hitherto unknown norm against naming a virus after its place of origin. The same media outlets that had called the Chinese coronavirus the "Chinese coronavirus" or "Wuhan flu" soon informed us that Trump's accurate naming of the virus was racist. The ChiComs themselves soon followed suit, picking up the meme to cover for their own disgraceful and devious handling of the Wuhan outbreak by leveraging the media's wokeness.

When confronted by huffy journalists at his daily pandemic press briefings about his alleged hate crime—again, he was doing something that the media itself had been doing just weeks before—Trump predictably doubled down. And, also predictably, the media looked like a bunch of fools for parroting commie propaganda and catering to the obsessions of neurotic, elitist weirdos when people were dying, economic activity was grinding to a halt, and the stock market was tanking.

Despite the huge challenges facing the American people, the lies keep coming. At one point, the media falsely imputed that the president was urging people to inject disinfectant, and then predictably began a search for people dropping dead from mainlining Lysol at his orders. The lying got more sinister when the liars turned on possible treatments simply as a way to own the Drumpf. Trump hailed a potential treatment called chloroquine that some French doctors had claimed was useful. The media muttered that Trump was no doctor and had no business making such assertions, as if the president were not surrounded by medical advisors.

The media routinely leaves out the information that hurts their narrative. Remember when they amplified the story of the couple of geniuses who self-prescribed chloroquine and drank down fish tank cleaner? They didn't find it relevant to mention that the wife, who survived, had previously been charged with domestic abuse against her husband. Those of us untrained in the mystical art of journalism might consider that important tidbit of information critical context, but what do we peasants know?

In fact, the media worries that we cannot be trusted with any information at all. The president's popular daily briefings were such an effective messaging tool when the networks showed them in their entirety—uncut, unedited, and unbent to the preferred narrative—that the leading lights of journalism began to panic as they watched the president's approval ratings climb. The media brain trust proposed halting the simple transmission of the briefings to the American people, since apparently only they are competent and capable enough to assess the information Trump provides. Those wise men and women want to determine what we need to know. Luckily, the would-be gatekeepers are on a fool's errand because the walls have already come tumbling down. Fox has kept running the briefings, as have several other networks, so only liberals are deprived of access to the primary source. As much as it wants to, the mainstream media cannot gag the president.

Another lie is that Trump's failure to take any action to prevent the pandemic is the reason America is gripped by this particularly formidable grippe. One media talking head issued a long and oddly popular Twitter thread about how Trump's negligence could—nay, must—lead to his prosecution for murder. This requires a revision to the old saw that a lawyer representing himself has a fool for a client: a lawyer bloviating on Twitter about arresting the president for homicide has a fool for a follower.

Of course, the bug burned its way through China, South Korea, Italy, Spain, and elsewhere without Trump's help, but like all the other lies they have thrown at him, the charge that Trump golfed while America burned is ridiculous. In fact, very early on Trump banned direct flights from the hotbed of infection, China, and was greeted with a flurry of racism accusations by the same politicians and media figures who now say he should have done more. Claims that Trump ignored the crisis are truth-optional, but the urge to go with "Trump lied, people died" is just too delicious to resist. These lies do not have to make objective sense. They just need to be repeated enough to be effective.

At least, that's how it worked in the old playbook. In the new playbook, Trump's allies began highlighting awkward tweets from the mayor of New York urging people to party away and running video of Nancy Pelosi assuring the world that all was well in crowded Chinatown. Because the walls of media power have come crashing down, conservatives were able to disseminate the truth to anyone willing to listen. The obviously false narrative couldn't stand up to reality.

But in the face of a catastrophe that has threatened to winnow away America's grandmas and grandpas and slash and burn our retirement accounts, there isn't much room for frivolous nonsense. Those screaming about the fact that Trump refused to wave his magic biotech wand and produce 20 million coronavirus test kits just seem foolish to people operating in the real world. The media pouts and the Democrats—stuck with an ancient presumptive nominee reduced to transmitting bizarre and amateurish hostage videos from his secret location—have panicked.

How the Chinese coronavirus pandemic pans out is, at this writing, still unclear. America has not reopened, and to the extent Trump keeps it closed, he is trashed for wrecking the economy he rebuilt. To the extent that he reopens the country, he's accused of plotting to let zillions die. But what is clear is that even if we find a cure for the Wuhan flu, we still won't have a cure for the pandemic of lies about Donald Trump and you (except to tell those lying schmucks to go to hell).

Afterword

As always, the words of Stiv Bators, the deceased lead singer of the Dead Boys and later the criminally underrated post-punk band Lords of the New Church, said it best. His song "Open Your Eyes" is all about waking up to the establishment's lies, and I hope this little trip down mendacity lane has helped you open your eyes to their lies. That was one of the two goals of this book. The other was to be the first conservative tome to cite Stiv Bators.

If you see the lies coming, they can't hurt you. They are big, dumb, and clumsy. Their power exists only until that moment when your face breaks into a wide grin, and you bust out laughing at the sheer silliness of it.

Racist.

Sexist.

Whatever.

Donald Trump doesn't care, and you shouldn't care either. Your caring and your decency are what the liars count on. Because you would never defame someone, you used to be vulnerable to imagining that no one else would do that to you.

But they can't count on that anymore. You're woke, as the hep kids say.

One amazing thing about the Trump era is the clarification, how the truth of things long suppressed has revealed the true state of play in American politics. Our establishment has shown itself to be as corrupt and self-serving as it is incompetent. Liberal ideology has been boiled down to its leftist essence, while conservatism was purged of those who were content to diddle while liberty burned.

The truth will win, if only we refuse to surrender it.

Donald Trump is not racist, and we are not racist.

Donald Trump is not sexist, and we are not sexist.

The same goes for being warmongers or corrupt or the tools of the rich or transphobes or Nazis or heretics in the eyes of the Great Weather Hoax Cult.

Well, maybe the last one is true. Yay climate heresy!

Donald Trump reminded us that we can fight. He didn't just encourage us to defend ourselves, he showed us how it is done. Refuse to accept their lies. Refuse to obey. Refuse to respect their authority.

As *Instapundit* Glenn Reynolds advises, punch back twice as hard.

Donald Trump might have been the right guy at the right moment to take this conservative-populist movement from the fringe into the Oval Office, but he won't be the guy who keeps it there. There will be other leaders to come, future conservatives who understand how the liars operate and don't fear the fight. But with or without leaders, we are the only people who will keep conservatives in power and ensure that we never again become an embarrassing afterthought to faraway snobs.

They can defame us without our consent, but they can't beat us unless we let them.

Acknowledgements

My number one critic, editor, and co-conspirator in this was my hot wife, Irina Moises. I could not have done it without her support and her picking up the slack around the house while I wrote it. Thanks!

My agent, Keith Urbahn, spearheaded the idea, and Harry Crocker of Regnery accepted the challenge. Paul Choix edited it as penance for his sins.

Lots of people helped me with this, mostly without knowing it. I got ideas, tidbits of insights, and inspiration from a bunch of people, including Larry O'Connor, Hugh Hewitt, Duane Paterson, Michael Walsh, Chris Stigall, Cam Edwards, Glenn Reynolds, Matt Betley, John Cardillo, Derek Hunter, Jack Posobiec, Evan Sayet, John Milius, Stiv Bators, and many others. Thanks!

I also want to thank the folks at Townhall.com, where I've been working on some of these themes for almost a decade.

I also want to thank my Twitter followers and those who have supported my writing all along—you rock!

And, finally, I want to give my customary shout-out to Andrew Breitbart. Without him, all might well have been lost.

KAS

About the Author

Kurt Schlichter is a senior columnist for Townhall.com. He is also a Los Angeles trial lawyer admitted in California, Texas, and Washington, D.C., and a retired Army Infantry colonel.

A Twitter activist (@KurtSchlichter) with about 250,000 followers, Kurt was personally recruited to write conservative commentary by Andrew Breitbart.

Kurt is a news source, an on-screen commentator on networks like Fox, Fox Business, and Newsmax, and a guest on, and guest host of, nationally syndicated radio programs talking about political, military, and legal issues. CNN and he are not on speaking terms.

He is the author of the USA Today bestseller *Militant Normals: How Regular Americans Are Rebelling Against the Elite to Reclaim Our Democracy* (2018) as well as *Conservative Insurgency: The Struggle to Take America Back 2013–2041* (2014). He is also the author of the Amazon bestselling novels *People's Republic* (2016), *Indian Country* (2017), *Wildfire* (2018) and *Collapse* (2019)

Kurt served as a U.S. Army infantry officer on active duty and in the California Army National Guard, retiring at the rank of full colonel. He commanded the 1st Squadron, 18th Cavalry Regiment (Reconnaissance-Surveillance-Target Acquisition) and is a veteran of both the Persian Gulf War and Operation Enduring Freedom (Kosovo). Kurt graduated from the Army's Combined Arms and Services Staff School, the Command and General Staff College, and the United States Army War College, where he received a master's degree in strategic studies.

Kurt lives with his wife Irina and his monstrous dogs Bitey and Barkey in the Los Angeles area. Kurt enjoys sarcasm and red meat.

His favorite caliber is .45.